IN THE EYE OF THE CHINA STORM

To dear Sam and Francesca:

Thank you for your friendship
and support through many
difficult times.

Eileen
2011

FOOTPRINTS SERIES
Jane Errington, Editor

The life stories of individual women and men who were participants in interesting events help nuance larger historical narratives, at times reinforcing those narratives, at other times contradicting them. The Footprints series introduces extraordinary Canadians, past and present, who have led fascinating and important lives at home and throughout the world.

The series includes primarily original manuscripts but may consider the English-language translation of works that have already appeared in another language. The editor of the series welcomes inquiries from authors. If you are in the process of completing a manuscript that you think might fit into the series, please contact her, care of McGill-Queen's University Press, 1010 Sherbrooke Street West, Suite 1720, Montreal, QC H3A 2R7.

IN THE
EYE
OF THE
CHINA
STORM

A Life Between East and West

Paul T.K. Lin
with Eileen Chen Lin

McGILL-QUEEN'S UNIVERSITY PRESS Montreal & Kingston • London • Ithaca

© McGill-Queen's University Press 2011

ISBN 978-0-7735-3857-3

Legal deposit third quarter 2011
Bibliothèque nationale du Québec

Printed in Canada on acid-free paper that is 100% ancient forest free
(100% post-consumer recycled), processed chlorine free.

McGill-Queen's University Press acknowledges the support of the Canada Council for
the Arts for our publishing program. We also acknowledge the financial support of the
Government of Canada through the Canada Book Fund for our publishing activities.

Library and Archives Canada Cataloguing in Publication

Lin, Paul T. K., 1920–2004
In the eye of the China storm : a life between East and West / Paul
T.K. Lin with Eileen Chen Lin.

(Footprints series ; 14)
Includes bibliographical references and index.
ISBN 978-0-7735-3857-3

1. Lin, Paul T. K., 1920–2004. 2. Chinese Canadians–British
Columbia–Biography. 3. Scholars–China–Biography. 4. China–
History–Cultural Revolution, 1966-1976. I. Lin, Eileen Chen, 1924–
II. Title. III. Series: Footprints series ; 14

DS779.29.L55A3 2011   951.05'7092   C2011-902225-7

Designed and typeset by studio oneonone in Sabon 10.2/14

Dedicated to a generation of idealistic Chinese youth and intellectuals
who in the twentieth century ventured upon
"an odyssey of purpose, pain, and hope"
to build a new China,
strong, prosperous, and democratic,
with social justice for all.

横眉冷對千夫指
俯首甘為孺子牛

鲁迅

With levelled brow I gaze at a thousand accusing fingers
With bowed head I serve the people like an ox

Lu Xun
Translated by Paul T.K. Lin

CONTENTS

AUTHOR'S NOTE

Paul T.K. Lin (1920–2004) was a Canada-born Chinese historian and intellectual who dedicated his life to the rise of an independent, prosperous, and democratic China, worthy of respect in the family of nations. After attending university in Canada and the United States, he moved to the newly established People's Republic of China in January 1950 and lived there for the next fifteen years. In 1964 he returned to Canada to share his experiences of New China and to advocate for rapprochement between China and the West – and particularly with the United States, which still maintained a Cold War blockade of the PRC.

Paul was a scholar but he was also an activist who, throughout his life, encouraged Canadians to reach out to China. He spoke at many conferences, wrote for newspapers and periodicals, and was frequently interviewed in the media. He took keen pleasure in having made a small contribution to the establishment of formal Canada-China relations in 1970, and there is no doubt he was there in spirit when the fortieth anniversary of this agreement was celebrated in the fall of 2010.

During his teaching career at McGill University, which spanned seventeen years, Paul had intended to write several academic books on the early period of the People's Republic, chiefly for his students. Yet the constant flux of the PRC's political scene, coupled with the unreliability of the data he had collected in China during the Cultural Revolution, frustrated his repeated attempts. It was not until near the end of his life, when his health began to deteriorate, that he decided to write his memoirs. Building upon a detailed 1997 resumé of his life and work, Paul chose the title *In the Eye of the China Storm*, prepared an outline of the chapters, and lived to write the preface and first chapter, "In the Beginning Was Father." To our great sorrow, he passed away in 2004, before he could complete the book.

The more than one hundred boxes of papers Paul left behind include manuscripts, speeches, class lectures, press reports, and interviews, as well as scrapbooks containing photos and news clippings from his student days during the 1930s and 1940s. Among his papers are correspondence with family, friends, colleagues, and public figures, an oral history, a set of diaries dating from 1964 to 2004 with entries of daily appointments, and copious notes on important conversations and events.[1]

From these voluminous sources, I drew together the pertinent documents for each chapter and worked them into a narrative that would illuminate Paul's life and work. Where necessary, I took the liberty of strengthening the historical context and editing documents for the sake of clarity. I have tried to keep direct quotations to a manageable length, although some full texts have been included to reflect Paul's ongoing analysis of China's development.

Paul did not live to write every word of *In the Eye of the China Storm*, but the vast majority of words are his. The book is written primarily in his own voice, save for chapters 3 and 4, which were written by me. Thereafter, I occasionally supplement the text with perspectives of my own, as Paul's journey to New China (and back) would have been far different if I had not been China-born and accompanied him for sixty years. My contributions throughout the book are introduced by 𝌀 and end with 𝍖.

The reader will observe that there is more discussion of my family's roots in China than of Paul's. The reason for this imbalance is explained by Paul in the first chapter: "I never had the opportunity to discuss with Father the details of his young life prior to coming to Canada." According to traditional Chinese practice, the patriarch of the family, especially one as authoritarian as the Rev. Lim Yuen, seldom discussed his past with his children. And it never occurred to Paul and his siblings, who grew up in remote Vernon, BC, far away from close relatives, to ask their parents about the details of their lives in China before coming to Canada. In my case, when my father passed away in 1953, my mother wrote half a dozen notebooks detailing her life before and after her marriage. Some of my family history is included to give readers insight into the semi-feudalistic and semi-colonial China that shaped my childhood, but that Paul only encountered when he arrived in Beijing in 1950.

---

1 Paul T.K. Lin's papers – letters, manuscripts, interviews, photographs – will be deposited in the Archives of the Hong Kong University of Science and Technology.

This is not the "academic" book Paul wished to write, but rather a more straightforward account of how Paul – in deeds as well as words – combined Canadian and Chinese universal and shared values and navigated both cultures during a politically complex period. Proud Canadian that he was, he identified himself most closely with the generation of patriotic Chinese intellectuals who helped to bring the People's Republic into being.

There is no single audience for this story. Paul had family and friends around the world. He had colleagues and students in universities, corporate board rooms, and government offices in Canada, the United States, China, Hong Kong, Macau, and Europe. A Chinese edition of this book is to be published, based on the English text.

Regarding the English pronunciation and spelling of Chinese names and places, Hanyu Pinyin is used throughout, except for a small number of people who never changed their names from earlier romanizations – Sun Yat-sen, Soong Ching Ling, Chiang Kai-Shek, Choming Tsai Chen, K.H. Ting, Walter Chun, and a few others.

Eileen Chen Shu Lin
January 2011

PREFACE

The proudest day of my life was October 1, 1950, New China's National Day. I marched with seeming multitudes across Tiananmen Square, exalting in China's independence from foreign controls. China had reclaimed its destiny – for better or for worse, the Chinese people had emerged from their 5,000-year history and would determine their own future.

I waved, I cheered, I celebrated. But, as we passed by the dignitaries on the podium and people raised their fists to Mao Zedong, shouting *Wansui,* "ten thousand years"– the traditional greeting for an emperor – I could not raise my fist. My euphoria lay not in finding another idol to bow down to, but in the fact that the Chinese people had "stood up."

I felt some discomfort but kept my hand by my side. At that moment I knew that I was a son of Canada as well as a son of China.

Paul T.K. Lin, July 2000

ABBREVIATIONS

AFP Agence France-Presse
APEC Asia-Pacific Economic Co-operation
APF Asia Pacific Foundation
BC British Columbia
CASS Chinese Academy of Social Sciences
CBC Canadian Broadcasting Corporation
CCF Co-operative Commonwealth Federation
CCHDTP Canada-China Human Development Training Program
CCP Chinese Communist Party
CFR Committee on Friendly Relations among Foreign Students
CFS China Forum Society
CIDA Canadian International Development Agency
CNCP Committee for a New China Policy
CP Canadian Pacific
CPA Cathay Pacific Airways
CPIRD China Program for Integrative Research and Development
CPPCC Chinese People's Political Consultative Conference
CSCA Chinese Students' Christian Association
CSIS Canadian Security Intelligence Service
CUSO Canadian University Service Overseas
CWI China Welfare Institute
CYA Chinese Youth Association
ECE Early childhood education

FBI Federal Bureau of Investigation
FYIO For Your Information Only
G&M *Globe and Mail*
IPR Institute of Pacific Relations
KMT Kuomintang
NDP New Democratic Party
NGO Non-governmental organization
PLA People's Liberation Army
PMO Prime Minister's Office
PRC People's Republic of China
RCMP Royal Canadian Mounted Police
RIW Ricci Island West
RMB Renminbi
SAR Special Administrative Region
SCLCFC Soong Ching Ling Children's Foundation of Canada
SCM Student Christian Movement
TVA Tennessee Valley Authority
UBC University of British Columbia
UCLA University of California, Los Angeles
UEA University of East Asia
UN United Nations
UNESCO United Nations Educational, Scientific, and Cultural
    Organization
UNICEF United Nations Children's Fund
US United States
USSR Union of Soviet Socialist Republics
YMCA Young Men's Christian Association
YWCA Young Women's Christian Association

Part One

1920–1949

Chapter One

IN THE BEGINNING WAS FATHER

My father, Lin Zuoran, was born in 1882 in Xinhui County, near the city of Guangzhou in the Pearl River Delta of south China. He often proudly reminded the family that Xinhui was the birthplace of the famous scholar-reformer Liang Qichao (1873–1929), who had worked closely with his mentor Kang Youwei to persuade the young Emperor Guangxu to launch the historic but short-lived Hundred Days' Reform in 1898. The empress dowager suppressed the reform, forcing the reformers to flee into exile, but their struggles heralded the final overthrow of the Qing Dynasty (1644–1912) by republican revolutionaries led by Dr Sun Yat-sen in 1911.

Father grew up in a China seething with portentous change. Since the first Opium War in 1839, when Britain forced international trade upon China with gunboats and annexed the island of Hong Kong, the country had essentially been occupied by Western powers – France, the United States, Tsarist Russia, Italy, and Germany – riding on Britain's imperialist coattails. China's sovereignty was deeply compromised by British control of customs revenue and extra-territoriality, which enabled foreigners to escape Chinese law. The final humiliation, however, was China's defeat at the hands of the Japanese in 1895. Under the terms of the Treaty of Shimonoseki, Japan not only exacted an outrageous indemnity of 200 million taels from a prostrate China, but also seized the province of Taiwan as a colony. This was the beginning of Japanese aggression and territorial ambition in China, which would not be checked until the end of World War II.

I never had the opportunity to discuss with Father the details of his young life prior to coming to Canada. In the years leading up to 1900, new ideas from the West were challenging patriotic Chinese intellectuals to find political, technological, and institutional methods – whether by reform or by revolution – to restore China's territorial integrity. Father had received a good grounding in the Confucian classics and even in his teens must have raged at the impotent plight of his country. His family, however, did not have the resources to enable him to pursue a scholar-official's career. Friends and relatives already in Canada urged him to consider overseas work, where he could earn a living, study English, and learn more about what made the West powerful. So with a smattering of English, and only enough money to pay the head tax of fifty dollars, Father arrived in Victoria, British Columbia, Canada, on March 9, 1897, aboard the *Empress of India*. The colonial authorities registered him as George Lim Yuen (Lin Ran), an abbreviated English transliteration of his Chinese name.

Father initially signed on with a salmon cannery on Lulu Island, but within a few months found a job as a houseboy for an English teacher who paid him two dollars per month and provided free English lessons in the evenings. Later he moved to Vancouver, where another cannery manager offered him a wage of fifteen dollars per month. Father, however, was intellectually ambitious and eventually found day labour, which freed him in the evenings to attend church-sponsored Bible classes in English. He saved his money and in December 1901 sailed back to China to marry Chiu Mon Som on January 22, 1902. She was a gentle young woman with bound feet from the neighbouring village of Xia Lu. Theirs was an arranged marriage, as was the custom at the time.

Unable to afford the head tax (now $100) and reluctant to bring his bride back to Vancouver, which was rife with anti-Chinese sentiment, Father returned alone to Canada in May 1902. His Bible teacher then introduced him to George Cowan – a lawyer and devout Christian – who paid him well as a houseboy and gave him time off in the evenings to continue his study of English. In January 1904, however, the shocking news of his father's death forced him to cross the Pacific once more to attend to family affairs.

Father returned alone to Canada in November 1905, just weeks before the birth of his first child in Xinhui – a daughter, named Lam Kam Pang. With a family to support, he now planned to establish a restaurant business with two friends. But fate intervened. The Diocese of New Westminster of the Church of England in Canada, which had sponsored his English and Bible classes, approached this inspired new convert about serving the needs of Chinese Anglicans. On his own initiative, Father had started a Bible class in Chinatown that had already brought several members into the fold. In 1907, the diocesan executive committee asked him to take charge of the Chinese Mission on Homer Street, as Chinese catechist and missionary under Vancouver's Christ

Certificate of landing awarded to Paul's father, George Lim Yuen, upon his arrival in Canada as a labourer in March 1897

George Lim Yuen (rear, second from left) attends Latimer Hall as an Anglican seminary student, 1912–14. (Archives of the Anglican Provincial Synod of BC and Yukon)

6

Paul's mother, Chiu Mon Som, upon her
arrival in Canada in 1912 at age thirty,
ten years after her marriage

Below
Family portrait in Vancouver, 1923.
Front: Paul, age three. Middle, left to
right: David, Mother, Andrew, Father,
Helen. Rear: Margaret

Church vestry. Father was responsible for thirty-two baptisms and twenty con-
firmations in the next five years, which resulted in the church underwriting his
studies at the Anglican theological college, Latimer Hall, in 1912.

By frugal living and with the support of the Anglican church, Father was
finally able to bring my mother and older sister to Vancouver in October 1912.
He graduated from Latimer Hall in 1914 and became a deacon soon after.
Ordained a priest in 1920, the diocese asked him in 1924 to move to Vernon,

BC to redevelop the existing Good Angel Mission into a Chinese parish. Father carried out this pastoral ministry in Vernon until 1941, receiving a monthly stipend of ninety-five dollars to raise a family of five children. He was the first Chinese to become an Anglican clergyman in Canada.

I was a child of four at the time of the move, the last of my beloved mother Mon Som's five offspring. In addition to my elder sister, born in December 1905 (named Margaret after arriving in Canada), Mother gave birth to four babies at Vancouver General Hospital: Helen arrived in August 1914, David in October 1915, Andrew in June 1917, and myself, Paul, in March 1920.

Unlike Vancouver, a bustling port city at the western end of the Canadian Pacific Railway, Vernon was a small town in BC's Okanagan Valley surrounded by lakes, orchards, and vegetable farms. Father ministered to the needs of scattered clusters of Chinese labourers, who tended to keep to themselves as protection against the deep-rooted racism of their white neighbours. The Chinese Exclusion Act of 1923, which would block entry of Chinese to Canada until 1947, had just been passed by Parliament. Perhaps Father thought that raising his children in the Interior would be healthier than in Vancouver, where the racism was more overt and sometimes violent. In any case, he moved his family to the Okanagan and soon became known to his Chinese brethren as a kind and reliable English-speaking friend, who would help to solve their problems without demanding that they first become Christians.

A CHINESE CONFUCIAN CULTURAL NATIONALIST

Father had received a strict Confucian education as a youth in China. In Canada, as the young father of a growing and increasingly Westernized family, he lost no time in imparting Confucian morals, etiquette, and values to his children. He was determined that we would appreciate our rich cultural heritage, as well as clearly understand China's current sorry state under the heels of Western and Japanese military imperialists. Although Sun Yat-sen had established the Republic of China in 1912, warlords and foreigners continued to battle for wealth and power, preventing any lasting national unity.

Father taught us children a patriotic "cultural nationalism," which also featured in his sermons. As his family, we had the somewhat arduous obligation of attending church services and Sunday school every week, which meant we frequently heard his exhortations. Even as a child, I noticed that in his Chinese sermons, Father always devoutly cited the Bible, but invariably strengthened his points by quoting Confucius or Mencius, philosophers who had lived four or five centuries before Christ. He seemed to regard Confucian teachings as a set of important pre-Christian humanist values and ethics, not at all in conflict with the teachings of Jesus. Father embraced the spiritual reality of Christianity as sincerely as he was convinced of the ethical truth of Confucianism. I think he fervently believed it was his duty to imbue his family and Chinese parishioners with not only an appreciation of Jesus Christ, but also the best human values of China's ancient civilization, which were ours by birthright.

Every day after school, Father gave us a Chinese lesson lasting an hour and a half that introduced us to the basics of Chinese ethics and culture. I began by reciting a simplified primer entitled *The Three-Character Classic* (*San Zi Jing*). The primer began with the line "The nature of man is originally good," followed by the five greatest virtues: human-heartedness (*ren*), righteousness (*yi*), propriety of conduct (*li*), wisdom (*chih*), and integrity (*lian*). A disciple asked what was meant by the word "ren" and Confucius replied: "Do not do unto others what you would not have others do unto you."

These teachings of Confucianism and cultural nationalism nurtured in me a passionate attachment to the values of my Chinese ancestry. In my early years, however, I was aware that socially, culturally, and linguistically I was more Canadian than Chinese. From grade school on, Father's insistence on disciplined study meant I was usually at the top of my class. I won spelling bees two classes ahead of my peers, my vocabulary enriched by the many volumes of English literature, poetry, and history I read outside of school. Whereas Father had grown up acting out the adventures of the heroes of *Water Margin* (*Shui Hu Chuan*), a Chinese classic novel, my friends and I acted out the adventures of Robin Hood in Vernon's densely green forests. I made lifelong friends in Vernon and was fortunate to have supportive teachers who encouraged me to excel.

In one respect, however, I was aware of being more Chinese than Canadian: racism. Because I spoke fluent English and was a Christian I was more acceptable to the mainstream. My experience with racial discrimination was not as bad as that experienced by the "peasant Chinese," scorned by most white Canadians. Chinese men had first come to British Columbia during the Fraser River gold rush of 1858. More were imported in the 1880s to build the Canadian Pacific Railway. Following the completion of the railway, white British Columbians began to complain that the Chinese were not only taking their jobs and undercutting their wages, but were infecting Canada with foul vices and disease. This resulted in anti-Chinese legislation that forced the men into crowded Chinatowns and marginal jobs as cannery workers, vegetable farmers, grocers, and laundrymen. They were rejected by white society because they

Paul, age fifteen, as a high school student in Vernon, 1935

were poor, uneducated, and could not speak English. They were denied the vote, which meant that certain professions were closed to them. Schools and swimming pools were often segregated. For their own security, they kept to themselves. Anti-Asiatic riots in 1907 led to the beatings of Vancouver-based Chinese and Japanese and the destruction of their shops, some by torching, others by throwing rocks through windows. The head tax, which had cost Father $50 in 1897, rose to $100 and then $500 before all Chinese were banned from coming to Canada from 1923 to 1947. As Chinese men were unable to bring their wives and children from China during this period, the Chinese community shrank in size.

Through Father, I knew all the Chinese in the Okanagan Valley – a community that never numbered more than three hundred. I also met all of Father's friends who continued to live in Vancouver's Chinatown. Father had lived in Chinatown for more than twenty-five years and was well-respected there, both as a clergyman and community leader. He also assisted in the building of the Lin Clan Association of Vancouver (first established in Victoria in 1908) and was elected the association's president in 1923.

Reverend George Lim Yuen leads a Chinese float in the Jubilee parade, 1935.

Father's career as an Anglican priest brought him a social prestige in white Canada that was denied to most of his Chinese countrymen. During this period of anti-Chinese hostility, the Church was perhaps the only avenue open to an ambitious Chinese youth who aspired to the respect due an educated man. Despite his achievements, however, Father remained a humble person and fiercely loyal to his Chinese friends. He taught me to honour them as elders and to always be courteous, because they were good, hard-working people who deserved my respect.

I empathized with the suffering experienced by so many first-generation Chinese immigrants. Canadians did not understand that these Chinese came from a country with a long and glorious history. They were discriminated against because China was sick – dominated and bullied by nations with superior military power. My hope then was for China to become strong one day, so that Chinese everywhere could regain their dignity. This intention, cultivated by my patriotic and morally demanding father, became my mission in life. My wonderfully wise and kind mother certainly nurtured my romanticism, sensitivity, and love of music and literature, but it was Father who shaped my destiny.

Chapter Two

A BUDDING SCHOLAR AND ORATOR

In 1919, the year before I was born, thousands of students from Beijing's universities marched into Tiananmen Square to protest the granting of Germany's colonies in Shandong Province to Japan by the Treaty of Versailles at the Paris Peace conference. This sparked the May Fourth Movement, a thirty-year struggle against foreign imperialism that would only be resolved with the founding of the People's Republic of China in 1949. The slogans of the day were "Down with the house of Confucius!" and "Up with Mr Science and Mr Democracy!" China's salvation required a wholesale modernization of politics, economics, education, and world view. Intellectuals and students would lead the way.

I grew up in the 1920s and 1930s always aware of China's political struggles, especially in the face of ongoing Japanese aggression that the Western powers tended to ignore, if not abet. Father and his friends followed events in China closely, having long supported the revolutionary party of Sun Yat-sen, who had visited Vancouver in 1897 and 1911 to raise funds. Chinese-Canadian newspapers hotly debated the issues. It was not until Japan's invasion of China in 1937, however, that I first spoke out publicly on these issues. As a Canadian of Chinese descent, I was deeply anguished by Japan's atrocities committed against the Chinese people. In January 1938, as Canadian foreboding of German and Japanese aggression grew, Rotary clubs in Vernon and Kelowna, as well as the Parent Teacher Association in Armstrong, invited me to address the Sino-Japanese conflict. I was only eighteen, a senior high school student, but my teachers knew that I was deeply informed on the issues and recommended that I speak.

The title of my speech was "The Background of the Present Situation in China." I will excerpt it at length here, for it records precisely what I was thinking and feeling about my ancestral homeland in January 1938.

Today, in the Far East, a struggle of tremendous magnitude is continuing to shock the senses of a world which thought it had known the most repugnant horrors of war after the paralyzing catastrophe of the World War. It is a saga of the heroic contest of an aroused people against aggression and tyranny. China, complacent Dragon of the ages, has awakened to new terrors ...

Never in ancient history had China met such a deliberate attempt to annihilate her, never before experienced the fullest horrors of modern warfare – of death rained indiscriminately from the skies, of deliberately planned massacres of defenseless women and children in congested areas by bursting bombs and scattering shrapnel, of wanton destruction of civilian property and educational centers. In the inferno of panic and terror that was once their villages, their homes, the hearts of old and young China alike turned to stone. For them the light of laughter had flickered out forever ...

As early as July 25, 1927, Japanese Premier Tanaka pronounced: "Japan cannot remove the difficulties in Eastern Asia unless she adopts a policy of Blood and Iron ... In order to conquer the world, we must first conquer China ... Then the world will realize that Eastern Asia is ours and will not dare to violate our rights."

From this, one can catch a glimpse of Japan's militaristic policy – this dream of an Asian Empire – of a world empire! [The Tanaka Memorial is no longer considered genuine.]

But what will be the consequences if Japan wins this war and dominates China? The contagion of aggressive militarism will spread rapidly to other nations. Democracy is gravely threatened today – but democracy and the peace of the nations are doomed if China falls ...

The Chinese people appeal to you, sane thinkers of a fortunate land blessed with peace and prosperity, to act before it is too late. China pleads not for pity – China scorns any pity – but China does ask for your humane and sympathetic understanding of a problem that affects us all – and to put that understanding into something concrete.

I am proud to be a Canadian – enjoying liberty of thought, of speech, of conscience – and I am also proud to be a Chinese – belonging to a civilization venerable with five thousand years of glorious traditions. I speak

China Defence League poster, 1938

for China because she needs the understanding, the moral support, and the invaluable assistance of this great Dominion whose shores are washed by the same mighty sea that crashes in ominous roar against the coasts of China.

I ended my speech by appealing for donations to the Red Cross, which would be forwarded to Hong Kong to assist in war relief.

Press reports on my speech were supportive and encouraging. Father said little, but I know he was pleased that the story of his war-torn China was being covered in the mainstream English media. Mother was quietly proud too, even if she did not entirely understand the speech. After more than twenty-five years in Canada, her English was still limited. I am glad that she lived to see her son stand before a Canadian audience and have his ideas about China received with respect. On May 14, 1938, Mother died of pneumonia at the age of fifty-six.

UNIVERSITY OF BRITISH COLUMBIA, 1938–1939

In sorrow and bereavement, I struggled through my final exams and was awarded both the Governor General's Medal for the district and a Royal Institution Scholarship to attend the University of British Columbia (UBC). In September I left Vernon for Vancouver, but was much concerned about leaving

Family portrait in May 1938, after Paul's mother had passed away. Seated, left to right: David, Father, Andrew. Standing: Helen and Paul

Father alone as a widower. My siblings had all left British Columbia: Margaret had married Peter Jue and now lived in Montreal; Helen was taking a nursing course in Alberta; David was attending medical school at McGill University; and Andrew was an aeronautical engineering student at the University of Minnesota. I promised Father that I would try to write every week and that I would always be more than glad to help, by typing his sermons, reports, or letters.

My first day at UBC was bewildering – thank goodness for several Chinese students who showed me about. I enrolled as an engineering student and attended three lectures my first morning, with homework already assigned! University was very different from high school in that students were expected to do everything on their own time. You either did the work or not, which was your own funeral.

UBC was a small school, but had a good reputation in several departments. The English course was reported to be among the very best in Canada and the engineering department was well respected, although it focused primarily on theory, with little practical training. Several Canadian friends from Vernon were at UBC and the Chinese students – all born in Canada – were quite friendly. There were twenty-three Chinese on campus and I was one of three freshmen. Automatically a member of the Chinese Students' Club, I much appreciated the reception they put on for new students.

When I first arrived, I spent two nights at the Hotel Stratford, where a room cost fifty cents per night. With Father's help, I then moved into the home of a fellow clergyman and paid five dollars per month for lodgings, not including meals. The house, while very nice, was on 13th Avenue just south of the new city hall, quite a distance from the university. I had lectures from Monday to Saturday, which required getting up shortly after seven o'clock, although I usually did not finish preparing for classes until after midnight. I walked four blocks to the streetcar line, paid seven cents fare to get to the university bus, paid another three cents fare, and finally arrived at the university about forty-five minutes later. If I needed breakfast, the cheapest was five cents worth of doughnuts and a five-cent glass of milk at the university cafeteria.

At noon I ate at a café, where a little roast beef and tea cost about twenty cents. If I had no evening classes and returned home to study, I would take another seven-cent streetcar to Chinatown to eat dinner at the Ho Sun Hing Restaurant, owned by Father's good friend Lup Hong. After dinner, it cost me a further seven cents to return. I could have eaten dinner locally for fourteen cents and saved myself the time of traveling to Chinatown, but Mr Hong's generosity was so kind that I usually made the trip. Coming from a small town, where I had slept, studied, and eaten all my meals at home, this was quite an adjustment. After a few weeks, however, I settled into a routine.

I thoroughly enjoyed my year at UBC and I made friendships that lasted a lifetime. Once I had my studies under control, I began to participate in campus activities, especially those focused on the political issues of the day. For me, that meant China under Japanese siege. I joined Vancouver's Chinese Youth Association (CYA) and participated in activities organized by the Student Christian Movement (SCM). I was attracted by the SCM's Social Gospel interpretation of Christianity and attended many of their events.

In the spring term of 1939 I was busy with several conferences. Over Easter weekend, five of us from the CYA attended the first Provincial Youth Congress, held in Vancouver. Two hundred delegates from various political, religious, cultural, and racial groups throughout the province gathered to discuss contemporary issues. I joined the Canadian Foreign Policy Committee, which verbally battled over principles of aggression, secret diplomacy, and the atrocious policy of appeasement. Arguing for a "Joint Embargo of War Materials to Aggressor Nations," my position was that moral, economic, and diplomatic censure was far more effective than war. If an embargo of scrap iron was placed upon Japan, the drop in US trade would be only 6.3% and the drop in Canadian trade would be only 2%. I felt sure that Western nations could sacrifice this piddling amount of revenue to assist China.

Several weeks later, the Pacific Northwest Embargo Conference was held in Vancouver, drawing delegates from Washington, Oregon, and British Columbia who represented a region of some 450,000 people. I spoke to the question, "Will the embargo not hurt the people of aggressor nations?" I said: "Permitting the shipping of war materials to aggressor Japan seems unwise in view of the fact that both the United States and Canada are concentrating their attention on Pacific Coast defenses ... We are now supplying materials, which may soon be used in extending aggression to this continent. The embargo cannot injure the Japanese people. Stopping Japanese militarists will serve to raise the Japanese masses out of their deplorable situation and allow the rise of democracy in Japan."

The final conference I attended that term was the Fourth Canadian Youth Congress for a United Canada, held in Winnipeg from June 30 to July 3, 1939. I was one of sixteen delegates chosen by the SCM from a dozen Vancouver youth organizations. Once again, the embargo issue was raised and once again I responded: "If the embargo did endanger the economic welfare of a few Japanese, that would be nothing compared to the millions of people who are being murdered, tortured, and raped in China. An embargo would be the lesser of two evils. It is a choice between a red war of bloodshed and a white war of economics!" I was in danger of becoming a broken record on the subject, but kept speaking up.

UNIVERSITY OF MICHIGAN, 1939–1943

Even before I arrived at UBC, I had begun looking for an American university with a large number of students from China. I wanted to know more about China firsthand and to learn Mandarin, but there were no China-born students at UBC. I searched American university catalogs; the Ivy League schools would naturally have Chinese students, but the tuition fees put them out of reach. I then discovered that the University of Michigan in Ann Arbor had welcomed Chinese students since 1893 and that eighty Chinese students were now studying there in many different fields. I applied in the fall of 1938 and matriculated the following September. Although I received a scholarship, money for room, board, books, and expenses was always a challenge. I paid for my first two years at Michigan by taking out loans and by working in the summer as the athletic director at Camp Birkett for Boys, near Ann Arbor. I enjoyed the work immensely and am proud to say that for two years in a row my cabin of boys received "Inspection Honours" for being the cleanest and tidiest in camp.

University of Michigan Chinese Students' Club, October 1941. Front, fourth from right: Paul (club president). Front, fifth from right: Dr Meng Chih (director of the China Institute, New York, which was set up during wartime to assist Chinese students in need)

During my third year, the university appointed me as staff assistant at a new men's dormitory to help first-year students and to keep the residence quiet in the evening. The annual stipend covered my room, but I still had to pay for my board. Such an appointment was considered prestigious for outstanding undergraduate and graduate students, so I accepted the offer. I supplemented my income by giving speeches on China and the war, organized by the university's extension department.

Father had firmly impressed upon his children, especially his sons, that in order to help China they had to learn concrete, practical skills at university. In his view, literature and history were for hobbies, not careers. After two years as an engineering student, however, I realized that my academic interests lay elsewhere. I thought that international law, which could be used to defend China's interests, might suit me and also be "serious enough" to satisfy Father. Fortunately, I had the strong support of my good friend and academic adviser Dr J. Raleigh Nelson, who wrote Father a moving letter on my behalf. It read in part:

I wonder if you can realize how greatly and wonderfully Paul has developed in his two years here. He has discovered in himself powers that none of us suspected. Much of this is, I believe, merely the natural fruitage of what you had given him both by inheritance and training. At least he has given you the credit for it all – his love for fine music and literature; his amazing facility in expressing himself; his real effectiveness as a speaker; his philosophical outlook and his beautiful Christian spirit ...

Knowing and loving China, knowing and loving him almost as my own son, I wonder constantly if he is not feeling in his soul the call to some spiritual or intellectual leadership for which his unusual gifts of mind and soul qualify him. I believe this is the case. I have greater confidence in this estimate of Paul because of the fact that for more than thirty years I was the adviser and guide of engineering students and I don't believe that is Paul's calling.

I certainly congratulate you on being the father of such a boy. One of the most beautiful things in his whole makeup is his respect for your wishes and his absorbing desire to realize fully all you aspire to see him achieve.

I was pleasantly surprised to receive an understanding letter from Father when I returned from my summer job at Camp Birkett in mid-August 1941.

My Son,

Dr Nelson praised you highly. From his words, I can tell that he is a very sincere, kind, and sensitive counselor, who tries to lead our Chinese students along the right path. It gives me great comfort to know that my son has the opportunity to be studying at a university where there are such professors with both knowledge and virtues to guide him.

As to which discipline you may wish to go into, please assess your own abilities and decide for yourself. But you must work hard no matter what field you choose, until you have reached your goal. Most importantly, is to study something solid that will be useful to the world, and benefit others as well as yourself. When you have made up your mind, please let me know.

Father

WAR RELIEF WORK AND PEARL HARBOR

In the fall of 1941, I was elected president of the Chinese Students' Club. Our first event was a formal dance in celebration of Double Ten (October 10), the thirtieth anniversary of the founding of the Republic of China. University faculty and students were invited to attend. The theme of the event stressed the need for closer political and cultural relations between the United States and China, as the fifth year of the Sino-Japanese War ground on. Proceeds from the dance were donated to United China Relief to purchase medical and relief supplies for China's 45 million war refugees.

After Japan attacked Pearl Harbor on December 7, 1941, the Chinese students at the University of Michigan immediately adopted a resolution to be presented to President Franklin D. Roosevelt through the university's president, Alexander G. Ruthven. The resolution pledged our wholehearted support to assist, by closely cooperating with the defense effort at the university and elsewhere, to prosecute the war against this common enemy. Further, we reaffirmed our belief, held by all Chinese students whether in the United States or China, in the immutable principles of freedom, justice, and democracy. We expressed our deep conviction that the people of China, with the people of America, Britain, and the other democracies at their side, would never falter until these principles had prevailed.

President Ruthven added his own endorsement, expressing his appreciation for the loyalty of the Chinese students, and submitted our resolution to the office of the US President. Within a month, he received a warm acknowledgment from the White House, which he forwarded to the Chinese Students' Club.

PUBLIC SPEAKING AND THE 1942 NORTHERN ORATORICAL LEAGUE CONTEST

Soon after I arrived at the University of Michigan in September 1939, I was asked to give public talks about China, as I had in British Columbia. Word of mouth led to more invitations than I could accept as a full-time student, and the university extension department kindly stepped in to help me organize speaking tours on the war. At that time I legally changed my name from Paul Lim Yuen to Paul Ta-Kuang (T.K.) Lin, which in Chinese means "Advancement of Light through the Forest." Having a proper Chinese name, spoken in Mandarin, was a major step in confirming my identity as a modern Chinese intellectual.

My audiences included high school students, parent-teacher associations, Rotary and Kiwanis clubs, business and church groups, and YMCAs. I traveled to large cities like Detroit and Grand Rapids and to small towns like Mount Clemens, Hastings, and Grand Haven. To save time, nearly all my talks were extemporaneous, without notes. Public response was positive. The president of the Mount Clemens Rotary Club, Harold Lindsey, sent me a letter in February 1942 thanking me for having "rendered a service to China and the Chinese people and to America and the American people, in promoting a better understanding of these two great nations and their peoples. We need more and more and yet more of such understanding in this world. You are a disciple of such promotion of understanding."

From these talks to grassroots communities in Michigan, I gained a firsthand understanding of the concerns and aspirations of people in middle America during those difficult war years. It also allowed me to refine my public speaking skills. In April 1942, I won the University of Michigan's speech contest in Ann Arbor, which enabled me to compete as the university's representative at the larger collegiate competition of the Northern Oratorical League, held near Chicago in May. Speakers came from the universities of Michigan, Minnesota, Iowa, Northwestern Reserve, and Wisconsin. I was awarded first place and received a $100 prize. The *Michigan Daily* headline on May 3 read, "Paul T.K. Lin Captures First in Oratorical Contest ... An Eloquent Plea for Faith in World Democracy Wins Every Judge."

I had chosen "The Pacific Charter" as the title of my address, echoing the declarations in the "Atlantic Charter" – a blueprint of the goals and aims of the Allied powers for the post-war world – drawn up by British Prime Minister Winston Churchill and US President Franklin D. Roosevelt. It had been published on August 14, 1941. "The Pacific Charter" pleaded for the liberation of all peoples, including those in Asia. These were issues about which I felt deeply and my speech was written at a time when the world increasingly was engulfed in murderous warfare. "The Pacific Charter" read in part:

> I must speak frankly to you today, not in bitterness, but because, having lived in America, I love America. And loving America, and hoping for the common salvation of both America and China, at this dark hour I must speak to you as I would to my own people, without reserve. If I offend, I shall ask your forgiveness. But I shall also be gratified that the offense will have attested to a truth sent home.
>
> I want first to tell you that my people have been fighting this war not for five months, but for ten years. For them, Pearl Harbor was not enacted on December 7, 1941. It was enacted on September 18, 1931, at Mukden, in Manchuria. It was enacted again for 88 bloody days in Shanghai, the following year. It was enacted again at Lukouchuao in North China on July 7, 1937. Pearl Harbor has been enacted ever since in every unholy

act of drug distribution, incendiarism, outrage, and murder in 800,000 square miles of Japanese-penetrated territory. How I could tell you the whole ghoulish tale of those ten years of agony – the Rape of Nanking, the sack of Hankow, the bombings of Canton and Chungking, where the casualty lists alone would dwarf the total of all the other bombed cities of the world put together ...

Imagine this great university bombed from the air, invaded by foreign troops, these great halls converted into military headquarters and torture chambers and enemy barracks. Imagine yourselves, together with students from your sister universities in the east and midwest, trekking on foot for over 1,000 miles to establish yourselves again in universities dug in the hillsides of Nevada. You can then appreciate what has happened to over 90% of China's universities and colleges since the Japanese descended upon them. Imagine fifty million starving refugees, over one-third of your total population, driven by war from the Atlantic and Pacific seaboards, into interior states like Utah, Colorado, Wyoming, and Nevada, there to find their only subsistence. You can then approach a correct view of the colossal migration into Free China ...

Ten years ago, in Manchuria, the Chinese nation filed into the front line trenches of democracy. At first, they too knew little what they were fighting for in terms of principles ... But when the Japanese bombers came and blasted the cities out of existence, when the Japanese tanks came and drove the peasant from the land that he tilled, the Chinese people suddenly found their false security destroyed. Then they knew that if they were to fight on, it would not be for the destructible institutions their hands had raised, not for an earth that could be rendered sterile, but for the deeper, elemental things of the spirit, indestructible and creative – freedom, democracy, equality and tolerance, truth and morality for all men – the final principles that must never be violated by the invaders ...

They turned hopefully to the Western democracies, which they had always deemed to be the stronghold of these principles of faith. They appealed for aid to save their idealism by stopping the Japanese. But the great Western powers literally rejected the appeal, and in effect helped turn the Articles of the League [of Nations] Covenant, the Kellogg Peace Pact, the Nine-Power Washington Treaty, into waste paper in which was destined to be wrapped and discarded nearly every international code set up by the nations. In the tragic years that followed 1931, while China pleaded for Western recognition of the global implications of Japan's expansion, America and the British Empire supplied on the one hand nearly 100% of Japan's war needs, while on the other, nearly 100% of China's medical supplies. It was as if the West were enjoying a sadistic drama in which the victim needed to be given new leases on life that the drama could go on. And to obtain places as spectators in the gallery of nations, they paid exorbitant prices in ideals ...

I know these are bold utterances. Forgive me if they pain you. But my people have a right to speak – however unworthily I represent them. Before any Atlantic Charter was set up to marshal the scattered moral forces of Atlantic nations (for such indeed had come to be its purpose), my people had written a Pacific Charter for their nation and all democratic nations without exclusion. It is a Charter, not a facsimile of the Atlantic Charter, not written in ink, but written in the blood of five millions of China's manhood. And the parchment is her scorched earth, the pen the indomitable will of her people. That Charter is not set up in eight meticulously worded points. It is etched deep into the daily thinking of her people, from the humblest peasant to Generalissimo Chiang Kai-shek himself. And the clear, unfettered terms of this Pacific Charter might well have said: "We hold these truths to be self-evident, that all men are created equal; and that they are endowed by their Creator with certain inalienable rights, and among these are Life, Liberty, and the Pursuit of Happiness"

China is at her Valley Forge. She is confident of final victory for this ideal, because she is confident of America, the America whence came the re-emphasized, dynamic philosophy for the moral resurgence of her people. If only America could see – could see herself as the Chinese people have seen her in the past one hundred years – the true America, in the role of mighty champion, towering among the nations, with justice and liberty and equality and democracy emblazoned on her escutcheon – names that spell neither national nor racial creed, but the creed of mankind ...

Not only China, but all Asia, is looking toward America. Let there be a definite assurance of her spiritual return to the dynamic, unalloyed idealism that we believe to represent the real America, and a thousand Asian armies would move with her and China to fight for a world empire of freedom. I adjure you to believe me, a continent and a billion men and women have cast you in the greatest role in the most soul-stirring drama of all times, O America! We are, in the words of Matthew Arnold, "wandering between two worlds, one dead / The other powerless to be born." The world of yesterday is dead indeed – cremated in the consuming fires of great-bombed cities. At this hour, reaffirm your faith, O America!

Upon you depend the light and the life of the coming world! This is the message, and this is the exhortation, of the Pacific Charter!

The first person I shared my good tidings with was, of course, Father. He rejoiced with me, but also imparted some words of wisdom.

May 2, 1942
Victoria, BC

Ta-Kuang, my son:

At 9:30 this morning, CP Telegraph delivered your telegram. When I read the good news that you were awarded first place by all the judges ... I was so happy and excited that I found myself clapping with pride and joy ...

But I hope my son will not become self-satisfied or conceited because of this wonderful success. I would like to see you continue to be a person of principles and virtues, and treat others with modesty, sincerity, and decency. I also hope that you will persevere in your studies until you have reached the final goal so that you could serve your country and improve the lives of the people.

With my blessings for a future of great progress,
Father

I was pleasantly surprised when Father sent me clippings about the contest from the English and Chinese media in Vancouver. The *Vancouver Daily Province* reported on June 13, 1942, "Vancouver Chinese Wins US Honour." Father was particularly pleased when he received a warm letter of congratulations from the Right Rev. Arthur H. Sovereign, Anglican bishop of the diocese of Athabasca, who commented: "The honour is so much the greater for he has had to compete with Anglo-Saxon students who have had the advantage of a [family] background of education in the English language." The Provincial Board of Missions to Orientals in BC even passed a resolution at the end of 1942, sending congratulations to both Father and myself.

Delta Sigma Rho bestowed upon me membership in their national honour society of orators, placing me in the company of scholars like Wellington Koo and many distinguished American leaders. Soon after, the Redpath Bureau in Chicago signed me on to give lectures across the country. In their promotional materials they quoted Professor C.C. Cunningham of Northwestern University, who wrote:

As the Unanimous Winner of First Prize in the Northern Oratorical League Contest at Northwestern University, May 1, 1942, Representing the University of Michigan, He Was Nothing Less than a SENSATION.

The Redpath Bureau's publicity sheet introducing Paul as winner of first prize in the Northern Oratorical League Contest, May 1942

PAUL T. K. LIN

Brilliant Young Chinese Scholar and Interpreter of the Asiatic Scene. One of the Outstanding Orators of His Race— "Should Be Heard Throughout the Length and Breadth of Our Land"

THE REDPATH BUREAU
1316 Kimball Bldg., CHICAGO, ILL., Telephone Harrison 8723

Never, in fact, during my thirty-odd years of experience of listening to student speakers have I heard one who surpassed Paul T.K. Lin. He is, indeed, a man with a message for American audiences in this period of crisis. I feel that he is better qualified than almost any other person, not even excepting those of greater maturity, to tell about the part that China has played and is playing in this war. Moreover, he has given thoughtful consideration to the problem of what the world should be like after the war, and what he has to say in this connection should be heard throughout the length and breadth of our land. Best of all, he presents his knowledge and ideas in perfectly ordered fashion, in language that is direct, forceful, vivid, and in speech that represents cultivated refined English at its best, as a medium of oral communication.

Redpath Bureau speaking fees would help to pay my bills during the next seven years of my graduate education.

I graduated in January 1943 from the University of Michigan with an Honours BA degree. In March, the University of Michigan chapter of Phi Kappa Phi elected me a member "in recognition of excellence in scholarship, participation in campus activities, and service to the university." I was

父親大人惠存

To Dad

男
蓬光敬贈

Palmer
ANN ARBOR

Affectionately
Paul
January 23, 1943
Ann Arbor

Paul graduates from the University of Michigan with an honours degree, January 1943.

awarded two scholarships to pursue further studies at the Fletcher School of Law and Diplomacy (jointly administered by Tufts and Harvard universities) and the Harvard University Graduate School of Government. Father made a special trip from Canada to Ann Arbor to attend my graduation, a difficult feat during wartime. Seeing him again, I felt profound gratitude for his constant support and recognized anew his pivotal influence in shaping my aspirations and achievements.

Prior to my graduation from the University of Michigan in January 1943, I had met and courted Eileen Siu-tsung Chen, a young Chinese woman from Shanghai. We married in Ann Arbor in June 1944 and she joined me in Cambridge, Massachusetts, where, after completing my master's degree at the Fletcher School of Law and Diplomacy, I was working on my doctorate at Harvard University. Eileen and her family were critical to the unfolding of my life's journey. Despite Father's training in the Chinese classics and history, I had never lived in China and was only slowly becoming proficient in Mandarin. In the next two chapters, Eileen recounts the story of her parents and her childhood, and the path that brought her in June 1941 to Chicago where we met at a Chinese Students' Christian Association (CSCA) conference.

Chapter Three

CHINA FAMILY

BY EILEEN CHEN SHU LIN

MOTHER, CHOMING TSAI

✑ My mother, Choming Tsai, was born in October 1889 in Dayu County, the hilly home of tungsten mines, situated at the southwestern tip of Jiangxi Province, central China. Her father was the magistrate of Dayu and, as the county chief, was able to provide his family with an idyllic provincial lifestyle. The Tsais had seven children, five boys and two girls. Choming was the younger daughter and the sixth child. A private tutor was engaged to teach the children the Chinese classics, literature, and calligraphy. All were taught the importance of education at an early age.

When Mother was ten years old, the family's comfortable life abruptly ended. My grandfather Tsai was dismissed from office over an unruly subordinate who had joined the Catholic Church to avoid being punished for extorting money from the villagers. Because of this man's foreign connections, Grandfather had hesitated to discipline the culprit, but mounting local outrage led his superiors to dismiss Magistrate Tsai for incompetence.

Since Dayu was no longer a haven, Grandfather Tsai moved his family south to a small town named Nanan, then departed alone for Guangdong Province to seek employment. With little news from him and no financial support, the family felt abandoned. They survived on money from the sale of their possessions at the pawnshops, but when nothing of value was left, they were forced to seek refuge at the home of Grandmother Tsai's widowed sister-in-law, Mrs Bao – an affluent relation in Nanchang, the capital of

Jiangxi Province. For three long years, the Tsai family had to endure the humiliation of living under someone else's roof. Not only did they experience harsh poverty, but they had to surrender their dignity in exchange for charity that provided them with life's essentials, but not much else.

The circumstances that befell my mother's family were a microcosm of the social upheaval taking place in China in the decades after the Sino-British Opium War. By 1899, China's door had been forced open for almost sixty years by the military might of the Western powers and Japan. In their wake came missionaries – some to do good deeds, others to share in the spoils. A weak and corrupt Manchu Dynasty was preyed upon by one foreign country after another over trade and territorial demands. China was forced to sign a series of unequal treaties that bankrupted the nation. The aggressors then branded China the "Sick Man of the East."

Finally, Grandfather Tsai found work in Anhui Province and was able to send two-thirds of his salary home to support his family. Although life was still hard, Grandmother Tsai was able to gradually pay off their debts to the Baos and restore the family honour.

After China's disastrous defeat by Japan in 1895, a yearning for change swept like a tidal wave across the land, including calls for the emancipation of women. Influenced by the missionaries, the reformers' first prong of attack was against the ten-century-old custom of foot binding. They next promoted modern schools for girls, to equip them with professional skills and to help them become the educated wives and mothers of the next generation. Mother and her elder sister Yimin desperately wanted to attend such a school, but limited finances forced them to continue their education through self-study at home.

Unexpectedly, the Tsai sisters' dream was realized in the spring of 1904, when they accompanied their mother on a visit to Dr Ida Kang, the only woman doctor of Western medicine in Nanchang. Dr Kang had been orphaned, adopted, and raised by an American lady missionary, who sent her to the University of Michigan to study medicine. She then returned to Nanchang to practice medicine and spread the Christian gospel.

Dr Kang cured Grandmother Tsai's bursitis after several treatments and in the process came to know Yimin and Choming well. She was so impressed by their good manners, intelligence, and fervent desire for further education that she arranged scholarships for the sisters to study at a missionary middle school in Jiujiang, some one hundred miles north of Nanchang. Their parents consented only after making the girls promise never to become Christians.

Yimin fulfilled her vow, but Choming, more curious and independent by
nature, converted soon after attending the school's church service. Her
parents were very displeased, gave her the biggest scolding of her life, and
forbade her to come home on holidays. To them, Choming's primary alle-
giance to God was an insult and a disavowal of the traditional value of filial
piety. Choming accepted her punishment in silence, but did not relinquish
her faith.

A year before her graduation in 1908, Yimin married Yao Qizi of Anhui
Province in an arranged marriage. Dr Kang was disappointed: she had
hoped that after graduation the girls would help with her medical and missionary work. However, Yao came from a large feudal bureaucratic family
and was chief of police in the Chinese sector of Shanghai. A man of wealth
and influence, his generosity to his wife's family helped to turn the Tsais'
fortunes around.

In June 1910, Choming graduated from the Rulison Middle School. She
taught school for two years to save enough to study in Japan for a year.
Then, with the help of her brother-in-law, she left for the United States in
1913 to attend college. She soon realized that the US$1,000 she had bor-
rowed from Yao would not last long. With one dollar, she bought a stack
of postcards and applied to as many colleges as she could find, looking for a
program that would allow her to study and also work part time. Finally, she
received a positive reply from Miami University in Oxford, Ohio. This small
college, without a single Chinese student on campus, welcomed Choming
with open arms in the fall of 1914. Recognizing her financial hardship, the
university not only granted her a full scholarship, but also found her free
lodging at the campus YWCA, allowing her to devote her attention to her
studies. She majored in sociology, specializing in juvenile delinquency.
During her senior year she took a Bible class taught by a Miss Elizabeth
Matthews, who took Choming under her wing.

Choming graduated from Miami University in the summer of 1917 and
entered Ohio State University in Columbus, to pursue a master's degree
in social work. In addition to a scholarship from Ohio State to cover her
tuition, Miss Matthews provided her with a monthly stipend to cover her
living expenses. Gratefully, she accepted her mentor's generosity as a loan
to be repaid at some future date.

FATHER, JIANAN H. CHEN

Father was born in January 1890 in Zhejiang Province, on the east coast of China. He was raised in the village of Diankou, Shaoxing County, renowned for China's best rice wine. Jianan was the youngest of a large farming family of nine children, three boys and six girls.

Their father, my grandpa Chen, was determined to give his sons the good education denied to him due to the tragic deaths of his parents during the Taiping Rebellion (1851–64). He groomed his eldest son to run the family business and paid for his second son to be tutored in the Chinese classics and martial arts. Sadly, this promising young man died at twenty from consumption. Grief stricken, Grandpa Chen soon passed away, reducing the family to poverty.

Although very bright, Jianan was not interested in studying until he was fifteen years old, having too much fun playing. Around 1905, in the aftermath of the Boxer Rebellion, a modern primary school opened in Diankou village, attracting many of his playmates. Suddenly alone, Jianan began to worry about his future, and decided he must go to school. The principal refused his application, because he was known as an unruly pupil. Jianan begged his mother for help and through the intervention of his uncle, a school trustee, he was accepted. It took him only two years to complete all the courses in the primary school.

Since there was no local middle school, village elders sent Jianan to Japan to learn papermaking, for there was an abundance of bamboo in Diankou. A bad harvest the following year emptied the village coffers, however, and the paper project was abandoned. Jianan returned to China, managed to get a scholarship, and graduated with distinction from a public school in Shanghai.

He then spent a year teaching at a middle school in Kaifeng, Henan Province, to earn some money before taking the university entrance examinations in China. He hoped to attend Qinghua University in Beijing, which offered opportunities to study abroad. However, due to his financial straits, he became trapped in a loveless engagement in Shanghai with a Miss Yen Shufeng, whose parents had no son but four daughters. They offered Jianan financial help through college, provided that he would become their son and support them in their old age. Jianan promised to take care of them, but neither he nor his mother was willing for him to be adopted as the Yens' son. Accepting his terms, the Yens then insisted that Jianan remain in Shanghai to attend St John's, an American missionary university.

The engagement soured early on, not least because the Yen girls took every opportunity to humiliate the poverty-stricken Jianan. Seeking solace from his misery, he attended the college's church service one Sunday, where he found a degree of peace and comfort for his troubled heart. He soon became a Christian.

Just before Father's graduation in 1917, Dr Francis H. Pott – president of St John's – encouraged him to apply for a Zhejiang provincial scholarship (derived from the Boxer Rebellion Indemnity Fund) to continue his studies abroad. The university lent him the train fare to Beijing to take the examination. He was third among the top ten students selected and was awarded a scholarship to study for a master's degree in the United States.

Jianan was a happy man in 1917 when he boarded a steamer in Shanghai to carry him across the Pacific Ocean to San Francisco. Nightmares of debt gradually ceased to haunt him and he eagerly awaited the dawn of a new life in America. Upon learning that Ohio State University was noted for banking and chemistry, the two subjects he wished to pursue, he headed for Columbus, Ohio.

CHOMING AND JIANAN – PARTNERS FOR LIFE

Shortly after arriving at Ohio State University, Jianan received a letter from Miss Yen in Shanghai bluntly telling him that she had never loved him and wanted their engagement annulled. This was followed by a blackmail attempt from her wealthy brother-in-law, who threatened to have Jianan's government scholarship withdrawn if he did not return immediately to be married. The family's machinations infuriated Jianan, who immediately ended the engagement, while promising to repay his debts to Miss Yen's parents when he returned to China. Disagreeable as this episode was, Jianan felt great relief at being a "free man" again.

Of the seventeen students from China at Ohio State, the only woman was Choming Tsai. Jianan and Choming met in a banking class and became friends through the Chinese students' club. Their friendship blossomed into love and they became engaged. By the summer of 1918, each had completed a master's degree. Jianan then enrolled at Columbia University in New York City to study banking under Dr Henry Parker Willis, first secretary of the US Federal Reserve Board. Dr Willis became his mentor and employed him to collect data for the US government on how France had preserved its currency system during World War I. When the project was completed, he

Eileen's parents, Choming Tsai and Jianan Chen, at Ohio State University, 1917

arranged for Jianan to do a six-month internship at the New York Foreign Exchange Bank, starting as a junior clerk and working his way up to the general manager's office. Meanwhile, Choming took courses at Columbia's Teachers' College and worked part-time at the university library.

Soon after World War I, the Chinese government sent Xu Rong Guang to the United States to negotiate a loan from the US government to set up a Sino-US bank. Xu turned to Willis for advice, asking him to suggest the names of promising young men who might be willing to work for his private bank in China. Willis recommended Jianan, who was offered a job as department head of business operations at the Shanghai branch of Xu's Mouye Bank. Upon his accepting the position, Jianan and Choming were married in New York. Their first baby, my brother John (Yunsheng), was born in New York City in December. The family left for China in February 1921 on a Canadian *Empress* liner.

Setting foot in Shanghai after so many years abroad was a rude awakening. Little had changed since the founding of the Republic in 1911 by Sun

Yat-sen. Foreign powers were still entrenched in all the major cities, each
with its own concessions and legal jurisdictions outside of Chinese law.
Internally, China remained partitioned among the warlords; as a country
it was weak and riddled with corruption.

Now that Jianan was gainfully employed, the couple's first task was to
pay off their debts, beginning with the sum owed to the family of Jianan's
former fiancée. They also had a duty to support their aging parents. The
only housing they could afford in Shanghai was in the Chinese sector, without electricity and running water. The few savings they had brought back
from America were soon exhausted. Jianan took on a second job, teaching
chemistry at Fudan University's night school three evenings per week.

A year later, the Mouye Bank's head office in Beijing sent Father to Hankou, Hupei Province, to audit the books of the local branch. Two weeks of
intensive investigation uncovered the loss of millions of yuan from bad loans
and corruption. Jianan was promoted to manager of the Hankou branch,
with instructions to restructure the bank and make it profitable. In September 1922, Choming closed up their home in Shanghai and with their baby
son joined Jianan in Hankou. By the end of 1925, the bank had netted a
handsome profit and Jianan was given a bonus of five thousand yuan. By
this time Choming had also given birth to three daughters – Mary Siu-fen
in 1922, Eileen Siu-tsung in 1924, and Louise Siu-duan in 1925.

During the period when my parents lived in Hankou, from 1922 to 1925,
warlords backed by various foreign powers wreaked havoc in different parts
of the country. Sun Yat-sen, who in 1919 had reorganized the nationalist
party – Kuomintang (KMT) – was based in Canton and had formed a fragile
alliance with the fledgling Chinese Communist Party (CCP), which had been
established in 1921. He still hoped to unify the country through peaceful
means and agreed in late 1924 to attend a conference in Beijing hosted by
three leading warlords – the "Christian General" Feng Yuxiang, Duan Qirui,
and Zhang Zuolin. Sadly, before any agreement could be reached, Dr Sun
died from liver cancer on March 12, 1925. Fifteen months later, Chiang
Kai-shek, commander of the KMT army, launched the Northern Expedition
to rout out the warlords and unify the country under a single government.
As the flames of war drew ever closer to Hankou, Jianan and Choming
agreed that she should take the children to Shanghai to ensure their safety.
By November 1926, KMT forces had captured Hankou, and established
the seat of the new government in Wuhan, the tripartite city of Hankou,
Hanyang, and Wuchang. In an effort to control all financial resources, the

KMT then froze the assets of all the local banks. This presented Jianan with a major dilemma, as the Mouye Bank's new chairman of the board defied the order and continued to release fixed deposits for better returns – a crime punishable by death. Jianan refused to carry out this directive and was ordered back to Shanghai. He immediately resigned. Subsequently the head office appointed a new Chinese manager to sit alongside a foreigner, whose major purpose was to scare off the warlords and KMT with the implied threat of "extraterritorial" military force.

Soon after, an acquaintance contacted Jianan at home and told him that the new KMT finance minister, T.V. Soong, had learned of Jianan's banking expertise and wanted to consult him about the ongoing devaluation of banknotes issued in Guangzhou. Soong was also considering setting up a central bank, a proposal that very much interested Father. In his view, a strong financial system was vital to the defeat of the warlords and the unification of China.

Finance Minister Soong asked Jianan to begin work immediately on founding a central bank. Jianan became general manager of the bank and, concurrently, director of the mint. On the new bank's opening day, crowds rushed in to exchange their Guangzhou banknotes. The bank had sufficient funds to meet its obligations and there was no run on the bank, as feared. The government had stabilized the currency, at least for the time being.

While excited by the idea of making a contribution to the revival of China, Jianan and Choming knew there were enormous risks in aligning themselves with the emerging Nationalist government; the warlords had yet to be defeated. Only later did they realize that they would also be pulled into the vortex of bitter power struggles within the KMT which lasted for several decades.

Jianan and Choming belonged to the generation that had grown up in the dying years of the Qing Dynasty. They had witnessed the degradation and suffering of the Chinese people at the hands of foreign powers and unscrupulous warlords. Their sympathy was always on the side of the Chinese people, but both had missed the May 4, 1919, patriotic youth movement due to their studies in the United States. They were strong nationalists, but not political activists.

Despite its successes in Wuhan, the KMT government was riven by intrigues, as Sun Yat-Sen had not designated a clear successor prior to his death. Chiang Kai-shek, president of the Whampoa Military Academy and commander-in-chief of the Northern Expedition, eventually emerged as the

supreme "strongman." In addition to his military "brothers," Chiang also
enjoyed the backing of powerful secret societies and wealthy bankers in
Shanghai and Zhejiang Province, who distrusted the KMT's alliance with the
CCP. Throwing in his lot with these supporters, Chiang unleashed a surprise
massacre in Shanghai on April 12, 1927. Thousands of workers, intellectuals,
and young Communists – who had helped Chiang's troops enter the city –
were killed or went missing. A week later, Chiang set up a rival KMT regime
in Nanjing. When the Wuhan KMT government expelled him from all his
positions, Chiang launched a blockade of the Yangtze River, which cut off
Wuhan's industrial base from its markets in Shanghai and disrupted its
supply lines of necessary raw materials. The subsequent economic chaos
alarmed foreign investors and Chinese industrialists, and radicalized workers
and unions in Hankou. The latter struck for higher pay; some even waged
class struggles to settle scores with their bosses. Owing to a shortage of
silver, the mint could not produce enough currency to meet demand. A new
financial crisis loomed.

Finance Minister T.V. Soong left Wuhan on business, but was prevented
from returning by Chiang Kai-shek. In view of these unsettling political developments, Jianan urged Choming to take the children and find refuge in
Shanghai. They rented a house in the French Concession and Jianan resumed
teaching at Fudan University.

Chiang Kai-shek detained T.V. Soong for personal as well as political
reasons: he wanted to marry Mei Ling Soong, T.V.'s youngest sister, but T.V.
did not trust Chiang, and opposed the union. Under Chiang's political and
economic pressure, however, Soong succumbed and was reinstated as minister of finance and governor of the Central Bank of the Nanjing regime,
effectively controlling its treasury and economy.

T.V.'s widowed mother, Mrs Charlie Soong, was also against the marriage
because Chiang was not a Christian and had previous marriages. She gave
her consent only after Chiang declared to her that he had renounced his former nuptial relationships and also promised to study the Bible and become
a Christian.

In July 1927, Wang Jingwei of the Wuhan KMT government capitulated
and, following Chiang Kai-shek's example, purged the Communists from the
Kuomintang and massacred militant workers, peasants, and intellectuals. He
then brokered a deal to merge the Wuhan KMT government with Chiang's
new regime in Nanjing. Only a few holdouts in the Wuhan government
refused to cooperate with Chiang Kai-shek, including Sun's young widow –

A banknote issued by the Central Bank of China in 1930, featuring a sketch of Sun Yat-sen's mausoleum in Nanjing. The seals were those of the bank's governor and deputy governor; Jianan's seal is on the left.

The Chen home in the French Concession, Shanghai, pictured here in the 1930s

Madame Soong Ching Ling. She declined Nanjing's offers of high office and went abroad in protest.

In 1928, the Central Bank in Shanghai formally opened on the waterfront Bund, alongside the big foreign trading houses and banks. T.V. Soong appointed Jianan as deputy governor of the Central Bank and, again, director of the mint. At thirty-eight years of age, Jianan had reached the apex of his banking career. Gone were the days of economic insecurity. To accommodate

一九三七年十二月十日在漢口留影

The last reunion of the Chen family in Hankou, December 1937. Standing, left to right: Eileen's two brothers, father, mother, and two sisters; Eileen stands second from the right.

a growing household of children, nannies, and servants, Jianan and Choming bought a house in the French Concession, No. 20 Rue Portier. It was a two-story English Tudor, surrounded by a well-tended garden on three sides that included a goldfish pond. This was the house I grew up in until the summer of 1937, when Japan attacked Shanghai.

Choming's fifth and last child was a son born in 1928 – George (Chen Lisheng). She was not content to be just a wife and mother, however. When the Japanese first attacked Shanghai in 1932, she volunteered at hospitals to care for the sick and wounded. Our home became a mini-workshop where she and her friends gathered to make bandages and clothing for the front. In August 1937, following Japan's brutal invasion of China, she shepherded us children to safety in Diankou and then initiated a fundraising drive to expand the village's only primary school (where Father had been a student in his youth), to accommodate the hundreds of refugee children flocking to Diankou with their families.

Despite my parents' turbulent life, my childhood was happy and free of worries. Father was a good provider, generous, kind, and mild in temper. He left the education and discipline of the children entirely to Mother, who was caring but strict. She exhorted us to study hard, finish our college education, and conduct ourselves by a code of Christian ethics. She shielded us not only from the horror of war, but also from her own pain over Father's occasional philandering. She never quarreled with Father, nor criticized him in front of us. We were taught to respect and appreciate him as head of the family. Father was the love of Mother's life and she was his tower of strength. ⚘

Chapter Four

TWO LIVES ENTWINED

BY EILEEN CHEN SHU LIN

Poor health in infancy and childhood left me a class behind my age group when I began my formal education in 1932 at McTyeire's Number Two Primary School, founded by American Southern Methodist missionaries. Although it was a private school for the daughters of Shanghai's elite and was located near our home in the French Concession, my sixth-grade teacher, Miss Yang Guangmin, was a passionate patriot. She gave her students a solid grounding in recent Chinese history, teaching us about the suffering and humiliation imposed on the Chinese people by foreign predators for more than a century. She instilled in me a fervent desire to help China become strong, so that foreigners would never again bully the Chinese people.

My high school education was rudely interrupted in August 1937, when Japanese gunboats and aircraft bombarded Shanghai's Chinese sector to gain a foothold for their invasion of central China. Father remained at his post as deputy governor of the Central Bank in Shanghai, but later retreated with the Chinese government to Hankou and eventually to the wartime capital of south-central Zhongqing. He lived there throughout the war, leaving only when the Japanese surrendered in 1945. Mother was in charge of our safety. After a brief stay in Father's childhood village of Diankou, she took us to Hong Kong and then, one by one, sent us abroad to study in the United States. In May 1939, I left Hong Kong on the *Empress of Japan* to continue my education in California.

Mother placed me under the guardianship of two missionaries who had co-founded the Bethel Mission in Shanghai. Dr Mary Stone was Chinese; Miss Jennie V. Hughes was an American. Their mission was nondenomina-

tional and focused primarily on evangelical work, but Dr Stone, an obstetri-
cian trained at the University of Michigan, also maintained a hospital in the
mission's Shanghai compound. When my mother was stricken with typhoid
fever in the early 1930s, Father had engaged day and night nurses from the
Bethel Hospital to care for her at home.

After Japan invaded Shanghai, the Bethel Mission moved to Hong Kong
to establish a bible school, but in 1939 Dr Stone and Miss Hughes decided
to return to the United States with their three adopted daughters: Mary
and Grace were both Chinese; Norma was a Caucasian from Nicaragua. Dr
Stone was related by marriage to Mrs T.V. Soong, who asked her to take her
teenage daughter, Loretta, to the United States. My mother figured that if
the Soongs trusted the two missionary ladies to take care of their daughter,
so could she. Where Loretta was treated like a "princess," however, I was
treated more like a paying ward.

So it was that I left my warm and loving home for the first time, at age fifteen, to live among strangers in a Pasadena, California bungalow. Dr Stone
was gentle and reasonable, but Miss Hughes was unpredictable – fanatically
religious with a domineering streak. The two women addressed each other
affectionately as "darling" and "dearie," each playing a different role in the
household. Dr Stone made speeches about China to church groups, which
generated fees and donations. Miss Hughes took care of reports and correspondence and supervised us girls. She made sure we thanked the Lord for
our daily bread at every meal, attended her evening Bible class, and said
our prayers before bedtime.

I was enrolled in a public high school, which I quite enjoyed. Although
I spoke limited English, the teachers and my classmates were friendly and
helpful. I did my best to fit in, studied diligently, helped around the house,
respected my guardians, and befriended the other girls. I wanted to be a
credit to my parents. There was, however, no privacy under Miss Hughes'
probing eye. She insisted on knowing everything about me, which included
reading letters from my family. To keep my parents truly informed, I re-
sorted to using a classmate's home address for my private mail. Beneath the
apparent calm of our daily routine, I became increasingly fearful of Miss
Hughes. She would suddenly lash out with wild accusations and force the
unfortunate victim to admit her "sin," whether she had committed a wrong
or not. I found this behavior shocking as I had never felt the need to hide
anything from my parents. Increasingly unhappy, I wrote home and was
rescued by one of Father's friends in Los Angeles, who enabled me to leave
California in late December 1939 to join my sister Mary at Western College

Eileen as a student at St Margaret's Hall
School for Girls in Versailles, Kentucky, seated
with Mother's friend Elizabeth Matthews,
spring 1940

Below
Family reunion in Cincinnati, Ohio, 1941.
Mother, Mary, Eileen, Louise, and George

for Women in Oxford, Ohio. We spent Christmas and New Year's holidays
with our brother John and his wife in Fort Knox, Oklahoma. John was
a graduate of the Whampoa Military Academy and had been sent by the
Chinese government for further training at the US army base. What a joy
it was to be with family again.

In January 1940, my mother's friend Elizabeth Matthews accompanied
me to St Margaret's Hall, a boarding school for girls in Versailles, Kentucky.
It was a high church Anglican school run by nuns, with many rules and
regulations, which applied to everyone. I had no difficulty adjusting and
gradually regained my emotional composure.

When the Sino-Japanese War intensified and threatened Hong Kong in the fall of 1940, Mother brought my younger sister Louise and brother George to Cincinnati, Ohio, to provide a haven for us all. Sheltered under her protective wings, I felt secure again, and the following May I graduated from high school.

MEETING PAUL LIM YUEN, JUNE 1941

It was a hot evening in June 1941 when I first set eyes on Paul Lim Yuen at the University of Chicago, where we were attending the midwestern conference of the Chinese Students' Christian Association. Wearing a light blue shirt with the sleeves rolled up neatly above his elbows, Paul was reviewing the progress of the war ignited in China by Japan in 1937. He spoke eloquently, with charisma. What impressed me most was his compassion for the suffering of the Chinese people. His rich baritone, impeccable English, and courteous manners attracted me. Discreetly, I tried to find out more about him and learned that he was a delegate from the University of Michigan, a second-year student from Canada. The imprint of his dual cultural background intrigued me; I decided I had found my Prince Charming.

I could not wait to share my stroke of luck with Mother, who had brought her teenage children to this conference of university students and scholars to broaden their horizons, while enriching her own intellectual and spiritual interests. I rushed upstairs to share my secret with her. She smiled and said in jest: "You are talking nonsense, my foolish girl. You have just graduated from high school. What do you know about marriage at seventeen?" I explained to her that I had heard Paul speak about China with eloquence and passion, and coaxed her to come downstairs. Mother wanted to know more about him first. "He is twenty-one, going into his junior year at the University of Michigan. His father is an Anglican minister of Chinese descent in Canada." I told her all I knew. "In that case, he wouldn't look at you," she said. Nevertheless, she went downstairs with me and listened intently when he spoke. "Yes, he does look promising," she observed, but did not further indulge me. No one was more aware than Mother of the gulf between her innocent and immature teenage daughter and this intelligent, serious-minded young man, who seemed already to know his mission in life.

The four-day conference was packed with events of interest and fun. In addition to early morning prayers, Bible studies, and church services for devout Christians like Mother, the program included formal lectures by noted speakers on current affairs and philosophical and moral issues. Afternoons were devoted to sports and recreation, early evenings to panel discussions organized by the students, and the last event of the day was a social, where the young people could dance and mingle.

Mother was right, of course. I made absolutely no impression on Paul Lim Yuen at any of these activities. Our chance encounters were fleeting and from stolen glances I noted that the young women who clustered around him were much more mature than I. So I tucked my "Prince Charming" deep in my heart and at the close of the conference accompanied my family home to Cincinnati.

After leaving Chicago at the end of June 1941, I was under no illusion that I would see Paul again. In August, I was accepted at Ohio Wesleyan College. Mother believed that I would master English more quickly if there were not many students from China on campus. As it turned out, the only other Chinese student at Ohio Wesleyan that year was Larry Zhang, an engineering student from northeast China.

SECOND ENCOUNTER, CHRISTMAS 1941

After Japan's attack on Pearl Harbor on December 7, 1941, the United States declared war on Japan, Germany, and Italy. Mother was elated, thinking that the war would soon be over. But before long, Japan succeeded in invading Malaya, Thailand, the Philippines, and Burma. The progress of the war in Europe was equally dismal. Devastated by the Allies' setbacks, she could neither sleep nor eat, glued herself to the radio, and would burst into tears whenever she heard bad news from the war fronts. This went on for a few weeks until she realized that if she did not make a change she would have a nervous breakdown. So when my sisters and I came home from college for the Christmas holiday, Mother took us all off to Chicago to attend an international Christian students' conference, where she hoped that learning more about the world situation would allay her anxieties.

I was excited by the possibility of seeing Paul again, but he was nowhere to be found. Disappointed, I turned my attention to the conference where the war was the main topic of interest at all the workshops. An atmosphere of gloom pervaded in the wake of the Allies' defeats. The prevailing analysis was that the United States was unprepared for war after so long a period of peace, that it underestimated Japan's military might, and that it regarded the war in Europe as more important than the war in Asia. A major concern among the Chinese students was the US military draft, since the Chinese government had offered President Roosevelt the services of Chinese students studying in the United States. While many students genuinely looked forward to an opportunity to serve, some felt threatened.

Four days slipped by. On December 24, Paul suddenly appeared at the conference. What a Christmas present!, I thought to myself. Despite my thumping heart, I kept my composure. He walked over to our table and greeted us warmly, as he did his many other acquaintances. That night, as we were all seated around the Christmas tree waiting for Santa's appearance, Paul came and sat down beside me. He conveyed greetings from my school-mate Larry Zhang, who had lent Paul his car to drive to Chicago. Then, when Santa gave me my Christmas present – a half apron in a delicate purple print – Paul offered to tie it on for me. Before the end of the evening, he asked if I would accompany him to see a matinee showing of *Citizen Kane*, the next afternoon.

Soon after the movie began, I felt Paul's arm stretching out behind my back as he rested his hand lightly on my shoulder. Gently, he nudged me toward him until my head was resting on his shoulder. This innocent closeness electrified our young hearts and neither of us could remember much of the film afterwards, except the name "Rosebud," uttered longingly by the hero in the final scene.

The next evening, Paul invited me to the conference dance. The ballroom was dimly lit, with a spectacular dome of stars and moon shining above. When the band played the enchanting melody of "Star Dust," Paul asked me to dance. From that evening, "Star Dust" was our song.

Mother invited Paul to visit us over the holidays and we spent two days together. This visit, although brief, saw the blossoming of our love.

Mother liked Paul because he was a thoughtful and considerate budding scholar. His responsible way of handling debts also impressed her. He had borrowed five dollars from Mother for his bus ticket and returned it immediately afterwards, enclosed in his note of thanks.

COURTSHIP, 1942–1944

In fall 1942, I transferred to the University of Michigan to be with Paul, although the shared interlude was brief. Paul graduated in January 1943 and immediately left for Boston to begin his master's program at the Fletcher School of Law and Diplomacy.

During our months apart, we wrote to each other daily, spoke at the
weekends by long-distance phone calls, sent telegrams and flowers, and made
the occasional visit. I entered Paul's world from a sheltered life of some
luxury in Shanghai. Paul's handsome features and special charm, nurtured
by the cultures of East and West, mesmerized me. I admired his compassion
for China, his intellect, idealism, and leadership qualities. But I was totally
unprepared for his mission in life.

I came to understand that in Paul's mind his "ideal girl" would be China-
born, modern yet respectful of traditional Chinese values, and well versed
in Chinese language and literature. He had dated several young Chinese
women at university, but found them puzzling and difficult to communicate
with. He had little understanding at that time of the importance of social
status to these girls' affluent families. In their view, the son of a preacher in
Canada was not an ideal match for their daughters. Fortunately, Mother
liked Paul for his passion for China, his integrity, and his intellect. She
sent Paul's 1942 prize-winning speech "The Pacific Charter" to Father in
Zhongqing. He showed it to his esteemed friend, Madame Soong Ching
Ling, who after reading it asked Father to send this young man to her
when he came to China.

I had left Shanghai at fifteen, young enough to escape total contamination
by the often shallow values that prevailed among children of wealthy families. Paul appreciated my sincerity and agreeable nature, but was so conscious
of the social and intellectual divide between us that early in our courtship
he tried to end our relationship. Bridging our differences seemed too daunting a task. I was heartbroken and he relented. Then he tried to "mold" me
according to his ideals. I regarded Paul as my teacher and idolized him but
did not like his criticisms, often accompanied by flashes of impatience and
temper. During the summer of 1943 when we began talking about marriage
and thinking of guests we would invite to our wedding, Paul suggested two
Chinese men who ran the Liberty Café in Ann Arbor. They were old friends
of his father from Vancouver. I must have raised an eyebrow, because suddenly Paul became very angry and told me they were *his* friends and every
bit as worthy of attending our wedding as the other guests! I was shocked
at his vehemence and broke up with him. We made up in the fall after he
promised to contain his temper. Mother was relieved and proposed that we
formalize our relationship as soon as possible. Years later, when I came to
know his father and had lived for some time in the new China, I better understood Paul's demand that all Chinese, all people, are deserving of respect.

Paul's father was surprisingly supportive of our plans to be engaged. He
wrote:

I am most delighted to learn that you and Miss Siu-tsung Chen will be
engaged in December this year. When I met her, I found her to be upright
in character and attractive in appearance, with a gentle disposition, and
a good education. Her parents are Christians; so she also has a proper
upbringing. She is definitely eligible. If she truly loves you, and if her
parents are happy to give their consent, then I shall also endorse this
union wholeheartedly. May God bless you both with happiness and
a bright future.

I first met the Reverend George Lim Yuen in January 1943, when he came to
Ann Arbor to attend Paul's graduation. Although their relationship seemed
quite formal, Paul loved and admired his father. Father Lim's reserve never
intimidated me, for his eyes were kind. Paul told me later that his father had
liked me because I was brought up with traditional Chinese manners. Father
Lim had noticed that when we crossed the street, it was natural for me to
gently take his elbow and guide him through the traffic. To be honest, I think
Paul's father only really approved of me after he met my mother, who was
then studying for her doctorate at Ohio State University. He was most impressed by this. After his graduation, Paul had taken his father on a road
trip to the eastern United States, and Mother had invited them to stay at her
home when they came through Columbus. In his letter of thanks, eloquently
written in Chinese, the Reverend Lim praised Mother for her "nobility of
character and tireless pursuit of knowledge." He told her she was a role
model for womanhood and was gratified that she was willing to give Paul
her guidance.

We were engaged in December 1943 and set our wedding date for the
afternoon of June 24, 1944, to be held in Ann Arbor. I was to receive my
bachelor's degree that very morning from the University of Michigan. Paul
was on a break between terms at Harvard, where he was pursuing doctoral
studies. Because of wartime restrictions, Paul's father encountered many difficulties in obtaining his travel documents from Canada to the United States,
but to our joy he arrived in time to officiate at our marriage in the Episcopal
Church of St Andrew's. The wedding ceremony was intimate, attended by
several family members who were studying or working in different parts of
the United States and Canada, plus a few close friends from Ann Arbor,

Paul and Eileen relax on the lawn at the University of Michigan on 23 June, 1944, the day before their wedding.

Eileen graduates from the University of Michigan with a bachelor's degree in sociology on the morning of June 24, 1944.

The bride and groom cut the wedding cake, June 24, 1944.

Chicago, and Boston. My mother headed up the Chen clan. Unfortunately, Father was still working in China's war capital of Zhongqing. The celebration that followed was simple, in keeping with wartime austerity. After the tea reception, Paul and I left by night train for Boston. We had a wonderful honeymoon in New England, beginning a journey of life together that would last for sixty years. ※

Chapter Five

FROM ACADEMICS TO ACTIVISM

After our honeymoon, Eileen and I returned to Cambridge and set up our first home in an apartment on Massachusetts Avenue, within walking distance of Harvard University. I was working on a second master's degree that summer, before becoming a doctoral candidate in Harvard's School of Government. My master's thesis explored problems in the policy of the British Commonwealth towards the Japanese Empire, between 1921 and 1936. Having taken a range of courses in the fields of international law, international relations, modern political theory, and international economics, I proposed to write my doctoral thesis on the Far Eastern policies of the British Commonwealth and problems of Pacific security between the two wars. Professor William Yandell Elliott was my adviser for both degrees. I hoped to complete the PHD by the end of 1946.

CHINESE STUDENTS' CHRISTIAN ASSOCIATION
OF NORTH AMERICA

At the same time, I became increasingly involved with the Chinese Students' Christian Association of North America (CSCA). Founded in 1909 by Chinese students, the CSCA aimed to promote Christian fellowship, provide services to Chinese students studying in the United States, and enhance mutual understanding between Americans and Chinese. The Young Men's Christian Association (YMCA) became aware of CSCA's work and in 1917 its Committee on Friendly Relations among Foreign Students (CFR) agreed to provide an office in the YMCA's New York City headquarters and cover expenses for a general secretary. The YMCA had long been a leading proponent of "Wilsonian internationalism," which promoted international integration and interracial assimilation under the canopy of US democracy. With corporate philanthropists like John D. Rockefeller, Jr. and college presidents from Stanford and Harvard, the YMCA was also instrumental in establishing the Institute of Pacific Relations (IPR) in 1925. For several decades, the IPR and its publication *Pacific Affairs* were the pre-eminent forums for the exchange of views on political and cultural issues among academics and policy-makers in Pacific nations. IPR scholars often gave keynote addresses at our CSCA conferences.

My association with the CSCA had begun in June 1941, when I attended its midwestern conference on "Human Rights in China and the World." Ninety delegates from thirty-six American universities participated; all the speakers had worked in China and included well-known international statesmen. I was so impressed by the CSCA's moral leadership and mission of service to China that I agreed to serve as vice-chairman of the midwestern department for the following year. During the next three years, attending to CSCA business was my major extracurricular activity.

In the fall of 1944, I was elected CSCA national president and concurrently was chairman of both the eastern department and the Boston chapter. These duties, which included monthly trips to New York for central board meetings, kept me very busy. I was destined to become even busier, however, as I was preparing to take general examinations for my PHD in early 1945 and Eileen was due to give birth to our first child in May. Once I finished my dissertation, we intended to go to China. Eileen was taking post-graduate courses in child welfare at the Boston Nursery Training School, to prepare herself to take care of our own baby, as well as to organize child welfare centres in China. I expected to find work in my specialty of international law.

CSCA NATIONAL PRESIDENT, 1945

The year 1945 was a turning point in world history. US President Franklin Delano Roosevelt died unexpectedly on April 12. The final major battles in Europe led to Germany's surrender on May 8. Two weeks later, delegates from fifty nations met in San Francisco to draft the charter of the United Nations. The United States dropped atomic bombs on Hiroshima and Nagasaki in early August, and Japan made an informal surrender on August 15. This last event, of course, was what patriotic Chinese everywhere had been waiting for: the end of the War of Resistance against Japan. Technically the war had begun in 1937, but in truth Japanese territorial aggression dated back to 1895, when Japan took the island province of Taiwan as war booty.

I was frantically busy as CSCA national president. In addition to the day-to-day tasks of working with local chapters, meeting with the central board, and planning the eastern CSCA conference, scheduled for September 1945, I received many invitations to participate in events hosted for Chinese scholars and dignitaries. In New York I met with Meng Chih, director of the China Institute, and the diplomat P.C. Chang; at Harvard I met with resident Chinese scholars Dr Hu Shih, China's former ambassador to the United States, and Chang Chi-yun, one of China's leading geographers; and I crossed paths a second time with the Chinese financier Dr H.H. Kung, who had spoken at our CSCA conference at Yale University in the summer of 1944. On the home front, Eileen and I welcomed our first child, Christopher Lin, on May 16, 1945.

CAMP NORTHWOODS CSCA CONFERENCE, SEPTEMBER 1945

My year as president of the CSCA culminated in the eastern conference, which was held at Camp Northwoods by beautiful Lake Winnipesaukee in New Hampshire in September. The opening date of the Northwoods conference turned out to be an important day in history. I noted in my welcome address that the formal surrender of Japan by Emperor Hirohito had occurred just the day before, and signaled the advent of a crucial period in China's history.

As Chinese students, looking back on eight years of war, of devastation, of mental and physical terror, we cannot but think at this particular moment most appropriately of our individual responsibility toward our homeland. For many, this is the first moment in many long years that we have breathed freely. Some are eager to go home. Yet our joy is restrained. Our people have waged a bloody struggle to make victory. But last month, victory happened to us. Has victory come too soon?

Our problems today are as great as they were before we had victory. The task of solving them would stagger the minds of others who plan the destinies of nations. And now, we are faced with peace – a peace opening up the wilderness of these unsolved problems and untried opportunities. Where do we stand? How can the new China be brought about reasonably soon? Wherein lies our duty?

CSCA Northwoods Conference Preparation Committee, 1945. Front, centre: Paul holds infant Christopher. To the left of Paul is Pu Shouchang.

Let us defeat any allegation that our generation of students has shown great hesitance to express their views and convictions and therefore must have no solid or positive convictions on the great issues of our times ... I think you will agree with me that to move our people forward, we must feel ourselves genuinely as one of them. I am not suggesting in these remarks that we should all produce views on politics here. Rather, we should all take into our realm of thinking and feeling those problems and issues, which are the common concern of our people and which we must understand and evaluate, in order that we can serve adequately.

Our week at Northwoods was packed with plenaries, student panels, devotionals, and religious services, all addressing the conference theme, "China's New Horizons and New Purposes." Topics included "China Under Constitutional Democracy," "What Is Min Sheng Zhu Yi? (People's Liveli-hood)," "Our Christian Duty in Postwar China," "China Among the Powers," and "China's Relations with Asiatic Peoples." The program was created by a hard-working discussion committee, led by Pu Shouchang, my old friend from the University of Michigan who was now a doctoral student in economics at Harvard.

After the defeat of Japan, the Chinese Nationalist government put out a call for Chinese nationals studying in the United States to return home to assist in rehabilitation efforts. Personnel were needed to organize and manage public works projects, distribute relief, administer camps for displaced persons, work on child welfare, compile statistics, and produce publications. It was announced at Northwoods that the CSCA had established a placement service for these jobs in our New York office; students were encouraged to apply.

We closed the week with the adoption of various resolutions on the main issues, the most important being a demand for a truly constitutional government under which the Chinese people could enjoy social, political, and economic democracy to the fullest. The conference was reported by the *Granite State News* of Wolfeboro, New Hampshire, on September 14, 1945:

For the past week, Camp Northwoods on the edge of Lake Winnipesaukee has been the scene of one of the most unusual gatherings seen in many years. One hundred Chinese students and twenty speakers have participated in the annual Chinese Students' Christian Association's Eastern Conference. In addition to enjoying unusual New England camp life, the students have discussed some of the most fundamental problems facing China and the World.

On Saturday night, the students heard Dr Owen Lattimore, noted author and director of the Walter Page School of International Relations at Johns Hopkins University, speak on "China's Future Relations with Asiatic Peoples." Dr Lattimore pointed out that China, for the first time in a hundred years, has enjoyed freedom of political action in Asia and it is up to the Chinese people to fully utilize that unusual opportunity ...

In addition to Dr Lattimore, the students heard from such distinguished speakers as Dr C.L. Hsia, director of the Chinese News Service, Dr Y.P. Mei, chancellor of Yenching University in Peiping, William H. Dennis of the State Department in charge of Chinese students, Rev. Earl Ballou, secretary of the Associated Christian Colleges in China, and many others.

The students, many of whom had never seen the New England countryside, lived in the rustic atmosphere of a typical camp. They lived in cabins with no lights, enjoyed swimming, tennis, and other sports, and held most of their meetings outdoors. The discussions and arguments were heated and many were the time that the chairman was forced to call for order. They argued earnestly about China's internal political problems, including the current communist question, discussed China's economy, and talked about China's position as a future world power. The climax of the discussion was reached on Friday morning when the groups

got organized into a Model parliament and the Leftist party defeated the
Rightist party by a 38 to 36 vote ...

CSCA GENERAL SECRETARY, 1947

The Northwoods conference was a great success, but I was happy to step
down from the CSCA presidency to concentrate on completing my doctoral
thesis. I did attend the 1946 eastern conference in New Jersey, where debates
became more intense regarding the corruption and repression under KMT rule,
as well as US support for the KMT in the civil war with the Communists. One
of the speakers was Liu Liangmo, a former China YMCA secretary, who taught
us songs he had recorded during the Chinese War of Resistance (1937–45),
including "March of the Volunteers," which later became New China's
national anthem.

In the summer of 1946 I was confronted again with financial difficulties.
With the war over, US government grants to students had terminated. By
accepting numerous speaking engagements sponsored by the Redpath Bureau,
I was able (barely) to support my little family, but these activities interfered
with my academic work. I accepted the delay of my thesis and in January
1947 undertook a one-year appointment as general secretary of the CSCA.
My monthly salary was $250. Frankly, what enticed me was not the meagre
stipend, but the challenges now arising from the winds of change in postwar
China and the United States.

We moved from Cambridge to New York City. Affordable housing in postwar New York was hard to find, but we spotted an interesting advertisement
on a student bulletin board at Columbia University: "Looking For Students
Willing To Care For And Live On My Chinese Junk Rent-Free For Six Weeks."
The owner was the assistant of a famous *New York Times* columnist; the junk
indeed had been sailed across the Pacific, repainted, equipped with modern
amenities, and was now moored permanently in Long Island Sound. We were
delighted to be accepted as tenants. I commuted to work every day at the CSCA
office, located in the YMCA on Madison Avenue. Eileen remained on the junk
with two-year-old Chris, who enjoyed playing on the open deck. Only a plain
wooden plank connected the boat to shore.

Now that we had temporary shelter, we had more time to look for a real
home. Soon we found an affordable apartment at 380 Riverside Drive, around
the corner from the subway and shops at Broadway and Tenth Avenue. Shortly
after we moved in, we met a charming couple, the Rev. K.H. Ting and his wife,

Siu May Kuo, originally from Shanghai. K.H. was an Anglican priest who had just finished a year's posting with the Canadian Student Christian Movement in Toronto. Both were taking courses at Union Theological Seminary and Columbia University before returning to China. Fiercely patriotic and increasingly disgusted with Chiang Kai-shek's government, they favoured a coalition government between the Nationalists and the Communists. Their Social Gospel emphasis on justice for the poor and marginalized resonated with me. We enjoyed their company and became lifelong friends.

CHINA'S CIVIL WAR, 1945–1949

Postwar events in China require a little background. The Chinese Communist Party (CCP) was founded in Shanghai in 1921 and briefly allied itself with the KMT in 1926, to launch the Northern Expedition in an attempt to unify the country. However, Generalissimo Chiang Kai-shek, who had led the KMT army north from Guangzhou, ordered a massacre of CCP members and followers in 1927. Chiang then spent the next nine years trying to exterminate the Communists, making it a higher priority than fighting the Japanese who were steadily encroaching on Chinese territory. In 1934, finding themselves cornered by the Nationalist army in eastern China, the Communists set out on an 8,000 mile Long March across China. A year later, Mao Zedong emerged as the leader of the CCP and established the Party's headquarters in hilly Yanan, Shanxi Province. In December 1936, Zhang Xueliang, the Manchurian warlord who had joined his forces to Chiang's, revolted and took Chiang captive. He demanded that the KMT and CCP form a united front to resist the Japanese; under threat of death, Chiang acquiesced. In theory, the KMT and CCP became partners in the fight against Japanese militarism. But hostilities between the two parties simmered beneath the surface and after V-J Day in 1945 flared into a civil war for control of China.

In late November 1945, 6,000 university students held a rally in Kunming, southwestern China, demanding peace, democracy, and a coalition government. Prominent intellectuals such as the anthropologist Fei Xiaotong and political scientist Qian Duansheng addressed the crowd. The government's answer was to send in military police to break up the meeting. The students staged a boycott of classes and issued a manifesto against the KMT government's suppression of democracy and its preparations for civil war. The manifesto also called for the withdrawal of US forces, which seemed to be siding with Chiang Kai-shek's KMT against the Communists.

On December 1, Chiang's military police broke into college campuses with bayonets and hand grenades, killing four students and injuring many others. This became known as the December 1st incident and provoked a massive wave of protest across the country against KMT bloody repression. On January 4, 1946, US President Harry Truman sent General George Marshall to China to broker a ceasefire agreement between the KMT and the CCP. But with the two sides deeply suspicious of each other, all-out civil war broke out within half a year. In July 1946, KMT secret police assassinated the poet Wen Yiduo and writer Li Gongpu, two well-known patriotic intellectuals who had been living in exile during the war in Kunming. Their deaths deepened the people's animosity against the repressive regime. Meanwhile, inflation was causing immense hardship for a population exhausted by more than a decade of war.

Most Chinese studying abroad initially took a neutral position, tending to blame both the KMT and the CCP for this drift toward war. Anti-US feeling began to grow, however, as Chinese detected American duplicity in supplying Chiang Kai-shek with arms and logistical support. Viewing the situation from afar, as we did between 1946 and 1949, it was difficult to distinguish the "good guys" from the enemy. Yet there was a clear consensus that China needed peace and democracy to rehabilitate the economy and rebuild its society.

From 1945 to 1948, an influx of students from different parts of war-torn China arrived to study in the United States. Most of them joined the CSCA in search of friendship and community. Some focused primarily on their studies, but others were deeply concerned and patriotic activists who felt that their studies could be of no use to the reconstruction of their homeland if China continued to be torn apart by civil strife, corruption, and tyranny. Probably there were a small number of KMT and CCP party members in the mix, but most students were simply patriots.

As general secretary of the CSCA, I was on the road a great deal helping students to organize regional summer conferences to discuss the pressing issues they faced as Chinese living abroad. Their foremost concerns were the KMT-CCP civil war, postwar reconstruction, and Sino-American relations. My message was to encourage democratic procedure, freedom of expression, and genuine friendship based on mutual respect. I also experimented with another way of expanding the horizons of Chinese students who had little opportunity to experience grassroots America. In June 1947, I led a CSCA travel seminar of twenty-two students to explore the newly established Tennessee Valley Authority (TVA).

The TVA was an integrated, comprehensive, scientific program for the development of an entire river valley. Behind the science and the practical "know-how," however, was a larger political, economic, and social vision, which focused not merely on technical achievements, but on improving the total welfare of the people of the region. This was an eye-opener for the Chinese students, who knew that this kind of holistic planning was necessary for democratic reconstruction in China, but who also appreciated that the TVA ideas and methods would need to be adapted to Chinese conditions to be effective. The seminar promoted intellectual cooperation among highly specialized students, some of whom had prior experience as teachers and administrators. Notwithstanding their particular specializations, they took an interest in all aspects of TVA, following a fundamental tenet of TVA methodology: coordination and cooperation among physical and social scientific disciplines. Our visit also served to promote Sino-American understanding and friendship. Numerous invitations came from local organizations and individuals in the Knoxville area, leading to meaningful personal exchanges across cultural lines.

The theme of the CSCA eastern conference in Chester, Connecticut in September 1947 was "Sino-American Relations and China's Reconstruction." Journalist Israel Epstein and Canadian missionary James G. Endicott were two of the speakers who harshly critiqued Chiang Kai-shek's Nationalist government. Several resolutions were adopted after lengthy and heated discussion. One called for a coalition Chinese government to build an independent, democratic New China. Another demanded an end to US financial and military aid to the Chiang Kai-shek regime.

By 1948 I was ready to return to Harvard, but had to carry on with the CSCA until a suitable successor could be found. I was delighted when the search committee chose Siu May Kuo (Mrs K.H. Ting), who brought to the job both a keen intellect and recent experience working with students and the YWCA in China.

COLD WAR ARISING, 1948

China was now at a turning point. The introduction of the gold yuan (paper currency) by the Nationalist government, to control skyrocketing inflation, led to even greater economic hardship for the people. Private hoarding of gold was forbidden and citizens were ordered to turn in their gold bars on pain of severe punishment. The gold yuan was issued with the supposed security of the national government, but within months had depreciated to such an extent that millions were deprived of their life savings. This financial ineptitude, in addition to rampant corruption and heavy repression, alienated not only the

K.H. and Siu May Ting, New York, 1947. Siu May succeeded Paul as general secretary of the CSCA the following year.

workers and peasants of China, but also the bourgeoisie, the intellectuals, and even many of the industrialists. Disillusioned and destitute, they were desperate for change.

By now, I too had become disenchanted with the KMT and began to examine Mao Zedong's early essays on the building of a New China, including the "New San Min Zhu Yi," "Land to the Tillers," "On New Democracy," "On Coalition Government," and "Economic Reform." I was impressed by Mao's analysis of China's political and social problems. He appeared to have a viable plan to address the poverty of the peasants who constituted most of the population.

Soon after V-E Day in May 1945, the Western powers had begun to maneuver to contain Communism, beginning with the Soviets. Winston Churchill's "iron curtain" speech on March 5, 1946, at Fulton, Missouri, led to the Truman Doctrine of global anti-Communism. By the end of 1948, CSCA conferences had become outspoken and critical of US involvement in China's civil war. Senior leadership in the YMCA was increasingly uneasy with what they saw as our "radical politics" and one of my Harvard professors spoke to me privately, criticizing what he felt were my extreme positions.

In early 1949, I completed the first draft of my doctoral thesis. Although Professor W.Y. Elliott wanted me to do more research on the original documents now available in the newly opened Japanese archives, I was no longer interested in working on British-Japanese relations in the 1930s. I wanted to focus on the emergence of New China and would have been willing to research this key turning point in China's history. I dared not even raise the possibility, however, because I had already been named in the American press as a subversive. In December 1948, the *Saturday Evening Post* wrote an editorial attacking the CSCA and me for being sympathetic to the Chinese communist movement. The KMT press in the United States also maligned us.

Eileen and I had been planning to move to China after I finished my PHD, but the increasingly hostile political climate in the United States forced my hand. I decided to go as soon as possible. With Eileen and our two young sons (Douglas was born May 7, 1949), I resolved to seek out my ancestral roots and to participate in China's historic transition. I shared the hopes of the long-suffering Chinese people for freedom from war, poverty, and injustice in the New China.

EN ROUTE TO NEW CHINA

I wrote to Father regarding our decision to go to China, telling him "we do not have any illusions about the circumstances in China. We do not wish to become high officials and are prepared to suffer hardships ... You have nurtured my love for China since my childhood, and it was your teachings and guidance that have prepared me for service to the Chinese people." He raised no objections and before we left on the first leg of our journey, Father came to New York to see us off. On October 2, 1949, we flew to San Francisco and boarded a Danish Maersk freighter for Hong Kong.

The journey across the Pacific took thirty-five days. The freighter was truly "a slow boat to China," but was the most economical and comfortable transport I could find. Due to the rough November seas, Eileen was immobilized with seasickness most of the way. I turned out to be a good sailor, which was fortunate, as I had to look after an energetic and curious four-year-old, as well as be part-time nanny to our six-month-old infant. Washing diapers in the cabin bathtub was a new experience for me! After weeks of monotonous sailing we finally reached Hong Kong. Eileen's family surprised us by hiring a taxi boat to take them to the mooring of *Marchen Maersk* and coming on board to welcome us. Eileen was elated to embrace her parents, especially her father, whom she had not seen in more than ten years. I too was excited (and slightly nervous) to meet my father-in-law for the first time. Both of us, of course, were

Christopher, four years old, holds his brother Douglas, five months old, in October 1949, just before the Lins embark on their journey to China.

delighted to see Mother Chen again. We had last seen her in the fall of 1945, before she left the US to rejoin Eileen's father, now back in Shanghai from the wartime capital of Zhongqing.

I left the United States in 1949, when loyalty to the Chiang Kai-shek regime was being equated with loyalty to the United States. The question "Who lost China?" echoed through the halls of Congress and patriotic Chinese students like myself suddenly were no longer welcome. Rabid "Cold Warriors" in Washington saw only a faceless Communism in China, while we saw our people, our land, our culture, and sovereignty in turmoil. We had family members, friends, and academic colleagues across China, all willing to work with the new CCP government of Mao Zedong to build the New China. We would join them.

Had I not left when I did, I might have been swept into Joseph McCarthy's security hearings and been persecuted – as happened to scholars like Owen Lattimore and State Department China personnel like John S. Service, whose father had been a YMCA secretary in China. I struggled with the decision to leave the United States, but knew in my heart it was time to "go home" and offer my skills for my people's future.

Part Two

1950–1964

Chapter Six

JOURNEY TO NEW CHINA

FIRST IMPRESSIONS

In my first letter to family in North America in early January 1950, I described our first weeks in Hong Kong.

> Hong Kong has been a life of extreme ease for us, almost enervating. The rounds of sumptuous dinner parties, the marvelous food, mild climate, and relatively cheap daily necessities can easily encourage the unwary to stay indefinitely in this almost cultureless, colonial-minded community. There are no libraries, no museums, no theaters but plenty of movies (mostly American), the famous Lido dinner dance at Repulse Bay and many amazing restaurants like the Aberdeen, where we ate a delicious seafood dinner of live fish we selected from baskets hung over the sides of the floating restaurant.
>
> From reports here, it appears that many friends are already in Beijing, Tianjin, and Shanghai, working terribly hard with adequate but very simple food and living conditions. Opinion among Chinese businessmen is one of guarded optimism toward the New China. While people fear the strict, puritanical morality of the Communists, most non-Communist Chinese view the new government as not a definite good, but the last best hope for the country and a new era of progress for the people. They just hope this will not be denied by stupid, blundering foreign intervention from any quarter ... Present reports are that British recognition will come soon.

HISTORIC JOURNEY TO THE LAND OF MY FOREFATHERS

Eileen and I agreed that I would go on ahead to China to scout out the political situation and to find a home for us in Beijing. She would stay for several months with her parents and our boys in Hong Kong. So, on January 4, I boarded a PNE coastal liner for Tianjin in the company of two businessmen, acquaintances of my in-laws. I left my Canadian passport with Eileen's mother, bringing only my birth certificate, and entered the country with the travel papers of an ordinary Chinese. Traveling in steerage, the trip was not particularly comfortable, but I made many new friends on the boat, all Chinese. One was Lao She, the noted author, whose writings included the famous short stories "Rickshaw Boy" and "The Tea House." We had long discussions about art and politics, and he invited me to accompany him to a Peking Opera performance when I arrived in Beijing.

Ten days later, as we crossed the Taku Bar into Tianjin harbor, my new friends called me up to the deck. "Paul, this is your first sight of China – the China you have wanted to see all your life. You must drink to it!" I was so moved that I could not speak. "Look, we have pretty good liquor here," they said. "One usually drinks to China with *bai gan*." I had no idea that *bai gan* was as strong as vodka, so when they handed me a bowl and insisted I drink it *gan bei* (bottoms up!), I gulped it down. What a disaster! Five minutes later, I was running for "the head" in steerage. My friends had a good laugh over my misery.

Our baggage cleared customs promptly; mine was hardly touched. I feared they might tax the typewriter, considered a "luxury," but one of my Hong Kong companions quickly gave the inspector my life history, in capsule, including the fact that I was on my way "home" to serve. The inspector welcomed me warmly and waved us through without charging us a penny.

It was impossible for me to gauge the extent of the change since Liberation, but I was told that even a year ago bribery at the customs house had been rampant. There was no sign of it, and onshore we were accosted by only a couple of beggars, whereas previously we would have been swarmed as we came off the boat.

My Hong Kong companions and I stayed in one large room at the Tai Lai Hotel. Relatively clean, it was also well heated which, after ten days at sea, was a luxury. We tumbled into bed (I was still feeling the effects of the *bai gan*) and slept soundly. At about 3:30 am we were jolted awake by a loud knock on our door. In barged two armed soldiers, demanding we show them identification and state our purpose for coming to Tianjin. At first I was shocked, but they explained: "You must understand that the city is still under martial law, which requires that we check every visitor. Your papers are in order. Good night."

Our breakfast of five orders of ham and eggs, toast, butter, and milk totaled RMB 21,000 (about US$1), including room service. I was told that for as little as US$50 per month, a family of four could live quite adequately. A maid and extra milk for a baby would probably increase the cost by only six dollars. After breakfast, we walked the streets of Tianjin, which were crowded with Sunday pedestrians and bedecked with the flaming crimson flags of New China. The swish of the pedicabs was often punctuated by the tympani of a *yangko* (folkdance) troupe coming up the street, and I caught my first glimpse of the famous Liberation Army troops (PLA) – healthy looking country boys, warmly clad in US uniforms.

A few days later, we visited Nankai University on the outskirts of the city. The small campus had a few good buildings and comfortable quarters for the teaching staff, but otherwise was empty; the Japanese had destroyed the library and most of the dormitories in 1937. Nankai's chief secretary explained to us the new form of university administration, including salaries, which were not paid in cash but in grain. Associate professors earned from 800 to 900 catties of millet per month, while full professors earned as much as 1,300 catties. A catty weighed about 600 grams. He estimated that 320,000 catties of millet were needed to maintain the university on a monthly basis. This translated into the labour of 120,000 Chinese farmers merely to keep the university going, which was a basic reason why the Chinese universities could not hope to expand until agricultural-industrial production was increased.

Nankai was now a national university. Tuition was free and students were accepted on the basis of examinations. Only one out of four was accepted and poor students were given sustenance grants. International law (my field) was now being taught according to new principles of Marxist analysis, while the departments of political science and sociology were gradually being abolished as tools of "imperialist hegemony."

In the gathering dusk, on the long trip back to our hotel, I could see both China's weakness and strength in the long lines of heavily laden carts pulled by straining donkeys and men. The scene touched me profoundly, as if a 1930s woodcut had suddenly come to life. How long would it take to turn these millions of willing human hands into humane and infinitely more productive labour?

After much coolie helter skelter, we departed next for Beijing on the Express train. I was impressed with its punctuality – better perhaps than rail service in the United States and infinitely more efficient than KMT days. The train was reasonably clean and comfortable and we arrived in Beijing on the dot.

Arrival in Beijing was an experience. There was a sense of orderliness and dignified efficiency at the station. The red cap porters had set fees, so there was no haggling. Once outside the station, however, this discipline broke down. Met by a friend of a friend, we hailed two pedicabs and negotiated a fare of RMB 1,000 per cab. But when we arrived at our hotel, the drivers demanded RMB 4,000. One little "liberated" fellow swore at one of my companions, accusing him of being a "capitalist oppressor." To be done with them, we paid RMB 3,000. Life on the streets had not yet been entirely sorted out, but this was a minor mishap.

The broad streets of the capital, lined by imposing edifices, breathed an air of timeless serenity. We rode silently. I reveled in the ancient elegance and was speechless with pride … until we arrived at our hotel. It had been chosen for being inexpensive and conveniently located. I ended up sharing a straw pallet on a single bed with one of my companions, along with numerous tiny critters. After a few days I was very happy to move on.

We were guests at Dr Chen's home for supper. I was encouraged by the lively conversation, the balanced progressiveness of his wife, and the straightforwardness of his nephew, who was a cadre. We talked openly about what we considered to be mistakes made by Party members, especially the overly suspicious attitude of some toward intellectuals and technical experts. This had resulted in a few unfortunate cases where surgeons had refused to operate, due to fear of criticism by cadres without medical training.

On January 20, I traveled to Shanghai on the Special Express. Heading south on the Tianjin-Pukou railway, I sensed I was retracing the course of recent revolutionary history, from the great capital city of Beijing through the countryside already under PLA control, and the vast famine area of Anhui. The changing scene from my train window made me sharply aware of the monumental tasks of the Liberation Army, which had to overcome so many obstacles. Repairing the rail arteries must have been one of their top priorities; we passed over many bridges restored in a period of time that would have astounded American bridge builders. At Pengpu, scene of a terrific CCP-KMT battle for control of the nerve centre of rail communications in China, we watched as a bombed-out steel bridge was raised from the riverbed, log on log, by hand labour. At Pukou, where we crossed the Yangtze, the entire train was shunted onto a ferry. The crossing was timed to occur in darkness, as was our arrival in Shanghai, to avoid ongoing deadly attacks by Chiang Kai-shek's air force. (Several days later, when I was the guest-of-honour at a dinner held by the YMCA National Committee at the Banker's Club on the Bund, twelve KMT B-24s roared overhead, delivering the worst bombing since the CCP's victory.)

Food in the train's diner was foreign-style, good and cheap. Peddlers sold hot food at every stop, but as we moved south this became significantly scarcer and dearer. There were armed guards at every station and junction point. Train platforms were neat and loudspeakers intermittently blared announcements and music for the edification of travellers.

Finally we reached the incorrigibly Westernized metropolis of Shanghai. I had never experienced "old Shanghai," but sensed little had changed since Liberation. The contrast with Beijing was startling. Along the famous Bund, the arrogant symbols of Western financial power still stood, although I knew these "machines of commerce" were slowly being directed into service of the people. Among the chic-looking women on the streets, fur coats and permanents abounded. The shops looked like those in Hong Kong, filled with luxury goods; there was no scarcity for people with cash. Business, however, was heavily taxed, leading to loud and bitter griping by businessmen who could no longer rake in huge profits. A campaign was on to sell government victory bonds, whose purpose was to address inflation, as well as to finance reconstruction.

Reforming Shanghai was proving very difficult for the CCP. Misinformation, insufficient training, lack of experience and, in some cases, sheer ignorance led to many mistakes. The job was tougher in Shanghai than in the north, because the cadres were surrounded by the "sly" men of commerce, the metropolitan socialites with their sophisticated manners, and the two-faced "cosmopolites" who accepted the new austerity by day and whispered conspiratorially against it by night.

While in Shanghai, I spent a most pleasant evening at Madame Sun Yat-sen's (Soong Ching Ling's) home. Father Chen provided me with a formal letter of introduction, although she and I were actually "family" due to my brother Andrew's marriage to Dr Sun's granddaughter, Pearl Sun. I had heard a great deal about Madame Sun's charm and graciousness, but still was surprised by her. It must take a deep, inner serenity – born of simple, clear convictions – for a person to grow to her age with such dignity and composure. Her home was comfortable and she appreciated fine wines, so what I brought was "on the button." We had a brief chat before two other guests joined us for dinner and conversation, which did not lack for some pretty earthy humor!

I told her that I was looking for a job. She mentioned the dearth of diplomats and suggested the Foreign Service. I knew that she had no definite offer in mind, however; individuals returning to New China generally offered their services for reconstruction and then were placed where they could do the most good by the government.

In early February, I boarded a late afternoon train for Nanjing, capital of

Family portrait at Pearl Sun and Andrew Lin's wedding in Shanghai, November 1947.
Front, left to right: Mrs T.K. Sun, Mrs David Lin, Dr and Madame Sun Fo, Madame
Sun Yat-sen (Soong Ching Ling), Pearl Sun (bride), Mrs T.P. Sun. Rear, left to right:
Tse Keong (T.K.) Sun, David Lin, Andrew Lin (bridegroom), Tse Ping (T.P.) Sun

the former KMT government, to consult with some other friends about the
situation in China. Seated in an uncomfortable second-class car, I contented
myself by looking out on the serene countryside flooded by eerie moonlight.
A tall American with a beaked nose sat opposite me; attached to the China
Inland Mission, he was hustled off the train in Nanjing and questioned
before being allowed into the city. Fearing to disturb my hosts, who had not
received the letter informing them of my midnight arrival, I spent my first
night in a shabby hotel outside the city gate, on a straw mattress and
unheated wooden bed.

The trip into Nanjing by pedicab was long and soldiers searched me at the
city gate. The streets exuded a sour odour of abandonment and defeat. Deserted
by Chiang Kai-shek's officials, the government buildings retained a sense of
the grandeur of the old regime, upon whose carpetbagger riches the city had
flourished. But Nanjing was shorn of its former glory; hotels, restaurants, and
tailors were devastated by the exodus of officials. Hundreds of mansions
belonging to former officials initially were a real revelation for the PLA soldiers

who liberated the city, because most came from poor rural backgrounds and some had never even seen a flush toilet before. Beggars who had been put in camps outside the city were making their way back to the streets. Conditions were in sharp contrast to the good order of the northern cities, which had been under CCP administration since the mid-1940s.

After Nanjing, I returned to Beijing. Friends at Yanjing University put me in contact with a team of college students heading out to redo the land reform on the outskirts of Beijing. The leader, a Party member, accepted me as a member of the team, saying it would take them at least two weeks to clean up mistakes made the first time.

Land reform was the redistribution of the large holdings of major landowners to the majority of dispossessed poor peasants. The process first required an evaluation of all the landholdings in the village, followed by their redistribution more fairly according to the status of each individual. The specific demarcation of each status was where mistakes often occurred and the need arose to redo the land reform.

During our visit to the countryside, we stayed in poor peasants' homes, which were heated only by coal burning stoves. My major challenges were to learn how to identify different degrees of exploitation, and how to differentiate between poor peasants, middle peasants, and landlords. The worst landlords had committed all kinds of violence against the peasantry and were easily identified as "vicious despots." Intellectually, I understood the issues, because I had read about the land reform before I came to China, but still I made some crazy mistakes. One day our team entered a courtyard where an old lady in black clothing was drawing water from the well. She could hardly have looked more miserable. I said to the leader, "I presume that is a poor peasant." He corrected me: "No, that is the landlord. Don't forget, although this area is close to Beijing, it is very poor. Most of China's peasants, including landlords, have a very low standard of living."

During class struggle sessions, the poor peasants encircled the landlord/lady, shaking their fists and shouting fierce accusations. Hitting was against regulations, but did happen sometimes. The most amazing thing to me was to witness the sudden change in the demeanour of poor peasants. From time immemorial they had grovelled before their exploiters, never imagining they could demand justice and relief for their sufferings. But now, encouraged by the outside teams, they radiated a new kind of dignity.

The most difficult task during this early period of land reform was to convince the peasants that they had the right to overthrow the authority of their oppressors. The Party could not liberate them; they had to do it themselves.

This meant overturning thousands of years of Confucian tradition, which had forced them to kowtow to a hierarchy of authorities and to accept their misery as fate. Backed by the PLA, the land reform process was designed to change the deeply rooted power structures in every village.

Returning to Beijing, I found that my field of international law had been expunged from the university curriculum as an "instrument of imperialism." I was disappointed but not entirely surprised. I subsequently found part-time work as a translator of short stories and wrote articles for magazines like *World Knowledge*. Freelancing gave me time to reflect on what was expected of intellectuals like myself in China's New Democracy. By March 1950, I felt my first impressions had ripened sufficiently to attempt to answer the questions of friends in the United States, who were waiting to return or were simply trying to understand events in China. What I wrote reflected the first steps in my own metamorphosis as a Western-trained intellectual in the maelstrom of the revolution. Although lengthy, I will transcribe it here in full as it records my unvarnished impressions of my first four months in New China.

METAMORPHOSIS

Where to begin? China, old and new, has been the subject of many notorious generalizations. Yet the most convincing lesson of travel in China for me has been the obvious complexity: development is uneven, cities differ greatly from villages and from each other, conditions change at an unbelievable pace under the pressure of need.

A one-eyed reporter can still record a black, terrifying picture. Suffering and poverty remain the lot of the majority; ignorance and inexperience retard reconstruction; old ideas are alive and new errors are born every day. And if you are looking for Totalitarianism (as defined by the Hearsts and Luces), it's really quite easy: confine your contacts to landlords or Shanghai businessmen, shattered by the demise of black marketeering and speculative profits; or to American missionaries who speak only English and can't travel to see what's going on; or to English-speaking Chinese with foreign-bred reservations. Talk with anyone whose way of life is still tied to the fast-fraying apron strings of China's old order and who has made no serious effort to understand the goals of the new leadership and the New Democracy, and you can collect a garbage can of "facts" to demonstrate the horrors of Communism.

On the other hand, it is also impossible to make sense of the country from the lyrics of those puerile, ultra-left "kindergarteners" (fortunately few though loud) who pour a beautiful sheen of doctrinaire lacquer over all the unmended dents, cracks, and scars of the new order. Doctrine has its place, but by itself, its froth and foam can cover up the virtues as well as vices of actual practice.

Black/white absolutes are the currency of ideologues. Yet truth is more than a heap of unrelated facts, and real objectivity demands that one also account for one's own subjective attitudes in analyzing data. For example, "progressives" must recognize that instinctively we still react to events as middle-class intellectuals whose starting-point is the individual. Only through conscious effort in living, thinking, and working here does one begin to accept the principle that the interests of the majority – the peasants and workers – come first in the priorities of the government.

We also must remind ourselves that no amount of explanation will clarify trends here without placing facts in historical, economic, and cultural perspective. Some businessmen claim, for example, that economically we are no better off than under the KMT. Actually, in a few parts of China, this is true. But how did this situation develop? Decades of war, famine, KMT devastation, and a bad 1949 harvest are the objective terms under which the government is working. The question then is whether the situation will be left to stand or to deteriorate, as under the KMT, or will current methods prove positive in the long run?

It would be a thankless task to try to provide a coherent picture of the actual situation here. I shall not try, but rather will suggest ways in which one who is preparing to return to serve our people may mentally prepare him/herself. I direct the suggestions chiefly to intellectuals, like myself, with middle-class or Western-trained backgrounds.

If one has already decided to return, it is likely that one has already acquired a generally favorable picture of the New Democracy, so I shall not waste words of encouragement. Regardless of how progressive one is, however, it seems necessary to acquire mental shock absorbers for the impact of actually working and living in the New Democracy. What must one expect to find different or even disagreeable at first? Speaking from experience, I would say that the intellectual's adjustments fall into two categories – physical and spiritual.

Physical Adjustments: Austerity is the necessary badge of public service in New China. For highly trained college graduates, work in government will disappoint if they anticipate a routine job, paying a comfortable salary. Indeed, government work has become a *mission,* not a "position." With any other viewpoint but of patriotic duty, one is unlikely to be attracted to starting salaries for engineers (technical personnel are by far the highest paid) of 600 jin [catty] of millet, or the equivalent of about US$25 per month. It must be remembered that this government is stripped for action, as if in a war, against the remnants of the old order.

It is difficult for those outside China to grasp that this is a real revolution, led by a revolutionary government, with a new class of government workers unknown in the history of Chinese officialdom. They are men and women sacrificing and fighting against time and huge odds with hardly time to think of their own interests, yet with the morale and esprit du corps characteristic of a conquering army. Here in Peking three do the work of five and five eat the food of three. From cabinet ministers to messenger boys, men and women in ill-fitting, sometimes frayed and faded blue uniforms stream in and out of Peking's government offices, which are bare of all but the basic necessities. Time and money are not available to repair broken windows and to pave Peking's more wretched hutongs. The government rolled up its sleeves only last October, inheriting a shattered economy from the KMT. Pioneers cutting a new path do not expect the comforts of home. But those who return to China today will have the chance to be architects of their nation's future and will receive the gratitude of their own people. It will be clear to all that neither money nor a privileged life, but only the desire to serve, to work hard to redeem the sacrifices of others and to realize the hopes of 400 million countrymen, were the incentives bringing them home to New China.

Spiritual Adjustments: What then of the spiritual obstacles to adjusting to the new China? Once inside liberated China, you will find that you have stepped suddenly from a relatively static world into a dynamic world of multifaceted change. No newspaper or second-hand accounts can replace personally experiencing this change, since one of the very objects of the revolution is thought itself.

From the moment you step inside China at Canton or Tianjin, you enter into a struggle with yourself. Whether acquired in old China or in America, you have established standards and habits of life and thought by which you automatically judge all that goes on around you. According to these old values, some aspects of the new order may strike middle-class intellectuals as anathema:

(1) Discipline: Perhaps we pride ourselves as being disciplined. Yet our discipline has often only served self-interest and always has been dictated by individual judgment. But here, discipline derives from social direction, conformity to the norms and needs of the majority, rejecting the idea that individuality per se has innate value of its own. Totalitarianism! But then you observe peasants and workers and see their dignity as individuals has been enhanced rather than violated. You meet the lofty though iron morality of the cadres and think: Police state! But far from a police state, you are reminded of Sunday school every day or a huge adult Boy Scout troop. Persuasion is promoted mainly by a powerful group process of criticism/self-criticism unheard of in China's old civil service and guaranteed to discipline integrity, teamwork, and efficiency into the most weak or individualistic. This new type of all-persuasive discipline is not easy for individualistic people to swallow in one dose.

(2) Mass action: It is difficult for middle-class intellectuals to resolve the paradox of going down to the level of the masses in order to progress – to elevate physical labour to the same status as intellectual endeavor and to learn from it. From long habit, they think of themselves as natural leaders by the mere act of higher cerebration. Yet a single experience of taking part in a land reform team teaches the lesson that, under favorable conditions, the broad masses of the people possess both the wisdom and the knowledge to solve their own problems. To cast off the intellectual's traditional aloofness from the masses will be an effort that cannot be entirely painless.

(3) The spirit of struggle: Peasants and workers have been the direct victims of aggressive war and feudal subjugation. Today the cadres are helping 400 million people to direct their hatred of injustice at an old system of power, which reduced their lives to an existence not far above the animals that tilled their fields. In this situation, the problem of the intellectual is that he is compassionate, but indiscriminately so. His habits of thought tend to direct his compassion to individuals closer to his way of life, rather than to the broad masses so alien to his daily contacts. He might instinctively extend pity to a weeping landlord writhing before the verbal cross-examination of a village meeting, while accepting as a matter of course the lifelong misery of millions of peasants. He may only achieve deeper compassion for the suffering of the great majority when he realizes that it takes the year-round toil and sweat of anywhere from 50 to 100 farmers to support the kind of life he enjoys.

(4) Community life: By contrast to life in a New York apartment, one's life here is an open book and anyone can turn the pages. Lack of privacy is not by malicious forethought, but a natural outgrowth of a close family community. One nurtures in such a community an acutely sensitive social conscience, which sets the limit for extravagances or thoughtless ways of living. An intellectual accustomed to regarding his lifestyle and behavior as strictly private property, like his money or house, will find it a bit awkward.

(5) Puritanism: The strain of severe Puritanism in today's government agencies extends from outer appearances to interior ways of thought. Awkward uniforms, dilapidated government buildings, and unsightly manners reflect the preoccupation of the government with immediate needs, but it is likely that the innate "façadism" of some middle-class intellectuals would rebel against such outer shabbiness. Then there is the earnestness of government workers who hold to a code of honour by which a small gift from anyone but close friend or relative might be taken as an affront to his character. No sense of humor? Yes, simple, sincere, sometimes boisterous humor. But not the humor of the old morality, which could be drawn upon to laugh away a little squeeze here and a little bribe there, or to indulge in lavish rounds of pleasure with a conscience drowned in cynical resignation to the "unavoidability" of official venality. For speculators, KMT carpetbaggers, and other feeders on human flesh, this must indeed be a joyless world. For an intellectual, it is a world whose joys he must train his ears to appreciate and gradually his heart to embrace.

(6) The Party's monopoly on information: This will be one of the hardest pills for old-type intellectuals to swallow. The first barrage of edited news, slogans, and propaganda from the liberated newspapers hits one square in the spot where an intellectual hurts most – his carefully nurtured mind, with all its huff and puff about freedom of inquiry. But the use of mass media for education is frank and gradually one appreciates its full significance in the context of: (a) the long feudal background of Chinese society, plus a low level of literacy; (b) continued acts of KMT sabotage; and (c) the tremendous power of negative reaction abroad. Until the advent of administrative orders, the newspapers also serve as conveyers of policy statements, reports, and educational information to cadres scattered across the country. With the picture of US newspapers fresh in mind – divorces, murder, comics, who had a con by whom in Hollywood, Republicans slinging mud at Democrats and the mud going

the other way again – one is inclined at first to find the newspapers here drably pedagogic. Then there is the political tone. Whence the "loyal opposition"? Is this not a "controlled press"? Perhaps. But the meaning of "democratic centralism" in China is in the constant objective demonstration that all forms of control are in the interest of all the people.

(7) The demise of face, fate, and favor: Intellectuals used to climbing to official position by old methods will be sorely disappointed. The revolutionary government puts a premium on the usefulness of what one knows and how effectively one can apply such knowledge. College degrees are respected, but not worshipped, and there is no place for the "overeducated" who disdainfully relies on his fund of diplomas, technical jargon, or family connections to gain status.

(8) Sense of movement, development, and historical stages: An appreciation of historical movement is key. Old intellectuals are apt to judge by absolutes and to be deeply critical of the wrongs, outrages, and individual errors, past and present, committed by the new leadership. Some of these mistakes are the legacy of years of oppression, war, and desperate struggle. They should be judged harshly, but they should never be judged absolutely unless and until mistakes are left unmended over a period of time. We are still recovering, not yet building. The new leadership is bound to make many false starts, carry out unsuccessful experiments, and produce policies which cannot immediately be understood. Old categories of thought often do not fit into the necessary flux and strain of guided progress toward concrete long-term goals. Intellectuals must learn to work and think together as an interrelated process.

These are some of the likely adjustments facing us as we enter this great era in China's history. On the whole, we intellectuals are pure of motive but have yet to acquire by direct experience vision enough to see that the building of New China may sometimes hurt our sensitivities or even our own interests.

I hoped that my observations would prepare and encourage my colleagues for the exigencies of life in New China, but knew that only direct experience would convince them of my words.

Chapter Seven

BEIJING LEARNINGS

During the four months that Paul was in China, the children and I remained in Hong Kong with my parents. Father especially adored baby Douglas and little Christopher, who was four and a half years old, curious and smart. We were so engrossed with our new adventure that we failed to appreciate the predicament my parents were in at this turbulent time. Their old world in China had collapsed; they had just been uprooted from their home in Shanghai and money was tight. Mother was not happy with our decision to return to China and was disappointed that Paul had not finished his PHD at Harvard. She feared for our safety and worried over the hardships awaiting us. Father was more philosophical and understood our dream to help build a democratic and prosperous new China. He was confident we would face no problems, for as far as the new regime was concerned our records were as clean as a new sheet of paper. Besides, he said, we could always come back to them if necessary.

Paul returned to Hong Kong in early spring 1950, having found us a home in Beijing. We noticed that he had lost some weight, but appeared fit and inspired by what he had experienced. We left at the end of April for Tianjin, leaving baby Douglas in the care of my parents. Our plan was for me to return to Hong Kong in a year to bring him to Beijing, when we would be more settled and he would be a little older.

In addition to our personal effects, we were allowed to bring in two English Raleigh bicycles, which would be our essential means of transportation. Since we were moving to China to live, clearing customs was a matter of routine, but there was no nonsense. To make sure we did not smuggle anything in, the inspector made me empty a bag full of dirty laundry. We spent one night in Tianjin before catching the morning train to Beijing. Similar to Paul's earlier experience, two armed soldiers awoke us in the middle of the night, demanding to check our travel documents.

I had grown up in Shanghai and had never been to north China. Paul asked the pedicab drivers to take us home via Tiananmen Square in the heart of Beijing. I was awed by the magnificence of the Forbidden City, renowned as the largest palace complex in the world. It was tightly guarded by a moat and an imperial square, walled in on the eastern, western, and southern sides. The roofs of the palace were tiled in gold; the walls and portals were painted vermilion red. The square's majestic grandeur evoked a sweeping sense of history, a vista of centuries of ancient Chinese civilization. The pedi-cabs wound their way northwards through streets and *hutongs*, a crisscross of lanes that dated back seven hundred years. Finally we reached the Drum Tower at the north end of the city, beyond which flowed the Houhai (Back Lake). Along its picturesque banks lined with weeping willows stood a row of *si-he-yuan*, compounds with living quarters built around a courtyard.

Paul took us to number 24E, which would be our first home in Beijing. Friends of the absentee Hong Kong landlord occupied the large and desir-able north wing, facing south. We rented the smaller east and west wings, unconnected but facing each other across the courtyard. We used the east wing as our bedroom, with an adjoining washroom equipped with a sink and Japanese-style flush toilet, but no bathtub. The west wing served as our living and dining room, attached to a separate cooking area. Because our liv-ing quarters were completely unfurnished, we camped with friends of a rela-tive for the first few days. Our host family was in turmoil when we arrived. Their newly constructed dream home, located near the Imperial Palace along the route to Beihai Park, was coveted by the new regime. It was a gated, Western-style concrete mansion with modern conveniences and a lush grass lawn. They were most reluctant to surrender it, but had little choice.

Soon, my mother's elder sister, Auntie Yimin, arrived to welcome us to Beijing, accompanied by my first cousins, none of whom I had seen in over a decade. Auntie Yimin was a scholar in Chinese classics and had tutored us at home when we lived in Shanghai. Her daughter, Cousin Jinxin, was the first Chinese student to graduate from the Berlin Conservatory of Music in the 1930s and was well versed in English, German, and Chinese. Her brother, Cousin Yilin, had always been a brilliant student with a genuine respect for the poor. Even as a young teenager, he would bow to thank the rickshaw-puller after each ride. While studying at Qinghua University in the 1930s, he had participated in protests against Japanese aggression and became a Party member at that time. When we met in 1950, he was the vice-minister of trade.

While we were catching up on old times, our host poured his housing troubles into the ear of my cousin, who listened patiently but made no comment, as the matter was not under his jurisdiction. In the end, when repeated negotiations with the authorities failed, our hosts decided to pack up and leave for Hong Kong. They offered to sell us their good-quality furniture at a reasonable price, but even then we could not afford to buy it. At the time I did not appreciate the unfolding historical drama I was witnessing. In a microcosm, it reflected the transfer of wealth and power from the haves to the have-nots after a revolution. I learned later that my parents' house in Shanghai, No. 20 rue Portier, was also confiscated, along with all the properties that had belonged to government officials of Chiang Kai-shek's regime.

We bought some inexpensive second-hand furniture, a coal briquette stove, and utensils at the street markets. If we had had the means, and the inclination, we could have picked up antique treasures and paintings by masters at rock-bottom prices. Our new home, though sparsely furnished, was comfortable and clean. In order to cook three meals a day, however, we had to keep the coal briquette stove constantly lit; otherwise we might spend hours trying to relight the flame. There was also no furnace to heat water for bathing or laundry. It became a necessity of life to engage a housekeeper, to free ourselves from the drudgery of household chores so that we could go to work.

Shortly after moving in, we discovered that our next-door neighbour was the well-known Dr George Hatem (his Chinese name was Ma Haide). An American-born dermatologist, he had come to China in 1933 to study tropical medicine and married a Chinese actress and film director named Zou Sufei. When we met him, he was working at the Ministry of Health, in charge of eradicating venereal disease and, later, leprosy. He was fluently bilingual and bicultural, charming, articulate, and humorous, as well as a smooth dancer to both Western and Chinese music. Being neighbours, we visited them frequently that summer.

I found a nearby kindergarten for Lin Kai (Christopher), staffed with professionally trained teachers. With a smattering of Beijing dialect, he easily passed the entrance IQ test. But many challenges of cultural adjustment awaited him even at his tender age of five. In New York, his black nursery school teacher had taught him how to fight back when bullied by a white boy. In Hong Kong, the English boys at the international school had regarded fist fighting as a sport. But here in China, children were taught not to fight. It took us years of loving patience to tame him to be "civilized" and disciplined according to Chinese standards. His teacher told us that his classmates liked to play with him, but were also slightly intimidated and nicknamed him the "big tiger."

Initially I took Chris to and from school on the back of my bicycle, cycling over unpaved lanes and a bridge that crossed a dry creek. The smooth stone bridge was often slick after rain and, out riding one afternoon, we toppled from the bridge into the creek bed. I hit my head and was knocked unconscious. When I revived, I found myself in a pedicab with Chris wailing on my lap. Fortunately, neither Chris nor I suffered any broken bones in this mishap; even the bicycle remained intact. After this incident, I decided to let our housekeeper shepherd Chris to school and I would find a job to supplement our limited income.

FIRST JOB IN CHINA

In May, Madame Soong Ching Ling arrived in Beijing from Shanghai on official duties. The previous year, she had been elected one of six vice-chairpersons of the Central People's Government by the Chinese People's Political Consultative Conference (CPPCC). Despite her busy schedule, she invited Eileen and me to her residence for a private dinner and introduced me to two senior diplomats in the foreign ministry. Qiao Guanhua was director general of Asian Affairs and concurrent director of the China Information Bureau. His wife, Gong Peng, was director general of the foreign ministry's information bureau.

Appreciative of the complexities of the new political culture, I did not expect an immediate job offer from them, despite Madame Soong's kind introduction. I had come to China to learn, not to climb a career ladder. I wanted to experience the tremendous transformation of China that was underway and to discover if I could integrate its revolutionary values into my identity. To that end, I spent my days reading Mao's works and later was quite pleased when Qiao offered me a job in the China Information Bureau. I would be chief editor of a daily English-language bulletin of international news, gleaned from the major wire services. Named "For Your Information Only" (FYIO), it catered to government offices and various embassies.

I began work at the end of May 1950, starting off on my bicycle at 6:30 am to reach the office at Xuan Wu Men, in the south end of the city, half an hour later. I often did not return home until after 8:00 pm, sometimes later. The work was not difficult, but the hours were long and the only day of rest was Sunday. By then, I was usually exhausted.

In 1951, I was transferred from FYIO to head the English broadcasting division of the Overseas News Department. Liu Zunqi, deputy director of the China Information Bureau, a veteran journalist, and an international affairs specialist whom I had met in New York in 1947, had asked specifically for my services. This new post involved teaching and training personnel in English broadcasting, hosting news programs, editing, and writing major news articles.

"SOFT LANDING" IN THE PRC

I wholeheartedly shared Paul's vision of the New China, which was why I returned with him to China without hesitation, despite the turbulent times. Practical by nature, however, I looked for a job that would provide us with enough income to survive. Paul's salary was minimal. The summer of 1950, I heard that the embassy of Czechoslovakia, a socialist country friendly to China, was looking for an English secretary and the pay was higher than at any of the Chinese organizations. I applied and was hired, supported by a reference letter from Gong Pusheng, a YWCA friend of ours in New York, who was now a senior staff member in the Chinese foreign ministry and the elder sister of Gong Peng, whom I had met at Madame Soong's the year before.

Although Paul respected my decision, I felt I was regarded by some of our peers as being "non-progressive" in New China's political culture, because my primary motive was not to advance the revolution, but to take care of my little family. Perhaps I was overly sensitive, but there were some "pseudo-revolutionaries" who seemed to avoid close association with overseas Chinese, intellectuals with Western training, and non-members of the Chinese Communist Party. Even a few "old friends" whom we had known well in New York fell into this category.

I enjoyed my time at the Czechoslovakian embassy, which provided me with a "soft landing" in China. The embassy staff was warm and helpful, led by a most impressive ambassador. I was one of three Chinese secretaries. The most senior was Mrs Mai, whom I later learned was a granddaughter of Kang Youwei, the leader of the historic 1898 Hundred Days' Reform at the end of the Manchu Dynasty. It turned out that the ambassador and his family had been in New York prior to this China posting, so we had many pleasant conversations about our days in the United States. A year later, I was ready to move on and face new challenges. Paul alerted me that the Overseas News Department of the China Information Bureau was looking for more English-language editors. I applied and was accepted.

BRINGING HOME BABY DOUG

In the summer of 1951, we moved house from Houhai in the north end of the city to a *hutong* in Dongcheng, the eastern part of the city, to be closer to our office. Our second home was in the north wing of a small compound owned by a tiny old lady with bound feet. She had once been the concubine of an old man, who left her their "love nest" when he departed. I then went to Hong Kong to collect baby Douglas from my parents. They were aging. Father was suffering from heart troubles; Mother wanted to move with Father and my sister Mary to Taiwan, where the cost of living was lower and they had a network of relatives and old friends who had accompanied Chiang Kai-shek and his Nationalist government to Taipei.

Travel from mainland China to Hong Kong was not easy, and was made more difficult by the Korean War, which had begun in 1950. Fortunately, the China Information Bureau facilitated my travel documents and, in return, I brought back some much-needed equipment and supplies for the office; they provided me with official requisition slips to show Chinese customs. When I arrived at the Guangzhou train station from Beijing, an armed PLA soldier suddenly appeared and brusquely said, "Follow me." Off the train, he passed me to a young female soldier, who minutely searched both me and my belongings. When she found the official requisition letters I was carrying, she dismissed me. I was not nervous, for I had done nothing wrong, but I needed an explanation for this unwarranted search. I politely asked why I had been targeted and was coldly told, "We have our reasons." Later it dawned on me that I had probably aroused suspicion by chatting on the train with a Soviet technical expert who had been invited to China to help in its industrialization. He and I had been the only two passengers in first class during the long journey to south China.

Entering Hong Kong was another hurdle, due to the quota system imposed by the British to limit the number of Chinese coming into the colony. My parents had advised me to exit China at Zhu Hai and take a ferry from Macau to Hong Kong. They said a "yellow cow" would take care of me, but did not elaborate further. I saw a boatman on the dock and without thinking blurted out, "Comrade, do you know where I can find the yellow cow?"

Shocked by my question, he angrily retorted, "Who is your comrade? There is no yellow cow here!" How could I forget that I was no longer in China? And even though I had no idea what "yellow cow" meant, I had obviously said something improper. I dared not ask any more questions and worried in silence. When the ferry docked in Hong Kong harbour, I was ever so relieved to see my parents, sister Mary, and nanny holding my baby in her arms. They explained that my entry to Hong Kong had been arranged through bribes to the "yellow cows" – middlemen.

It was wonderful to visit with my parents after a year in Beijing. They wanted to know all about New China, our work, family, and friends, and I wanted to catch up on all their news. Although we knew that Paul's father in Canada had recently remarried, we did not know any details. I learned that his stepmother's name was Shi Peixuan, a missionary from Guangzhou who was many years his junior. A relative had introduced her to Paul's father after he had expressed interest in a companion for his old age. Since China was still in a state of flux, they had married in Hong Kong and returned to Canada to live.

Finally the day of our departure came. It was wrenching to tear baby Doug away from his beloved nanny. He wailed all the way from Hong Kong to Beijing from a little broken heart. At the Guangzhou railway station, he caught sight of the back of a Chinese amah with a long braid and dashed over, thinking she was his Ah Sheng Jie, only to be sadly disappointed. His yearning for her brought tears to my eyes. I could only comfort him with my love and give him time to reconnect with me.

Otherwise our return trip was trouble free. Now that I had become more politically astute, I uttered not one word of English although there were foreigners sitting across from us on the train. When we arrived at the Beijing station, Paul and Chris greeted us eagerly. Our little family was together again.

FATHER CHEN'S PASSING

After my parents moved from Hong Kong to Taiwan in 1952, communicating with them became more difficult. By circuitous routes, we learned that Father passed away in early 1953 from a heart attack at the age of sixty-three. I sadly reflected that I had spent less than fifteen years of my life with Father. Beginning in 1937, war and revolution had torn our family apart. Yet he had always provided well for his children, ensuring all of us achieved good educations. When I later told Madame Soong Ching Ling of my father's

death, she consoled me on my loss, and said: "Mr Chen was a good man."
She had known Father in Wuhan in the 1920s, in Shanghai in the 1930s,
and as a neighbour in Zhongqing in the 1940s.

Mother and my sister Mary soon left Taiwan for California, to live near
my younger sister Louise and her family. My brothers and I were in the
People's Republic. Mother told me many years later that shortly after she
and Father moved to Taiwan, he was given an audience with Generalissimo
Chiang Kai-shek, in whose KMT government he had worked for nearly
twenty-five years. The Generalissimo entered the room, sat down, turned to
him, and asked, "Where are your children?" This appeared to be the beginning and the end of the audience.

Nearly forty years later, in November 1992, Paul and I finally had an
opportunity to pay our respects to Father at his tomb in Taipei. It had been
kept in perfect condition by a distant relative who, as a primary school
student, had been the recipient of a scholarship fund that my parents had
set up in his village of Diankou. I knew Father would be pleased that facing
his grave across the Taiwan Straits was his native province of Zhejiang.

LEARNING A NEW SKILL

I began work in the domestic news section of the Overseas News Department of the China Information Bureau in the summer of 1951. Having been
away from China from 1937 to 1949, working on domestic news helped
to reacquaint me with a China so different from what I had known in the
1930s. My work involved interviewing, writing, translating, and editing.
With no training in journalism, I learned the craft on the job. Several foreign
experts were engaged to polish our work and teach us the rudiments of
Western journalism. They included Douglas Springhall, Alan Winnington
and Michael Shapiro from England, Eleanor Chaidden from the United
States, Virginia and Colin Penn from London, and Dick and Lillian Diamond
from Australia. My Western education made communication easy and we
all became good friends.

In the early 1950s, the atmosphere in government organizations was informal and relations among colleagues were warm, irrespective of rank.
The leading cadres usually came from the caves of Yenan or other "liberated
areas." The staff was recruited from across the country, Hong Kong, and
abroad. We were united in the single purpose of helping to build the New
China. Pay for Chinese personnel was minimal and our living standard was

Eileen (second from left) shares a laugh with colleagues at
the Chinese Information Bureau in the early 1950s.

Eileen teaches Douglas to swim in the lake of Beijing's
Summer Palace, 1954.

at subsistence level, but no one complained. Paul and I gathered with
colleagues on Sundays to visit Beijing's parks and scenic spots; we had fun
swimming, ice skating, and social dancing at office parties. These were years
of warm camaraderie when we were still young and idealistic. It was also
wonderful to have family nearby. The China Information Bureau was only
a few blocks from Auntie Yimin's home and I often visited her during my
lunch hour.

THE "GOLDEN" REHABILITATION YEARS

The years 1950 to 1953 were the formative years of the People's Republic of China (PRC), during which Mao Zedong sought to create a "socialist" system and find a new path to economic development. The Kuomintang had left the national economy in a shambles, with industry on the verge of bankruptcy, mines flooded, railways paralyzed, and agriculture unable to supply enough grain and cotton. Prices in KMT-controlled areas had multiplied by 6 million times between August 1937 and August 1948. In February 1950, the Central People's Government issued its "Decision on Unified Control of National Economy and Finance," and within a year the galloping inflation and prices were mostly under control.

When I first visited the freshly liberated cities of China, the ugly scars of the old society stared me in the face. Scruffy dogs lapped up the excrement of equally hungry urchins in the streets; open sewers and fly-ridden latrines made passersby gag. Poverty, disease, and starvation afflicted millions. The national mortality rate was said to be twenty-five per thousand, the infant mortality rate 200 per thousand. The most dreaded diseases – smallpox, dysentery, cholera, typhoid, malaria, schistosomiasis, kala azar – claimed countless lives.

Yet incredibly, within a few years smallpox and cholera were eradicated and opium addiction and prostitution disappeared along with mass unemployment. These advances helped to reduce the incidence of mental diseases such as neurosyphilis and general paresis of the insane, which had comprised ten per cent of hospital cases before Liberation. New standards of personal and environmental hygiene became part of the new national ethos. Foreign visitors judged Chinese cities to be among the cleanest in the world and the country was well on its way to building a comprehensive healthcare system. How did it happen? Leadership and popular participation were key. Success lay in the willing mobilization of the entire population.

SOCIAL REFORMS AND THE PATRIOTIC HEALTH CAMPAIGN

Seven major social reform movements were undertaken during China's first three years. The most significant was the Patriotic Health Campaign, launched in March 1952 as a result of US germ warfare in the ongoing Korean War. The health campaign was a massive political movement. Millions of citizens were mobilized from the cities to the countryside, to clean up the environment and to set up a universal, if primitive, medical system. Old ladies with bound feet sat on their stools swatting their daily quota of flies, which they enticed with bits of salted fish. All pests that spread disease, like mice and mangy dogs, were eliminated. Primary schoolchildren roamed the streets politely asking their elders to refrain from spitting and littering.

Eileen was asked by her trade union to take charge of the department's spring-cleaning campaign. I teased her that this "honour" was due to her fastidiousness about hygiene, a product of her bourgeois background. She was remarkably successful in gaining everyone's cooperation – the windows sparkled, the floors were spotless, and the office furniture gleamed.

Other major social reforms included the suppression of counter-revolutionaries; eliminating bandits, spies, and reactionary cult leaders left over from the KMT regime; closing down brothels, opium dens and gambling joints; and re-educating prostitutes, petty thieves, and beggars for meaningful employment. Further movements included the Three Antis (corruption, waste, and bureaucracy) and the Five Antis (bribery, tax evasion, shoddy work, theft of national properties, and state economic secrets); reform of the old education system, including the remolding of intellectuals; and the proclamation of the new Marriage Law, which released women from the feudal bonds of landlords, clans, and husbands. Women could now hold land in their own names, arranged marriages were forbidden, and divorce was made much easier. Soong Ching Ling and her colleague He Xiangning had championed women's rights from the 1920s and were especially pleased to see this new law adopted.

The remarkable successes of the rehabilitation years stemmed from the collective efforts of the Chinese people, who were motivated by the government's inclusive policy of uniting not only with the workers and peasants, but with all who wished to serve the people and the nation.

THE KOREAN WAR

Half a year into China's all-out efforts to restore its national economy, civil war broke out in Korea on June 25, 1950. US President Truman declared that the United States would intervene on the side of South Korea and dispatched its Seventh Fleet to the Taiwan Straits. On July 7, the United States pressured the United Nations to pass a resolution to send troops to Korea under command of the American General Douglas MacArthur. After much debate seventeen countries participated, including Canada. The Korean War became the first hot war of the Cold War, fought partly by surrogate armies from the United States and the People's Republic of China.

By June 1951, Chinese volunteers and the North Korean army had forced the UN troops south of the 38th parallel and the Americans to the negotiating table. Two years of intermittent but fierce fighting followed, alongside difficult negotiations. The armistice was finally signed in Panmunjon on July 27, 1953, after both sides had suffered tremendous casualties. This was a major loss of face for the United States – the first time an American general had signed a peace treaty for a war he did not win. For China, it marked the first time in the nation's modern history that it had successfully stared down the world's number one imperial power, even with only a modest air force. This victory was a source of great pride for the Chinese people.

LIVING AS ONE OF THE MASSES

Since both Paul and I were earning low wages, we could no longer afford our rent and applied to the China Information Bureau for subsidized housing. Eventually we were assigned to the bureau's dormitory on the west side of the city. No. 41 Yang Shi Dai Jie (Sheep Market Avenue) was on a quiet street and the monthly rent was approximately five American dollars.

The compound was impressive: the central buildings displayed Western and Chinese motifs and were enclosed behind a set of vermilion red gates. Three main courtyards followed one after another down the centre of the compound, linked by long pavilions painted in traditional red and green. In the middle of the compound stood a large assembly hall, and behind the last courtyard lay a formal garden with grass, flowerbeds and miniature mountains made of rocks. The compound had once been the grand estate of a wealthy and powerful family; now it served as a dormitory for multiple households.

The bureau allocated quarters to each family based on rank and need. The rooms in the main courtyards had wooden floors, plaster ceilings, and glass windows. Our new "home," however, turned out to be the old horse stable in an unpaved side courtyard that had been used for parking rickshaws and cars. Inside, the stable was spacious, but the floor was mud and both the windows and ceiling were covered with rice paper. I was not thrilled, but did not complain because we had gone to China as private individuals on our own initiative, without invitation or "revolutionary" credentials. I was able to make the stable more livable by covering the mud floor with bamboo mats, which I also hung from the ceiling to separate our sleeping quarters from our living and eating areas. My worst fear was the rats

that lived above the rice paper ceiling. At night, we could hear them racing
back and forth overhead. I was terrified that one might fall on us. The rice
paper windows were useless against the cold and the rain, so we installed a
dusty coal-ball-burning stove to keep us warm during the winter. We cooked
our meals on a coal briquette stove outside, drew water from the courtyard's
cold water tap, and made do with an outhouse. We bathed at the bureau,
which provided separate showers for men and women, with hot running
water.

In April 1952, the China Information Bureau underwent several mergers.
Paul's division joined the Central Broadcasting Bureau. The Overseas News
Department became part of Xinhua News Agency, where I was assigned to
the North American and European section of the International Department.
No longer cadres with the China Information Bureau, we moved house to
the sparse comfort of Radio Peking's dormitories. Despite the cramped conditions, the floor was paved with easily mopped red tiles, the windows were
made of glass, and the ceilings were of white plaster. No more rat races!
Yet we still cooked on our coal briquette stove in the small courtyard and
shared the toilets with others. As usual, there was no facility to take a bath
or shower. Eventually we moved into a new Radio Peking apartment block
where we shared a unit of four bedrooms with two other families. The three
households used one kitchen, each with its own coal briquette stove. There
was a bathtub, but no hot water, and only one toilet was available for the
ten of us. Only in November 1961 were we assigned an apartment of our
own. Although it was still a coldwater flat, we had three rooms that we made
into a clean and cosy home. Due to Paul's added responsibilities, we also had
a private telephone, which was an uncommon luxury in those days.

RECTIFICATION CAMPAIGNS

Although we were ready to endure the physical hardships of China's poverty,
neither of us was mentally prepared for the incessant ideological struggles of
Mao's revolution. The new public ethos of selfless hard work, frugality, and
seemingly incorruptible "Serve the People" values moved me deeply when we
first arrived. This was sustained by the popular surge of hope for change and
by the Communists' didactic campaigns to generate a unifying socialist morality. This unity, however, was soon vitiated by excessive campaigns that often
found "class enemies" where they simply did not exist.

It was more than merely building a new state. The Party was intent on transforming not only the socio-economic system, but also the consciousness of human beings themselves. At first I accepted this. I had come to China to learn and although I was from a poor Christian family, I had been educated in elite American universities and knew that I consequently also had much to "unlearn" as I found my way in New China.

In my case, there was the added burden of having been born with the original sin of belonging to a family now classified as "bureaucratic bourgeoisie"– an enemy class – which had been nurtured by the "blood and sweat of the people." My parents were not vicious or despotic, but kind and considerate to those around them, having endured the deprivations and degradation of poverty during their childhoods. As Christians, they had instilled in us ethics of generosity, humility, and service.

After a period of agonizing soul-searching, questioning my very existence and self-worth, I managed to resolve these contradictions by separating the politics of the day from my personal life. I had not chosen the class into which I was born and could not reject my parents for their lives prior to New China. I could only be responsible for my own actions. Some others with backgrounds similar to mine became afraid of contacting their families outside China, but from the start I kept in touch with my parents and siblings to ease their worry.

ZHOU ENLAI ON THE CCP'S POLICY ON INTELLECTUALS

After Liberation, the Chinese Communist Party worked hard to "unite, educate, and remold" intellectuals to revolutionary values and to win them over to the working class. Yet even as early as 1951, Mao encouraged a succession of critiques on literature and art that targeted well-known intellectuals, like Yu Pingpo on his book *Studies of the "Dream of the Red Chamber."* Too often, instead of reasoned dialogue and debate, simplistic political negation and vicious personal attacks tarnished reputations and brilliant careers – injustices that were not acknowledged by the authorities for decades.

Fortunately the number of victims was limited and most intellectuals were left unscathed. Still, we were required to attend daily political study sessions and participate in the discussions. I was genuinely interested in the unfolding philosophical polemics, which exposed me to various schools of thought in Chinese literature and philosophy, but of course intellectual inquiry per se was not the point of the exercise.

A major breakthrough regarding the status and work of intellectuals came in January 1956 when Premier Zhou Enlai addressed a conference hosted by the Party's Central Committee. The meeting was timely, as China's dire shortage of scientists and specialists in all fields of knowledge was becoming increasingly evident. Speaking to an audience of over one thousand Party officials in government, universities, scientific academics, and literary and art associations, Premier Zhou emphasized the important role intellectuals must play in China's socialist construction. He acknowledged their outstanding contributions over the previous six years and expressed his confidence that the vast majority had succeeded in becoming part of the working class. He went on to criticize some in the Party for their sectarian attitudes and failure to appreciate the talents and skills that intellectuals could contribute to rebuilding the country. He urged the leadership to work more closely with non-Party intellectuals, to trust and support them in work appropriate to their experience, and to provide them with adequate living conditions.

Needless to say, intellectuals everywhere were exhilarated by the premier's important policy statement. Many intellectuals, myself included, had felt frustrated and unfulfilled in the tasks we were asked to undertake, which often had no relation to our training. Zhou Enlai made us feel needed and gave us hope that the Party would learn to value what we had to offer. Unfortunately, the implementation of such an inclusive policy ran counter to the unspoken and simplistic pragmatism of many cadres.

THE SHORT-LIVED "EUPHORIC PERIOD"

As the national economy grew and adjustments to the policy on intellectuals were implemented, our quality of life improved. In addition to receiving free medical care, we received salary increases; good harvests provided full food markets and basic department store products were affordable. Beijing was at that time a remarkably interesting place to raise a family. Crime was low and most people did not feel the need to lock their doors, day or night. The schools were good and teachers were dedicated and respected. In lieu of libraries, children were welcomed at the bookstores, where our two boys would sit for hours on the floor reading whatever interested them. As Beijing developed into China's cultural capital, we were able to go to plays, operas, concerts, movies,

The Lin family in Beijing, c. 1956

museums, and sport events for a pittance. When I came down with pleurisy in 1953, the office continued to pay my full salary, covered my hospital and medical expenses, and sent me to recuperate at Beidaihe, a famous seaside resort.

For anyone present during these first six years, there was no more colossal misnomer than the words "unchanging China." The pace of change was so rapid that if you did not read the newspapers daily, you were liable to wake up one morning surprised to find another big steel plant standing, automobiles rolling off a new assembly line, or a new romanization (*pinyin*) adopted for pronouncing *putonghua* – Mandarin Chinese. The Beijing skyline changed constantly. The plan was to catch up with the science and technology of the most advanced Western countries within twelve years. The country was booming.

Chapter Eight

A REVOLUTION IS NOT
A DINNER PARTY

BACKLASH: THE ANTI-RIGHTIST CAMPAIGN

With the success of the first Five Year Plan, which had rebuilt the Chinese economy based on the Soviet model, and pleased with the unexpected speed in completing the socialist transformation of the economy, Mao wanted to press China further in the direction of socialism. He was greatly upset, however, by Khrushchev's bitter exposé of Stalin's errors at the Twentieth Congress of the Soviet Communist Party in February 1956, which created waves of turmoil in the world's Communist movements. Paranoid about his own critics, Mao decided to "lure the snake out of the hole" by launching the campaign "Let a Hundred Flowers Blossom and a Hundred Schools of Thought Contend."

During my fifteen years in China, I managed to weather the frequent storms of ideological struggle through which Mao Zedong sought to instill his revolutionary values in intellectuals. During the brief "Hundred Flowers" movement of 1956–57, intellectuals aired their grievances over aspects of Party policy and behavior, encouraged by Mao. Shocked by the extent of this criticism, however, the Party quickly clamped down on those who had spoken out and unleashed an "anti-rightist" campaign, which grossly overstated the extent of "anti-Party" or "anti-socialist" feeling among the intelligentsia. The "anti-rightist" campaign lasted eighteen months and "unearthed" 550,000 "rightists," more than one hundred times Chairman Mao's original estimate. It took decades for many of the innocent to clear their names.

Paul rarely shared with me details about the political dynamics at Radio Peking, although I knew he was exhausted and under great stress owing to the countless struggle sessions and in-fighting among his colleagues. Not until I read parts of Sidney Rittenberg's 1993 memoir, *The Man Who Stayed Behind*, did I appreciate just how difficult the anti-rightist campaign had become for him. Rittenberg, an American "foreign expert" carrying a Chinese Communist Party membership card, tells the story of how he and another Party member determined who would be named a rightist in the English section of Radio Peking. Gerald Chen, wrote Rittenberg, was innocent of any real charges ...

> But he was the best we had. His real name was Chen Weixi, but he used the name Gerald, a souvenir of his Western connections. He was the son of a Zhongqing businessman who had cast his lot with the Communists. Living in Canada in the home of Dr James Endicott, a well-known left-wing preacher who once taught school in China, Gerald had grown close to the Canadian left wing and had returned to China after the Communist victory, a patriotic young man who wanted to do something for his country ... The specific action that Gerald was accused of was plotting to overthrow the leadership of the English section in favor of the deputy head of the section, the flashy son of a Chinese-Canadian minister and not a party member (Rittenberg, 217).

That "flashy son of a Chinese-Canadian minister" was Paul, who had won admiration and respect from his colleagues for his competence and dedication, as well as for being a person of principle, modesty, and generosity. But he also provoked the ire of those who envied him and were out to destroy him, if they could.

XIA FANG — "DOWN TO THE COUNTRYSIDE"

Merely to take issue with the unnecessary exaggeration of unjust conditions in the capitalist West was enough to earn me the stigma of having "rightist tendencies." In early 1958, therefore, I volunteered to participate in the first wave of "Xia Fang" (intellectuals sent down to the countryside), ostensibly to learn from the peasants. This meant a year living and working in a poverty-stricken village in north China. I actually did not mind this, because I had come to China to learn and seventy per cent of the Chinese people lived outside the cities. And frankly, it was a relief to remove myself from the poisonous cauldron of Radio Peking at that time.

I was a member of a team, led by a Party cadre, which moved into a village called Ma Luo Po in Cang Xian, a county near Tianjin. The peasants generally could eke out only enough wheat to survive four months of the winter, due to the saline soil. Their worst fear was *qing huang bu jie* – the time of the year when the green and the golden do not meet – meaning the new crop has not yet ripened and the old crop has been consumed.

Our team arrived in January, the dead of winter. I moved into a mud-adobe home of a poor peasant, where we ate "iron pizza" – a dish made of tough weeds – three meals a day. I slept on a *kang* between two old brothers. It was a heated brick bed, warmed by residual heat from the stove. We wrapped ourselves in our blankets, as we lay on top of straw mats. I roasted during the night and my skin felt like a piece of crisp toast in the morning. Wind howled through the paper windows.

The peasants distrusted the intellectuals from the cities. They assumed we were just pretending to be "comrades" and eventually would rob them of their grain. Their bitter experience of the old days encouraged them to keep their distance. We explained we had come to live like them, to eat what they ate, to share their joys and sorrows. We made every effort to prove the sincerity of our intentions. I climbed off the *kang* at five o'clock in the morning to sweep the yard and do household chores. Then I went with the men to the fields for heavy labour, much of it digging huge pits in frozen ground. In the evening, I taught the younger members of the household to read and write.

I remember vividly and with chagrin the cold February morning I tried to draw water from the well. The peasants used two huge wooden buckets that, when filled, weighed about sixty pounds each. The pump beside the well was covered with ice, as was the ledge. I dropped a bucket into the well and tried to lift it, but could not even fill the bucket with water. So I tried to drag up a half-filled bucket. When the household's daughter-in-law heard me struggling, she ran down shouting, "No, no, no, you mustn't do it. You can't do it!" With a flick of her wrist, she flipped the bucket down and drew it up full in a couple of seconds. She proceeded to gracefully carry the two heavy buckets, one on each end of a pole resting across her shoulders, to the house. I felt useless.

I witnessed the birth and upheavals of the "People's Communes" during my stay in Ma Luo Po. One night, members of my brigade knocked urgently on my door, to tell me that some bureaucrat had ordered them to plant rice, instead of sorghum, in their saline soil. If they did so, they said, they would starve. I was sick with dysentery, with a fever of 104 degrees, but they pleaded with me to talk sense to the village cadre. So I wrapped my shivering, feverish body in my blanket and braved the cold to pass on their concerns. Afraid to disobey his superior, the cadre muttered repeatedly that the matter was beyond his control. The brigade leaders were crushed by his response, but I pointed out to them that the village cadre had said nothing about *not* planting sorghum. "If I were you, I would go and plant sorghum immediately, tonight, and keep it quiet." They understood, rushed to the fields and planted sorghum. The following year, they did not go hungry.

Despite the physical hardships, I left Ma Luo Po with a sense of fulfillment. After a year working alongside these simple but honest and diligent peasants, I more deeply appreciated their sufferings and aspirations. When they eventually grew to trust and treat me as a friend, I was moved.

MY CLOSE CALL WITH TROUBLE

During the 1956 campaign "Let a Hundred Flowers Blossom and a Hundred Schools of Thought Contend," I was coaxed to air my grievances by a colleague, who had volunteered to edit our department's Big Character Wall posters (*Dazibao*). Not very politically inclined, I had only one minor complaint: I objected to being asked by the work unit to attend a diplomatic function at the Pakistani embassy, essentially as a "dance hostess." But when my complaint appeared in the *Dazibao*, I was horrified. The headline quoted me as saying: "I am not a Cabaret Girl!" This scandalous innuendo attracted much attention and drew suspicion that I was a potential "rightist." But soon after, when Chairman Mao reversed himself and launched the "anti-rightist movement," it was my colleague who landed in hot water. During another self-criticism session, a different colleague, Mr Xu, confessed under pressure that he had intentionally misled the gullible in the office, myself included, by telling us lies to savour our reactions. I was enraged and rose to denounce him. Much to my surprise, the next day I was invited to join a "core group" with a mandate to review and plan the progress of the anti-rightist movement in my department. Only then did I realize that under suspicion of being a "rightist" my criticism of Xu had vindicated me. The "anti-rightist movement" jolted me out of my naiveté and warned me to be more circumspect with my thoughts and words.

Unlike Paul, I never went down to the countryside, but did my share of physical labour – for a stretch of two weeks annually – either at Xinhua News Agency's reforestation project or on its farm near Beijing. We planted fruit trees at Ju Yong Guan in the Western Hills. There were no trails up the steep hills of rock and mud and we had to climb for nearly an hour to reach the spot, where we set about digging holes of one and a half meters in diameter and one meter in depth. We dug from morning until late afternoon, with only a few breaks in between. This was hard physical work and every morning my aching hands awoke me. My thoughts wandered … "What am I doing here?" But of course I never voiced this.

When assigned to work at Xinhua's farm at Fang Shan, a suburb east of Beijing, I sowed and harvested corn and yams, tended vegetable plots, herded pigs, and performed kitchen duties. I was spared from digging fish-ponds, which was back-breaking labour, after suffering a kidney infection. Herding pigs was not as tiring as digging fishponds, but in some ways was more harrowing. One lean year, when there was not enough food for both humans and animals, the pigs were skeletally thin and stricken with tuberculosis. When a pregnant mother pig suddenly miscarried, the other hungry pigs rushed in and gobbled up all her babies. I was traumatized and suffered nightmares for days.

During the hungry years following the Great Leap Forward (1958–61), I once briefly hallucinated that I saw chunks of dark chocolate when I was digging the rich brown soil. But harvesting corn was rewarding, for we were able to satisfy our hunger as we worked by eating the young, juicy, sweet corn just off the stalk. Being scrupulously hygienic, I found handling the un-treated, odorous night soil we used as fertilizer extremely distasteful. Unlike colleagues who came from the countryside, I failed in this task miserably and was ashamed by my poor performance.

Living conditions on both sites, Ju Yong Guan and Fang Shan, were basic, with cold water taps and outhouses. Hot water was available only in the boiler room. We slept on wooden beds with straw mattresses. Bedding, eating utensils, a washbasin, and a thermos bottle were the only comforts allowed from home. In 1957, before I became sick, I worked for a month on the construction site of the Great Hall of the People at Tiananmen Square. My changing roles – as editor, temporary peasant, and worker – sharpened my awareness of the difficult lives of the majority of China's people and I appreciated their invaluable contributions to society. ✒

THE GREAT LEAP FORWARD, 1958–1961

I returned to Radio Peking from the countryside in 1959 and was promoted to the position of artistic director of English-language services (a title without much power). I also edited and narrated English-language documentary films on China for the Central Documentary Film studio. Rumblings were heard about the dislocations caused by the Great Leap Forward, which began in 1958, but it was only much later that I had any idea of the political wrangling behind the scenes.

Of deeper significance was the growing division within the Chinese Communist Party leadership regarding the assessment of the domestic political situation and the need for continuing class struggle. The Eighth Party Congress in 1956 had taken the position that with the socialist transformation of agriculture, industry, and commerce, and with the necessary class struggles essentially over, there should now be an all-out effort to build up the economy. But in the ensuing years, Mao Zedong became increasingly disenchanted with Soviet politics and the Soviet model of development, which China had followed in the first Five Year Plan. Two concerns came to dominate his thinking: how to prevent the re-emergence in China of a bureaucratic stratum alienated from the people, and how to strike out on a self-reliant path of national development, untrammeled by dependence on an increasingly hostile Soviet Union? The politics of the first concern tended to radicalize the economics of the second, in a mutually escalating process.

In this atmosphere it was inevitable that political opportunists would attempt to capitalize on Mao's revived concern about class struggle. Their tactics were to magnify differences of viewpoint and present them as class antagonisms, wielding every available device of sloganeering demagogy, including a false concept of egalitarianism that had nothing in common with progressive social change. Critics of economic excess and errors committed during the Great Leap Forward and the People's Commune movement began to be stigmatized as class enemies opposed to the political and strategic orientation of the new policies. Little distinction was made between friend and foe. The atmosphere was hardly conducive to long-range planning and stable economic growth.

The problems of the Great Leap Forward illustrate this point. The conceptual approach was to inject at least three new variables into the development process to speed it up and to overcome hampering imbalances: maximum mobilization of the full potential of China's own human and material resources to effect a spurt in production and in capital formation; the adoption of new technologies, wherever possible; and institutional innovation to facilitate the operation of these two factors. For a country like China, this self-reliant, people-oriented approach might conceivably have succeeded, provided revolutionary enthusiasm was combined with rigorous science. Unfortunately, just prior to the Great Leap Forward, the "anti-rightist" campaign had snowballed into a sweeping denigration of intellectuals. This left the highly educated, who carried the necessary skills and experience of modernization, politically suspect. Subsequently, the Great Leap Forward was deprived of their moderating contribution and no technological revolution took place.

As a grand experiment in the use of mass movements to accelerate economic development, the Great Leap Forward had both successes and failures. The successes involved indigenous or intermediate but labour-intensive technology, such as the construction of numerous water conservancy and land reclamation projects, small hydroelectric plants and village factories, the expansion of transport networks, and the creation of rural health systems based on local paramedics (the famous "barefoot doctors"). The fiascoes were of two kinds: attempts to use indigenous technology to solve high-technology production processes, such as the nationwide "all out for steel" campaign using "backyard steel furnaces"; and programs to achieve immediate and spectacular increases in grain production, including attempts to alter the institutional structure of production and distribution, before productivity had risen to a level that warranted such structural changes. Examples were the oversized and managerially unwieldy People's Communes, which diluted the advantages of more efficient economies of scale, premature efforts to equalize the allocation of resources between rich and poor production units, and excessive limitation or outright abolition of private plots, cottage industries, and village markets. These actions increased neither production nor consumption.

The Great Leap Forward turned out to be a colossal failure. The full extent of the disaster was known for a long time only to the top echelon of leaders, however, because the Party feared full disclosure would destroy public confidence in the leadership of Mao Zedong, who had authored this quixotic experiment. When General Peng Dehuai wrote his forthright 10,000-character letter to Mao, criticizing his "ultra-left" policies, Mao launched a fierce counter-critique at the historic 1959 Lushan meeting. Clearly, it was a turning point in the inner-Party struggle, but at the time no one foresaw that events were leading to that pinnacle of ultra-leftism – the Great Proletarian Cultural Revolution.

FATHER'S VISIT TO CHINA, 1959

After nearly a decade in China, Father's visit was a happy respite. We had last seen him in 1949 in New York City, just prior to our departure for Hong Kong. In the fall of 1958, I received news that Father and my stepmother were in Hong Kong and we immediately invited them to visit us in Beijing. Father was eager to come, but was frightened by rumours he had heard in Hong Kong about persecution in the PRC. A clergy friend of his had supposedly been eaten alive by the "Communist wolves." Persuaded by my reassurances, he decided to take his chances and promised to come in April 1959.

I took a leave of absence from Radio Peking to meet Father and Shih Peixuen at the Gong Bei border near Guangzhou. Because Father was an Anglican Church of Canada clergyman and well-respected in Vancouver's Chinese community, the Overseas Chinese Affairs Committee not only helped us with the logistics of travel and accommodation, but hosted a welcoming banquet in Father's honour. Imagine his surprise when he spotted the very pastor who was supposed to have been murdered!

We had a comfortable train ride from Guangzhou to Beijing that enabled them to enjoy the lush countryside from Guangdong to north China, which Father had never seen. When the train pulled into the Beijing station, Eileen, Christopher, and Douglas were on the platform waiting for us. Grandfather's face lit up when his grandsons rushed forward to hug him and hold his hands, one on each side. Chris was now fourteen years old and Doug was ten. Both became expert "tour guides" of Beijing's historic and scenic sites for their grandpa's edification.

Father had last been in China in 1912, when he had brought my mother and sister back to Canada. Although he had always been a fervent patriot, Cold War rumours about the PRC had made him uncertain about the government. Gradually he began to relax and was genuinely impressed by the progress he witnessed – especially the absence of occupying foreign powers. He marveled at the better life of the people, the civic orderliness, and the fact that policemen on the streets did not carry guns. He was proud to see all the new buildings in the capital and to learn that China could now manufacture its own heavy machineries and light industrial products.

❧I introduced Paul's father and stepmother to my Auntie Yimin and her family: my brother George and his wife Julia who both worked in the Chinese foreign ministry; and my elder brother John, who came up from Shanghai. We had a grand family reunion at Cousin Yao Yilin's home.☙

The highlight of Father's trip was being received by Madame Sun Yat-sen at her residence. This was their first meeting, since he had been unable to be present at the 1947 marriage in Shanghai of my brother Andrew to Pearl Sun, granddaughter of Sun Yat-sen and Madame Sun. They also were received by Madame He Xiangning, an old friend of Madame Sun's and the widow of Liao Zhongkai, a close comrade of Sun Yat-sen's during the 1911 revolution, who had been assassinated by Chiang Kai-shek's men in 1925. Madame He was the recently retired chairperson of the Overseas Chinese Affairs Committee and had been succeeded by her son, Liao Chengzhi, who was largely responsible for the hospitality extended to Father.

After Beijing, friends in the Overseas Chinese Affairs Committee accompanied my father and stepmother on a tour to Hangzhou, Shanghai, and Guangzhou before they returned to Hong Kong. Father later wrote to thank us and to say how happy he was to have seen New China with his own eyes.

ECONOMIC CRISIS AND FAMINE

Fortunately, Father's visit preceded the disaster that occurred in the second half of 1959. Chairman Mao had launched the Great Leap Forward the year before in his quixotic but mistaken belief that China could speed up its economic development primarily through mass movements and indigenous technology. Instead of accelerating production, a severe economic slump followed the Great Leap Forward, caused by human error and natural disaster. The national economy lost 120 billion yuan and it is estimated that tens of millions of people died of starvation, malnutrition, and other unnatural causes. All essential items, including grains, edible oil, meats, sugar, and cloth, were rationed again.

The problems of the Great Leap Forward were compounded by the abrupt withdrawal of the Soviet engineers and technical specialists who had been hired to assist with China's planned industrialization. On July 6, 1960 the Soviet Union unilaterally tore up its high-tech aid contracts with China and withdrew all of its technicians, taking home the blueprints for 250 major projects, leaving them at a standstill. In light of this devastating split, Mao backed off his ultra-leftist policies, enabling the government to realign its economic priorities by putting primary emphasis on agricultural production, followed by light industry and, lastly, heavy industry. From 1962 to 1966, the economy rebounded and even attained a higher rate of growth than before the economic crisis, due to stringent government measures.

Madame Sun Yat-sen receives Paul's father and stepmother at her residence, April 1959.

Family reunion of the Lins, Yaos, and Chens in Beijing, April 1959. Front: children of Lins and Yaos. Middle, left to right: Eileen, Wei Popo, Father Lim Yuen, Stepmother, Auntie Yimin, Paul. Rear, left to right: cousin Yao Jinxin, niece Yao Mingrei, Eileen's brothers John and George, cousin Yao Yilin, Madame Yao (Zhou Bin), George's wife Chen Xiuxia

&' We had never experienced hunger before. Even in earlier years when basic commodities were scarce, we could supplement our diet with more expensive items not on the rationed list. But this time, there was nothing to buy – Beijing store shelves were empty except for a few bottles of orange and lemon drinks. Chris shot up in height as a teenager. Without proper nutrition, he developed tuberculosis of the lymph glands and had to recuperate at home for three months. Paul's work was very demanding, but because he was classified as a "high-level intellectual" he qualified for more meat coupons, which he shared with us. We could have asked for food parcels from our families abroad, as many overseas Chinese did, but we chose not to, out of pride and perhaps a foolish idealism – regarding hunger as yet another "learning experience." We also used the food shortage to teach our boys to share in times of scarcity. Once, at the dinner table, the four of us passed a scarce piece of meat from plate to plate, until Paul ordered that someone just eat it. ઽ

HOME LEAVE TO CANADA

January 30, 1962, was Father's eightieth birthday. To celebrate this milestone, my siblings and I planned a grand family reunion to be held in Vancouver in April. I applied and was granted a six-month home leave with Eileen. Unfortunately, our boys could not join us; Chris was finishing junior high and Doug was still in elementary school. We left them in the care of our housekeeper, Xu Popo, a wonderful elderly lady who served as a surrogate grandmother.

Since Father had not visited his ancestral village during his recent visit, I was given permission to tour Xinhui County and Gujin village at the end of 1961, in order to bring him news. I met relatives who still lived in the small homestead at the end of a narrow lane, as well as some of his old neighbours.

Eileen and I arrived in Hong Kong in February 1962. We stayed with one of her cousins, whose family graciously accommodated us although they were living in a crowded apartment on Kowloon's noisy Nathan Road. From there, we proceeded to apply for our entry permits to Canada.

When I left Hong Kong for China in 1950, I had brought only my birth certificate, giving my Canadian passport to Eileen's mother for safekeeping. Eileen did the same with her old Chinese passport when she joined me a few months later. When her parents moved to Taiwan in 1952, Mother Chen took our documents with her, knowing that Taiwanese customs would be lax due to Father Chen's official KMT connections. In 1953, however, following her husband's death, Mother Chen moved to the United States with her daughter, leaving our passports behind with a relative in Taiwan. It took me three weeks to retrieve my old passport from the Taiwanese custodian and Eileen's never resurfaced.

I went immediately to the Canadian High Commissioner's office in Hong Kong, exchanging the old for a new passport. With this valid passport and our marriage certificate, Eileen was qualified to apply for a British Subject Commonwealth Passport, as we had been married before 1947. We were told that it would take a month before a new passport could be issued to her, but with the help of Percy Chen, a well-connected lawyer in Hong Kong, she received it in one day.

With our passports in hand, we went again to the Canadian High Commissioner's office, where Eileen was given the option of applying for landed immigrant status. Not realizing the lengthy procedures involved – formal sponsorship, interview, medical checkup – we agreed. This resulted in Eileen being subjected to a four-hour interview, peppered with dozens of questions by two Canadian officials who seemed most interested in knowing what I was doing in China. Meanwhile, our Canadian reunion was getting underway; family and friends were beginning to converge on Vancouver from Montreal, Toronto, and California. The official birthday banquet for more than one hundred guests, including Mother Chen and Eileen's sisters, was scheduled for April 25. We finally decided that I would go ahead, while Eileen waited in Hong Kong for her travel documents. I told her I would try to expedite her entry from the Canadian side of the Pacific.

I arrived in Vancouver on April 20, 1962, and within days had sent letters and telegrams to the minister of immigration, the Honourable Ellen Fairclough, appealing for her assistance in expediting Eileen's admission. Her assistant replied that although the department had received reports from the immigration officials in Hong Kong and Vancouver concerning Eileen's application, additional inquiries had to be conducted before a final decision could be reached. On May 5, I wrote directly and pointedly to the prime minister of Canada, the Honourable John Diefenbaker:

My wife underwent an exhaustive interrogation in the Hong Kong office of Canadian Immigration on April 16, during which she was asked close to sixty questions. I fail to understand how any purpose can now be served by "additional inquiries," unless it is to further delay or bar her admission.

I have been given to understand that, in reality, approval of my wife's entry is being withheld on the grounds that I hold views which are not unfavorable to the present government of China. If this is true, I cannot see how such a position would redound to the credit of the Canadian government either in the eyes of the Canadian or the world public. I am sure you, Sir, would like me to feel that in coming back to Canada, I am not being required to beg or bargain for my rights, to barter my personal convictions, whatever they may be, for the opportunity to reside with my family in the country of my birth. I deem myself completely loyal to the interests of the Canadian people, and find nothing inconsistent with that loyalty if I admire the heroic efforts of the Chinese people to build a better life for themselves.

It is perhaps relevant to note that when the Hon. Davie Fulton referred in an election speech in Haney last Wednesday, to your administration's feat of turning Canada's adverse trade balance into a surplus of $182 million, he was referring to a happy circumstance which could not have been brought about without trade with China. In any case, I trust that no one's views on such issues … are being policed, that it is still the birthright of Canadians to think for themselves notwithstanding the prejudice of those few individuals – not necessarily Canadian – who arrogate to themselves the right to dictate what Canadians should think.

Paul and Eileen at Beijing Summer Palace, fall 1962

Aside from this aspect of the question, I have been forced to take note of the circumstance that my wife, as a person of Chinese extraction, has been subjected to such multitudinous "procedural" delays, while immigrants of Caucasian extraction are, more often than not, accorded gratuitous help to make their admission a speedy process and a pleasant experience. This contrast seems hardly to accord with principles of equality and fairness.

Finally, with the help of friends, including the first Chinese Member of Parliament, Douglas Jung, Minister Fairclough issued a special minister's permit, allowing Eileen to visit Canada for thirty days.

⫷ I flew to Vancouver on June 1. The reunion dinner was long over and family members who had come from out of town had all left. It was a disappointment, but my dear mother returned to Vancouver from California to see me, accompanied by my sister Louise. It was wonderful to see them after a separation of twelve years.

After spending some time with Paul's family and friends in Vancouver, we traveled east to visit his sister Helen in Fort Erie, Ontario, as well as his brother David and elder sister Margaret in Montreal, Quebec. In Fort Erie, we unknowingly picked up a tail one evening as we drove home. The following morning, when we came down for breakfast, we found a policeman waiting for us in the living room. He was a friend of Helen's husband, G.Y. Wong, and after briefly chatting with us confided that while on duty the night before, he had stopped a car for running a red light. The driver told him they were chasing a car that was carrying someone from "Red China." The policeman then pointed to the window – outside were four cars, one parked at each corner of the Wong property, keeping us under surveillance. The Royal Canadian Mounted Police (RCMP) was determined to prevent us from trying to sneak across the nearby border to the United States. They followed us when we left Fort Erie for Toronto, until Paul managed to shake them. As far as we know, we were not followed in Montreal. ⫸

We returned to Beijing in early July 1962 and I resumed work at Radio Peking. Not until December did I have time to share with Madame Sun a detailed account of our sojourn in Canada. I wrote:

Our trip took half a year, although we had only a little more than two months in Canada. Canadian Immigration did not exactly "facilitate" our entry, especially Eileen's, when they found nothing "refugee-like" about us – and indeed, when we arrived in Canada, the RCMP gave us a good deal of gratuitous "protection." We found Canada tightly held in the military-strategic and economic coils of the US octopus, and therefore under the sinister shadow of the American Security Council. Nevertheless, there were broad currents of bitter antipathy to US domination at all levels and enormous, albeit poorly informed, opinion friendly to People's China.

As soon as we arrived in Vancouver, we were besieged by relatives, former schoolmates, and old friends for a firsthand report by an overseas Chinese on life in "Red China"! We were literally beset by invitations from breakfast to nocturnal suppers and plied with questions (friendly with few exceptions) on the true state of affairs behind the "curtain," which a surprisingly large number of people know to be made of American bamboo. The queries ran the gamut, but it was noteworthy that the overseas Chinese took special interest in the grain situation; the foreigners in whether China is "warlike"; and the intellectuals of all races in political and academic "freedoms" and "brain-washing." Of course, smothered as they are in the welter of broadcast and printed lies, many people have no inkling of the most elementary Chinese position in regard to such issues as war and peaceful coexistence, Sino-American relations, Taiwan, the Sino-Indian border, so they are most grateful for any eye-openers.

Nevertheless, there is a deep, deep wellspring of goodwill for us among the Canadian people. Many people say nothing in public but privately confide their faith in China; I think all that 90% of the people need is the facts. I was asked to appear on television, to speak at public meetings, and to give a full semester course on contemporary China at the U. of British Columbia, but declined ...

My father and stepmother wish to be remembered to you. They retain vivid, happy impressions of their visit to China in 1959 ... He is in contact with a wide circle of loyal friends of People's China, including the devoted coterie of readers of the oft-quoted *China Reconstructs* ...

Three weeks later, Madame Sun replied:

Shanghai
December 24, 1962

Dear Eileen and Paul:

Your most welcome letter arrived sometime ago but my painful joints (also on fingers) prevented me from writing you sooner. And I wanted to write you myself. I wish, first of all, to express my deep appreciation and warmest thanks for your letter, which has given me an insight into the situation abroad and the various attitudes vis-à-vis China, which will enable me to assess events. For all probability, I shall return north in the spring, when I hope to have a long session with you both and learn more about related topics.

Last but not least, allow me to express my sincere thanks for your precious remembrances from abroad, and for bringing gifts from your parents, Pearl and Andy and dear Madame Chen [Eileen's mother], for whom I've always entertained fond memories, for she was among my first friends in Hankou, in 1926, when we arrived there on our Northern expedition. I shall write her shortly and ask you to forward it for me as it may not be convenient for her to receive mail directly from China.

With affectionate greetings,
Soong Ching Ling

DECISION TO RETURN TO CANADA

While we were in Canada in 1962, the Central Committee of the CCP convened a major conference in Beijing from January 11 to February 7. The conference was attended by 7,000 party secretaries from the county level up, heads of vital industries, and high-ranking military officers. The agenda was to find solutions to the serious economic crisis resulting from the Great Leap Forward and the People's Commune movement in rural areas. When I returned to Beijing in the summer, I was allowed to listen to a tape recording of a key speech made by Mao Zedong at this conference. For the first time he acknowledged some responsibility for errors made during the Great Leap Forward. He did not, however, offer a real alternative to the ultra-left direction of his policies. Furthermore, he began to hint at what he considered a "dangerous trend" toward revisionism that, if left unchecked, presented a grave threat to his whole strategy of development.

Having lived for more than a decade in the eye of China's stormy transformation, I had acquired a deep sensitivity to the government's public announcements and the nuances of the leaders' speeches. I felt a growing apprehension
that Mao Zedong's vision, despite his stated adherence to Marxist universal-
ism, was still conceptually that of an enclosed, culture-bound "modernization"
based on an overstated principle of "self-reliance." Viewed historically, Chinese
civilization prior to the "modern" age had contributed enormously to Europe's
modernization, via the Silk Route across Inner Asia and the Middle East. But
in the past few centuries, the West had outpaced China in complex processes
of economic, intellectual, political, and technological change. Could China
learn from these processes, telescope history, and quickly come to terms with
its crippling "modernity lag"? Could the nation once again revitalize Chinese
civilization, break through its isolation, achieve economic growth, and make
its own contribution to global development? These concerns seemed to me to
be paramount.

Nurtured in both Chinese and Western values, I felt a new sense of urgency
to help bridge the chasm of misunderstanding and encourage cooperation
between China and the West. I concluded that only objective and empathetic
dialogues, not confrontational shouting matches that ignored the dynamics
of historical change, could effect the understanding I sought. To create a new
framework for East-West cooperation, both sides would have to work on the
basis of equality and mutual respect for a set of "global values for development." This would require a difficult symbiotic process of seeking common-
alities while preserving healthy cultural differences. In this frame of mind,
I decided to return to Canada with my family in 1964.

I consulted with Madame Sun and told her that I had learned much by living
and working in New China, but now felt I could be most useful as a "friend
of the Chinese people" based in Canada. Madame Sun was understanding
and supported my decision, with the advice that not only should I go, but the
whole family as well. She immediately telephoned Liao Chengzhi, who was
then in charge of Overseas Chinese Affairs, to arrange for our exit. At last I
met the dynamic and affable Mr Liao, who was also director of the Foreign
Affairs Office of PRC's State Council. Still, it took some time to gain permission
– Radio Peking was reluctant to let me go.

Paul's decision to leave China and return to Canada came as a big surprise,
even to me, let alone to our teenage boys. Our journey to China had been
open-ended. Initially I was excited, but also anxious, anticipating the daunt-

The Lin family in their Radio Peking apartment in Beijing, Summer 1963, one year before leaving China for Canada

ing challenges we faced in starting life anew in another country. Chris, by nature adventurous, responded to the move with enthusiasm, even though by 1964 he was doing very well in one of the best schools in Beijing. He was a straight-A student, had been elected class president by his peers for two years in succession, and now belonged to the Communist Youth League. Our younger son, Douglas, was a milder and steadier personality. A good student from Grade 1 on, he was enjoying his time at school. His first response was "Do we have to go?" This was immediately followed up with "Of course I will, if the family goes."

Our sabbatical in 1962 to attend Father's birthday provided Paul with the opportunity to test the waters in the West. The overwhelmingly warm reception he received from family, friends, and academic colleagues had assured him that should he decide to return home, he would be able to make a living, despite the Cold War.

When I told Cousin Yao Yilin of our decision to return to Canada, he was not surprised. The Party, under the leadership of Liu Shaoqi, had issued a new policy allowing overseas Chinese to leave, if they felt they could survive in their countries of birth. Paul's timing in 1964 was fortuitous. Two years later, Mao Zedong launched the Cultural Revolution, which lasted ten long and bitter years. ✎

Part Three

1965–1982

Chapter Nine

RETURN TO CANADA AND
COLD WAR CHILL

We left Beijing in late September 1964 excited to begin our new life in Canada, yet not without a sense of foreboding due to the United States' ongoing Cold War blockade of China. We entered Hong Kong from the rural border town of Shenzhen without a hitch. After several nights at a modest hotel in crowded Wan Chai, we found a bright apartment on Ventris Road in Happy Valley, with the help of Walter and Junny Chun. Walter was the maternal uncle of my brother Andy's wife, Pearl Sun Lin. Before coming to Hong Kong to work for a Chinese bank, he and Jun had been our colleagues and friends in Beijing. This would be Eileen and the boys' temporary home while they awaited immigration approval to Canada. Judging from our 1962 experience, Eileen's admission could take several months. The boys, however, would not have difficulties, since Chris had been born in Boston in 1945 and Doug in New York City in 1949, and I had promptly registered their births with the Canadian embassy.

I took a couple of weeks to settle the family in Hong Kong, and then left for Vancouver in early October with the passport I had renewed in 1962. Father, my stepmother, and a host of friends came to the airport to welcome me home. It felt good to be back on Canadian soil again.

⚓ Not knowing how long we would have to wait in Hong Kong, Christopher and Douglas immediately began intensive study of English and enrolled in a Chinese high school to keep up with their other subjects. Although they could barely communicate in either English or Cantonese (Mandarin being their native language), sympathetic help from their teachers and fellow students soon put them at ease and I tutored them in English after school. On weekends, the Chuns – with their son Ping and daughter Yen – often took us to the beach to swim and fish.

It took six long months for me to gain permission to enter Canada to join Paul with our boys. I simply could not fathom why an application by the wife of a Canadian citizen faced such obstacles, delay, and political intrigue. Paul kept us posted on all the developments from Vancouver in regular letters, in which he expressed his growing frustration. ⁊

November 23, 1964

I had an interview at Immigration yesterday, accompanied by my lawyer Douglas Jung. My signed statement now goes to Ottawa; presumably the next step is Ottawa will notify you to get your medical examination … Doug says that such proceedings normally take over a month, sometimes several, hence we should be mentally prepared for a wait beyond the New Year. Sometimes, however, events move fast and if you hear from Ottawa let me know immediately. Don't worry, eventually all will be well …

Canadian Immigration requires that I give them evidence that I can support you. In addition to providing them with a bank letter on our (small) savings account, I told them I will be teaching at the University of British Columbia. I have accepted UBC's offer of a lectureship in their Asian Studies Department, dealing primarily with contemporary Chinese history. This will be part-time and because I have not yet received an official contract, I still do not know what the salary will be. Meanwhile, I am economizing as much as possible while trying to maintain good appearances … Fortunately, living at Dad's helps pare down expenses, but I am loath to place too large a burden on him. The two most worrisome expenditures are down-payments on a car and a house. Both are absolutely indispensable … Dave seems to be in a tight financial position and I have been unable to obtain a loan from him.

⚒ Paul and his older brother David were very close as youths. Paul had the highest regard for David, whom he looked up to as a role model and confidant. Gradually they grew apart, primarily over political developments in China. David remained staunchly loyal to the Kuomintang and became one

Eileen, Christopher, and Douglas remain in Hong Kong, awaiting Eileen's entry permit to Canada, October 1964.

The Chun family: Walter, Junny, son Ping, and daughter Yen, Hong Kong, 1960s

of their overseas representatives in Canada. By 1964, he was an established medical doctor in Montreal, but he seemed reluctant to help Paul rebuild his life in Canada. 🏵

November 28, 1964

It's a cold, foggy Saturday night and there's a gnawing ache in me, a yearning to have you beside me again and to hear the husky voices of our sturdy boys. How much I hope that we will spend Xmas together. Without you, a blazing hearth is cold.

I have good news, as you can see by the enclosures – the boys' passports. This means they are ready to travel at a moment's notice. Meanwhile, your papers for entry have been sent to Ottawa ...

Everything you touch here costs money, yet one has to solve the problem of house and car before the income begins to flow. The past fifteen years have, I suppose, maladjusted me to a life in which the onus of existence itself is a hectic and heavy burden ...

I am so glad the children are doing well in school. I am proud of their pluck, tenacity, and adaptability.

My days are busy; I often work late into the night on my lectures. Friends inquire after you and hope the three of you can get here by Christmas. Have not heard from Dave for some time.

December 16, 1964

There is no further word on your entry proceedings. December 8th, I sent a letter to the Hon. René Tremblay, Minister of Citizenship and Immigration, asking him to expedite matters for a Christmas reunion. I followed that letter with a telegram tonight ...

Your mother sent a cheque for $240 – $200 is to help you out in Hong Kong, then $20 each is for you and me as Christmas gifts. I appreciate her care and concern. I mentioned in one of my letters that I was having difficulty raising the cash for the down payment on a house. She offered to help, but it would have meant selling her house, so I wrote back to stop her and to say I would be able to solve the problem by other means. I intend to get a personal loan somehow, but the initial burden of debt is worrisome. It is also very tiresome to go that long distance to UBC on the bus, from Father's house in Chinatown. I must resolve the car question soon.

The high marks the kids are getting in school are a great comfort ... I shall not buy them Christmas presents here. Tell Doug that he can get a good flute and Chris an enlarger [for photos] as our presents to them.

My three dearest ones – we may not be able to enjoy a Christmas or even a New Year reunion – but you all know where my heart will be at that time. Despite everything, do make the best of it and enjoy a good holiday of cheer!

December 26, 1964

Did you have a good Christmas? How I yearned for the sight and sound of you! There were moments of sheer, excruciating loneliness for me in the last few days, despite the many holiday engagements.

Christmas Eve, I had dinner with the old folks. I bought a Christmas tree (the first they had had for many years) to bring a little more cheer ...

Keep up with your hobbies, kids, but whatever you do, do it well ... I shall be thinking of you at New Year's. We shall make up for all the good times that we could not have together as a family!

January 9, 1965

Worried by my silence the past few days? I've been very busy preparing for this semester's lectures ... It was a joy to hear from you so soon after New Year's; my holidays were an emotional ordeal without you three. This will be a difficult month financially, for I must make down-payments on both the house and the car ...

January 18, 1965

I have just received a letter from the Postmaster General in Ottawa assuring me he is looking into the matter of your admission. I was recently introduced to him here by a mutual friend. I also telephoned Doug Jung, who says if Ottawa has sent the papers to Hong Kong (as I have been assured by the immigration minister's assistant), that means the final okay may only be a matter of days ... so you should be prepared for fast action. Be packed and ready, dear ...

Chin up, darling ... and tell the kids I am very anxious to hear how they did on the examinations. I am very grateful that they have been good to you all this time, and they shall be rewarded when they come!

January 19, 1965

I just received your telegram with the good news your interview will be coming up next Tuesday. If things go well, you should be able to leave for Canada within days. I was unable to contact Doug Jung today, but first thing in the morning I shall get in touch with him or the Vancouver Immigration Office, to obtain the provisional approval letter. You can be sure it will be in the mail right away. I hope that your interview goes well and that they will not repeat the grueling interrogation of last time (which I protested). There will probably be the usual questions about former address, occupation, education, family. Please let me know exactly what transpires – all the details.

I have been quite busy. Hearing I had taught a seminar in international law at Hua Chiao University, Beijing, the International Law Association invited me to attend one of their meetings last night to hear a guest speaker.

January 20, 1965

Doug Jung got the letter of provisional approval from Vancouver Immigration. I am sending it herewith by registered airmail. I have had a copy made, in case this one is lost. Here's hoping your interview will be smooth ...

January 27, 1965

Yesterday's interview was quite simple. I was only asked about my family relations – name, age, date and place of birth or death – our addresses and my education. The answers were typed on a Statutory Declaration which I had to sign in court. I also handed in the letter of provisional approval you sent me. Thank you, dear. Now I must wait for a medical examination.

Your latest pictures show signs of strain and fatigue. You are working much too hard ... The children did well last term and are good company. Chris has matured quite a bit and thinks more and more of others ...

March 8, 1965

I just returned from the Immigration Office, where a Chinese secretary told me they are still waiting to hear from Ottawa. She said that they had referred my case up on February 12, soon after my medical exam.

On March 3, I met your new friend – the noted dermatologist, Dr Stuart Maddin – on his way to China to attend a medical conference. He was kind

Douglas Jung, lawyer and first Chinese-Canadian Member of Parliament, Ottawa, early 1960s (Larry Wong Collection)

enough to inquire about me with the Director of Immigration Office in H[ong]K[ong]. He was told the delay was due to the local medical doctor, who is behind in his work by two or three weeks. Dr Maddin introduced me to Dr David Baltzman, who is also going to attend the China conference. Dr Baltzman is the personal physician to Canadian Prime Minister Diefenbaker. When he learnt about my predicament, he immediately telephoned his influential Tory friends in Canada to help. I was deeply moved by their concern.

However, at this point, I really don't know what to believe. All I know is that I have every right to join my husband who is a Canadian citizen by birth. Furthermore, my two sons have Canadian citizenship too. I have been very patient, but can Mr Nicholson [the new minister of citizenship and immigration] help to speed up the process a little bit?

March 9, 1965

I went to the Immigration Office again this morning and spoke with a Canadian official. He said my medical examination was OK and that it is Ottawa which is sitting on my case now. He kindly offered to cable Ottawa for me today and hopefully can give me an answer in a few days. ᴈ

March 13, 1965

It is now possible to tell you quite definitely that a middle-echelon level of authority in Ottawa has blocked a favourable decision on your admission, for political reasons. This is a very foolish action on their part, whose gross short-sightedness they are not yet aware of. Of course, I think the matter has not yet been considered at the highest level. We are giving them until next Monday to make a favourable decision. If none is forthcoming, I have asked Douglas Jung to go all out. We shall ask Ottawa to show cause for their decision, and if necessary fight the case through the courts. Prominent university and community figures here are ready to back me up to the hilt. And it seems clear that there is very little that Ottawa can do in defense of their position. If the Canadian immigration authorities are in their right minds, and not abjectly intimidated by a foreign government, they will lose no time to recognize the rights of a Canadian citizen in this matter. Otherwise, it is likely to become a public, ugly mark against the present Liberal administration, with wider repercussions.

Until now I have been patient and tried to exercise the greatest restraint. But recent developments have made me furious and unless the Immigration Department changes its course immediately, I shall bring pressure to bear from every possible source. Please do not worry, dear, I am sure the outcome will be a healthy one; practically speaking, it will more than likely be a rapid one in our favour, unless there is more stupidity in Ottawa than I had imagined. Stay calm and keep up your inquiries as you think fit at the immigration office. Undoubtedly you are under surveillance in H.K., but live as if those monkeys never existed! When you arrive in Vancouver with the boys, you will be surrounded by friends and we shall try to make up for the long months of stress and strain imposed on you by small-time bureaucrats responsible for your suffering – the little men devoid of humanity and a true sense of responsibility to Canada's interests.

I think of you and the boys night and day, especially in the solitude of contemplation by the seashore and in the midst of my long nocturnal vigils over my typewriter. But a man's life is as he lives it and it is at least a satisfaction that we do not have to grovel and crawl and compromise with political malice in order to live. Yet Canada is full of wonderful, decent people, whom you will find heart warming and hospitable indeed.

Cast off your burden of worry, my dearest – the destruction of nerve cells is not worth it. We *shall* and *will* be reunited, soon!

March 17, 1965

The Minister, John Nicholson, has decided to issue a Minister's Permit for your entry into Canada and is notifying Canadian Immigration in Hong Kong to this effect. Undoubtedly, you have received my cable and are now preparing to leave on the earliest CPA flight to Vancouver, after getting your papers.

The decision to issue you a Minister's Permit was the result of a sharp struggle in Ottawa, after I had obtained information that your admission application had been turned down on grounds of "security." I authorized my lawyer to ask for a reversal of this decision and to warn that if a reversal was not received by Monday (the deadline was extended 24 hours at the request of the Vancouver Immigration Office) he was to take legal proceedings (issue a writ to "show cause"), which would have made the case public. Because the government had no leg to stand on and an open court fight might have had embarrassing political repercussions for the present Liberal administration, they backed down. The Vancouver Immigration Office received a telegram yesterday morning stating your admission had been approved, and this morning I received a special delivery letter from the Minister saying a Minister's Permit had been issued to you for "temporary entry for a period of one year," after which your case would be "reviewed" and "if circumstances warrant" your stay in Canada "may be extended." Doug Jung says this is only Department jargon and at the end of a year, you will automatically be given permanent immigrant status.

Coincidently, I met Minister Nicholson again at a dinner party given by the Chinese community. As we shook hands to say goodbye, Nicholson said he had finally solved your entry problem and so-called political reasons did not exist, but he planned to investigate. "Maybe someone is spreading rumours, to create problems for me," Nicholson commented.

So, in spite of all the obstacles and delays and pressures (some undoubtedly from un-Canadian sources), the fight has been won ... Cable me your departure date and we'll be at the airport to receive you! Be sure you get the proper papers declaring that the children are returning citizens and you are entering Canada with the intention of residing here; the papers will be useful in exempting you from customs duties for your personal effects.

Come with full confidence, dear. On my behalf, please thank all the friends who helped you in Hong Kong. Waiting eagerly ...

Eileen's first Canadian passport photo, 1965

We arrived in Vancouver on a bright, sunny day in late March 1965, into the loving embrace of our dear family and friends, who came to welcome us to Canada. It was like awakening from a nightmare of endless uncertainty and anxiety. I was granted landed immigrant status in Canada on February 15, 1966. As the wife of a Canadian citizen, I had to wait only a year before applying for citizenship. I became a Canadian citizen on June 12, 1967.

SURVEILLANCE IN VANCOUVER

Eileen's arrival with the boys sparked a hectic chain of events and rounds of invitations, while I tried to keep on top of my teaching load at UBC. We moved into a bungalow at the corner of 54th Avenue and Oak Street. Chris and Doug were especially delighted with their new rec-room where they could play ping-pong. The kitchen, living, and dining areas were bright and spacious.

The house looked great after nearly two months of endless chores by us all; fortunately, we had two hefty young fellows to help with the heavy jobs. Owning a house is an enormous burden, labour-wise and finance-wise, when you are starting out from scratch. Friends helped us buy furniture and appliances at wholesale prices, but even so the expenses were appalling. Eileen's mother sent us a trunkful of useful household appliances, like a vacuum cleaner and a bean cooker, to get us started.

The boys enrolled in New Canadian classes at a public school on April 13 and made friends quickly. Eileen gave them extra English tutoring at home. Besides organizing the household, she was also busy cooking and entertaining, to reciprocate some of the many invitations to dinner. I devoted all my time to writing and teaching at the university. In Canada, writing and publishing were essential to maintaining one's academic standing.

Our first houseguest was Mother, now seventy-six years old, who flew from California on June 20 for an extended visit. Chris and Doug were especially happy to be with their grandma and she was amazed at how much they had grown since she had last seen them in Hong Kong, nearly fifteen years before. She liked our house and enjoyed the guest room, with her own washbasin and a little nook to read and write. She was also pleased to find a church within easy walking distance of our house.

Her minister dropped in one morning, ostensibly to call on his new parishioner. Paul was away at the university. After a brief chat, he informed Mother and me that an officer of the RCMP had visited him with questions about "the Lins," who had recently arrived from Communist China and were under a cloud of suspicion. I was dismayed to hear of this official surveillance by the Canadian government, but kept my thoughts to myself and thanked him for letting us know.

Canadian friends in Vancouver also reported that the RCMP had interrogated them after associating with me; they were warned that Paul Lin was an "enigma."

The Vancouver Kuomintang consul general James Ling went so far as to pronounce in the *China Times*: "If there is a war between Canada and the Chinese Communists, the enemy would be only the Chinese Communist Party and not the Republic of China, with whom Canada still has diplomatic relations. There is a small group of Chinese living in Canada who are Communists and Communist sympathizers. The Canadian government has long been keeping a close watch on their words and deeds, and is bound to take harsh measures towards them." We had no doubts about to whom he was referring.

Eileen's sister Louise, who lived in Oakland, California, told us that the FBI had paid her several visits to inquire about my activities. They suggested that I should visit the United States as they would like to chat with me, but that I would not be "obligated" to answer any questions since I was a Canadian.

I had no intention of making such a visit and when they offered to come to Vancouver to talk with me, I declined.

THE UBC "ISSUE"

Shortly after I returned to Canada in October 1964, Professor William L. Holland, director of the University of British Columbia's Department of Asian Studies, offered me a part-time teaching position, beginning in January 1965. I had met Bill in New York City in the late 1940s, when he headed up the Institute of Pacific Relations (IPR) and I was general secretary of the Chinese Students' Christian Association.

Bill also asked me to give a few lectures that term. I delivered my first lecture at UBC to a class of about fifty in November and by the Christmas holidays had lectured five times in different classes. I enjoyed academic life all over again, but preparing lectures was a great deal of work, so I frequently had to burn the midnight oil.

Just prior to the arrival of Eileen and the boys in early spring, I gave the second Thea Koerner Memorial Lecture, called "Perspectives," designed to broaden UBC students' world views. This was my first public address since returning to Canada and at quite a prestigious venue. I entitled it "Changing China: Human Values and Social Purpose."

My theme was the contemporary revolution in China in the context of sweeping changes around the world. At the outset, I stated that no power on earth would succeed in its policy toward China, unless and until it reconciled itself to the interests and aspirations of the Chinese people and to the rules of China's historical development. The polarization of political loyalties during the Cold War had set up formidable barriers to communication, blocking a rapprochement of minds and often colouring our view of reality. Distortions, exaggerations, and easy dichotomies had created a lurid mythology about China.

I briefly traced China's recent history before describing the New China since 1949:

> To most Chinese, China's present is seen as the sequel to a long nightmare that lasted a whole century. This nightmare began in the middle of the nineteenth century, when a proud, far-flung empire and a grand ancient culture, hitherto secure in its self-assurance that civilization itself was

coterminous with its own boundaries, was shockingly humbled in the Opium War and subsequent encounters by so-called barbarian powers, which had somehow, somewhere in history, leapt ahead of her in science and technology. From then on, once they had tasted their advantage in predatory might, these invaders pounced voraciously on the flabby carcass of Imperial China. They carved her up and divested her of all but the external vestments of sovereignty.

In the process, the decay – the utter putrefaction of the old feudal order – was gradually exposed to view, repelling increasing numbers of the population from the symbols of authority. This alienation was accelerated when segments of the landed gentry and officialdom allied themselves with the foreign invaders, to seize their share of the spoils from increased extortion of the Chinese masses, now further facilitated by the inroads of foreign commerce. China groaned under the double weight of foreign and domestic oppressions – national humiliation, lethal poverty, and frustrating backwardness. The old Confucian structure of values, with its institutional concomitants, began to crumble from sheer inadequacy in the face of national crisis. This historical dislocation had a profound effect on the political and socio-psychological outlook of the modern Chinese.

There began the long, agonizing quest for the instruments of national salvation, through technical modernization, and for a new national identity, through reappraisal of the cultural heritage and adapting it to the modern world.

Both modernization and a new national identity proved elusive. Neither the predatory foreigners nor the domestic gentry and officials would abdicate their positions of privilege and power to allow the reorganization necessary for genuine industrialization. Reformers like Kang Yu-wei and revolutionaries like Dr Sun Yat-sen tried to fashion institutions after the ideas of Jeremy Bentham, John Stuart Mill, and Henry George. These ideas and institutions failed primarily because there was no resonance with the political, social, and psychological experience of the Chinese people, and also because they could never get a fair trial in an economically backward country where the urban middle class was pitifully weak.

Dr Sun's revolution of 1911 overthrew the Imperial dynasty but founded a republic only in form. As long as the previous social structure remained intact, the breakdown of the monolithic empire could only bring in its wake schismatic political feuding, warlordism, a paternalistic political tutelage close to Fascism, the denial of elemental human rights, widespread carpetbagging, exploitation and intensified impoverishment of the masses, and further national degradation. The victims were scholar and peasant, merchant and worker, nearly all segments of Chinese society. China was ripe for revolution.

This was the setting for the promise and program of the Chinese Communist Party (CCP).

For the first time in history, the nation stood at the confluence of two great streams of social ferment – the left wing of China's traditional "elite" (the intelligentsia), and the seething, downtrodden masses of workers and peasants. What remained to be done was to organize and channel this enormous flow of human unrest into the main stream of revolution.

Mao Zedong and the Chinese Communist leaders borrowed from the West Marxian tools of analysis, but answers to China's problems came from a deep delving into China's own national experience. The grand design for China's revolutionary course was to be a continuous but phased revolution. First the old social fabric had to be ripped apart, shattering the power structures controlled by foreign exploiters, landlords, and corrupt officials linked with imperialism. Next would be the establishment of what was termed the New Democracy – a system which would give land back to the tiller and permit the operation of private enterprise within the framework of national planning. Finally the nation would make the transition to Socialism, based on increasingly large-scale production owned by the State and collective enterprises. This was the stage China was going through today. Within these clearly marked lines of advance, China was taking giant strides towards the building, in the shortest possible time, of a strong, advanced country with modern industry, agriculture, and culture.

Such was the promise and the program. How good or bad it is, how well it will be carried out to the end, only history will tell. For us, the important point here is not whether we agree or disagree with such a grand design, the point is the vast majority of the Chinese people accepted it as the only viable option for the nation, other alternatives having been tried and found lacking. And no one who visits China can fail to be impressed by the scope and power of the forces that have been unleashed to achieve these goals.

Man changes himself in the course of changing his environment. In Chinese society today, both economic realities and the pressure of social sanction and moral education are bent on showing that individual interests can only be satisfied in the context of community interests.

But it appears to be a long, difficult struggle and one likely to be way-laid by many errors and excesses before it achieves its goals. In actual fact, there have indeed been some errors and excesses in China.

My own creed is that the summit of all Beauty is man's humanity to man, but in real life this calls for the suppression of man's *inhumanity* to man, or this ideal would remain an empty dream. This means the denial of certain values cherished by the minority who used to deny human values to the majority. If this is inevitable, then every such denial of values must be judged, not in isolation, but by its necessity for social progress, and perhaps also by the degree of severity deemed necessary. It would be self-delusion, however, to decry such acts made in the name of social justice with a blanket epithet of denial of human freedom or of human dignity, and to conjure up a scale and a popular resistance to them that does not exist.

After all, the observer looking at social change in China has his own problem of identity, too – for him the question might well be, where does *he* stand in the ranks of humanity?

During the question period, many issues were raised – the Sino-Soviet dispute, Tibet, the treatment of anti-Marxist dissidents. I spoke from the heart, but knew my sympathetic views toward the Chinese revolution would elicit diverse reactions, both for and against, from the audience.

The moderator of the lecture was Dr F.H. Soward, dean emeritus of the Faculty of Graduate Studies, who had been one of my professors at UBC in 1939. His closing statement was diplomatically frank:

Ladies and Gentlemen – your close attention and your applause indicate how much you have enjoyed this address of Mr Lin's. I think we must be grateful to him for the care he has taken in preparing this address. I have seldom listened to such polished prose from a lecturer as we had from Mr Lin on this topic. I don't expect he would want us to agree with him in entirety in his views – that would be too much to ask of any person, but I think we are impressed by the conspectus which he has tried to give us of the Chinese scene. I may enter one personal caveat and exercise the Chairman's privilege – I can't take the long view of the Tibetan revolution that Mr Lin does and I shall still subscribe to the Tibetan refugee society. The meeting stands adjourned.

Overall, response was surprisingly positive from both students and university colleagues, but almost inevitably a Cold War mentality intervened. On March 6, Professor Bill Holland asked to see me. After inquiring about my work in China, he said that a *Vancouver Province* reporter had threatened to attack UBC for hiring a professor fresh from Red China.

Two months later, on May 6, UBC president John B. Macdonald invited me to lunch at the Faculty Club. He bluntly said he could not employ me. The *Vancouver Province* had sent a reporter to investigate Bill Holland's background as director of the Institute of Pacific Relations (IPR) in New York City and discovered that Holland had been forced out, following accusations in 1950 by Senator Joseph McCarthy's Un-American Activities Committee, which claimed Professor Owen Lattimore (once editor of the IPR journal *Pacific Affairs*) was a Soviet spy. Now Holland had hired Communist sympathizer Paul Lin, who had lived and worked in China for fifteen years. Macdonald told me that if UBC hired me, the *Vancouver Province* would publish a denunciation of the university and its Asian Studies department.

When word leaked out, students threatened to stage a protest in my support. I thanked them but said that as a newcomer just back from China, I did not want to be a *cause célèbre* or harm Bill Holland in any way. Furthermore, I told the students that China was a huge and ancient civilization going through a crucial and difficult transition. It was absolutely vital for Canada and Canadians to understand, whether we approved or not. Neither demonology nor euphoria about China's course would help, but only honest inquiry into the realities of her past and present. Meanwhile, I would exercise my right to express my own convictions and did not intend to lose my soul, regardless of pressures from any government or media source on the China issue.

The issue continued to bubble at UBC and I heard from several graduate students during the fall of 1965, when I was already teaching in Quebec. One of them wrote, in part:

The details of your leaving UBC, involving [the *Province* reporter's] threat and Macdonald having Bill Holland officially make the decision, have been spreading widely here.

The Toronto *Globe and Mail* has picked up the threads of it – wants to break it – and a reporter named either Martin Knelman or Mike Valpy may be around to see you.

I have told them it is utterly out of the question to break any part of it, because *unless* Holland is put on the stand to repeat Macdonald's

William L. (Bill) Holland, mid-1970s

"Harvard can resist community pressure – we can't" conversation, Dr Macdonald is in the clear.

… The *G&M* realizes [the implications], but says if they can get you to talk and implicate the others they'll break it. Otherwise, they'll keep silence.

Of course, I never spoke about this issue to the press and continued to see Bill Holland whenever I was in Vancouver.

SEEKING EMPLOYMENT

I completed my semester at UBC in May 1965, with future plans still uncertain. Harvard University offered me a fellowship for research and writing. It looked like a great opportunity; I could write on a subject of my own choice, whether it was published or not. The main thing was it would give me a position and much-needed income, but it meant I would have to spend part of the year in the United States. On June 7, Dr Ezra Vogel of Harvard University's Center for East Asian Research telephoned long-distance and tried to persuade me to come, suggesting I visit Cambridge to discuss the matter with them. When I said that present circumstances would not permit a visit, they finally said they would leave the offer open for me.

By then, I had received an offer of a teaching position at Lakehead College in Port Arthur, Ontario. After consulting with Eileen, Chris, and Doug, I declined because it meant moving to a remote part of Canada. I also turned down an offer from the University of Saskatchewan.

In July, Bill Holland asked if I would be interested in a position at McGill University in Montreal – to teach Chinese history and head up a new Centre for East Asian Studies. I flew to Montreal in August for an interview. McGill offered a three-year contract, beginning at $9,000 per annum, plus $1,000 for moving expenses. Starting in September 1965 as an assistant professor, I would give three courses in the History Department: The History of China, The Modern Transformation of East Asia in the Nineteenth and Twentieth Centuries, and The History of Japan. After checking with the family, I accepted. Chris pronounced it the best option, because of McGill's superior academic reputation.

Chapter Ten

BRIGHT BEGINNING AND TRAGEDY

FROM VANCOUVER TO MONTREAL

As grateful as I was to have a job, the McGill position required pulling up stakes and making a trek across Canada, just after we had begun to settle down in Vancouver. Rather than disrupt the boys' schooling again, we decided that they would stay with Eileen in Vancouver for two or three months, while I went on to McGill to start my courses and find a home in Montreal. I flew out in September to assume my new appointment, lodging temporarily at McGill's Faculty Club.

Mother returned from California to keep the three of us company in Paul's absence. The boys and I worked hard during those three months and I spent hours translating the difficult English words in their textbooks into Chinese. English soon ceased to be a major difficulty and by Christmas they no longer needed my help. They could even correspond with Paul in English.

In December, Paul came home for the holidays and in early January Doug and I returned with him to Montreal. Chris was a freshman at the University of British Columbia and decided to move into campus housing. So we sold our house and car and headed for Montreal on January 8, 1966, arriving three days later. Paul had rented a small and dingy flat on Drummond Street not far from the university. Before our household goods arrived, we rented three beds and borrowed pots and dishes from Paul's sister, Margaret. Moving was always a fearful business, but was worst in the dead of winter.

Since we were living downtown, the only school Doug could attend was Montreal High School. On his first day, Doug was told that all boys were required to wear neckties. Someone was kind enough to lend him one, but when he mistakenly wandered into the staff bathroom to put it on, a teacher impatiently shouted at him, "Out! Get out!" We concluded that Montreal High was not the right place for Doug. Thankfully, the wife of one of Paul's colleagues recommended we check out Westmount High School, which had just initiated a new system called "subject promotion." Doug could take his strong subjects, like mathematics and physics, at his own grade level, and the weaker ones – English and French – temporarily at a lower level. This was ideal, but admission required residence in Westmount. By a stroke of luck, we found a wonderful apartment with a sweeping view of the city. We moved in immediately and Doug was able to transfer to Westmount High.✺

In mid-January, we received our first letter from Chris written in English. Thereafter, he wrote at least once a month to assure us that he was well:

I miss you all so much, but my line of vision is blocked by the huge mountains and great distance between us ...

Recently, I have been with Professor [Jack Weichen] Lin every Sunday. His whole family is so kind to me and I truly don't know how to thank them enough. I am not too lonely, except sometimes, a little bit. But this is good for my character forming ...

Baba, how are you? I was so happy to receive your letter, but I am also very concerned about your health. Please take good care of yourself. And, Mama, are you still as healthy as before? I am waiting most anxiously for good news about your work. Only after you find a job, will our family become financially independent. Xiao Bei [Doug's nickname], has this term been as difficult as the previous ones? I am confident that you can overcome all difficulties ...

My final exams will end on May 4. I got a ride from my schoolmates and will drive across Canada to see you. Please, will you find out for me if I could find a job in the evening, on a night shift perhaps, so that I could study and work at the same time ...

Chris arrived in Montreal in late May to spend the summer. He registered for an evening English course at Loyola College. On June 21 the two of us drove up to McGill's summer resort at Mont-Saint-Hilaire, a beautiful 1,200-acre

The *McGill Daily*'s photo of Paul, taken for its profile article on the new professor of Chinese studies, spring 1966

nature sanctuary. He deserved a proper break after working so hard during his first year at university. We enjoyed the peace and tranquillity, relaxing and chatting while walking the trails, swimming and rowing a boat on the pristine lake. Chris had matured. He seemed to argue less and to listen more. Part of this change was natural – he was no longer a child. However, I think the shift in our relationship was also due to our move from China: Chris was coming to recognize and respect me as a Canadian. Although I had had a significant job at Radio Peking while the boys were growing up in the 1950s, I was not a Party member and therefore had little status in the broader society. Chris actually spoke better Chinese than I did. Once in Canada, and forced to wrestle with the English language and the Canadian political system, however, he appeared to better appreciate my strengths. As a citizen and a native speaker, I had the power to speak out on public matters and be taken seriously. We increasingly discussed the Chinese-Western divide that I was so intent on bridging.

Toward the end of August, it was time for Chris to return to UBC. We wanted him to take a train back, but there was a strike on, and plane tickets were scarce. One afternoon at my office, Chris met a McGill graduate student who was also the director of the Montreal Drive Away. The company delivered cars from coast to coast, often making use of student drivers whose compensation was a free trip. Chris was enthusiastic and arranged to be one of three drivers to deliver a station wagon to Vancouver.

⪼ When Chris told me of his plan, I objected immediately on the grounds of the risk involved. I reminded him that the FBI had targeted us as suspicious new arrivals from Red China. But his mind was made up. Paul and I then warned him not to cross into the United States, because of this danger. Chris promised he would not, but could not vouch for the other drivers. I asked him: "What if you get killed?!" With the arrogance of youth, he replied: "So be it." The last phone call I received from him was from Chicago. He called person to person to his father, knowing that Paul had already left for Banff. This was his way of letting me know where he was, without having to pay for long distance charges. My heart sank, worrying for his safety.⪼

THE BANFF CONFERENCE ON WORLD AFFAIRS

Before Chris left Montreal, I flew west to address the week-long Banff Conference on World Affairs, sponsored by the Canadian Institute of International Affairs. I had arranged to meet Chris in Vancouver following the conference, so I could help him select courses for his coming year at UBC.

The title of my Banff address was "China and the West" and my remarks provoked some controversy. The *Herald* quoted my speech on August 24, 1966 without much comment, headlining its report "Montreal Professor Leads Attack on US Policies":

The most damning of several attacks on the US stand in Vietnam to emerge so far from the Banff conference on Asian affairs, came Tuesday in a volley by Professor Paul Lin of the history department at McGill University, Montreal ... He said the US appeared to Asians as a power so impressed with its own array of preponderant military and technological might, that it deems it possible to impose a Pax Americana on the rest of the world. This is an image established in Asian minds not by Communist propaganda, but by the record of nearly two decades of US power plays in Asia.

Asians find the facts to be these: There is not a single Chinese soldier or military base outside of China anywhere in Asia. It is understandable that they find it hard to conceive how Washington, thousands of miles away, can be far more certain than they of the Chinese threat to their security. Asians just cannot accept the assumption of evil Chinese intentions, especially while US napalm, gas, defoliants, and canisters filled with razor darts rain down on an Asian land where Chinese soldiers are not even present, and while US military leaders seem eager to bomb them back into the stone age.

The image of China as a bloodthirsty, conspiratorial incarnation of yellow peril, simply does not fit in the Asian view. The prime fact of China's history in the last century has been a long, agonizing experience of being the victim, rather than the author, of aggressive imperialism – an experience only too easily understood by other Asian peoples. The Asian viewpoint expresses the feelings and aspirations of more than half the people of the world. If we wish, we can dismiss them as pawns – but we act on this basis at our own peril.

The *Calgary Herald* article took a more Cold War approach, delivering a sharp defence of US policy in Vietnam:

Although the United States has been the target of sharp abuse during the Banff conference on Asian affairs, the conference has nevertheless had its productive moments in illuminating the complexities of Asian problems. Some of the speeches, however, failed to show up the broader implications of the situation. A case in point was the bitter attack on US Vietnam policy launched by Professor Paul Lin of McGill University. This speaker painted the United States as a war-mongering aggressor, intent on remaking the rest of the world in its own image. Unfortunately, Prof. Lin was careless with some of his facts. For example, there was the implication that, while the US may maintain a military presence in several Asiatic countries, there is no Chinese soldier or military base outside of China. It appears that Prof. Lin has forgotten about an oppressed little country called Tibet.

Much of this suspicion of Washington has been fostered by the Communist government in Peking, which views the continuing US presence in Asia as a threat to China's own nationalistic drive to re-establish its power. This attempt to paint the US as the arch-villain has, regrettably, made considerable impact in Asia and also among some Westerners who ought to know better. Complicating the situation is the fact that Peking gives every evidence of having been brainwashed by its own anti-American propaganda. The fact of the matter is that the US is not conducting a war of aggression in Vietnam but that it is merely attempting to preserve the peace and to give an unhappy people some opportunity for eventual self-determination. If the US has made serious errors in Vietnam, the reasons for its presence there remain valid.

Curiously, neither report mentioned my appeal to Canada to take initiative in establishing relations with China. I had said:

Let me again take note of what Senator Cameron observed in his opening address. Canadians have a unique opportunity in the present situation. They have an enormous fund of goodwill in China. The name of Dr Norman Bethune is the symbol of the best "internationalism" to all Chinese ... But we cannot go on forever drawing on the capital of goodwill built up by Dr Bethune ...

What is an independent Canadian policy? I certainly do not pretend to be a specialist on this complex subject. But it would seem to be eminent good sense to say simply that Canadian policy is based on Canadian interests, for Canadian objectives – not one based on the interests and foreign policy objectives of another country. An important immediate objective would be to formally recognize, for our own sake, the existence of 700 million Chinese; to develop friendship and normal relations with them, including the expansion of two-way trade and cultural exchange. To be sure, this calls for the most courageous, the most discerning of statesmanship. It calls for a far-sighted view of the stakes involved for Canada and the world.

I wrote to Eileen from Vancouver on August 28:

The Conference was far more important than I had at first imagined – indeed, it seems to have been a Fulbright-type hearing. In the end, Paul Martin summed up his position with considerable embarrassment, having to address pointed questions from an audience that by week's end had become overwhelmingly pro-China. Many have told me my speech made a tremendous impact, some sharp disagreements notwithstanding. The interesting thing was that the ambassadors of Indonesia, Burma, and Japan all agreed with my point of view, as did Chester Ronning, Canada's last ambassador to China until his departure in 1952.

I met many people and was besieged every free period with invitations for further conversation, including a demand that I speak to the ladies of the conference one evening after the reception. In the afternoons, I was invited for field trips by car to the surrounding lakes and mountains – the scenic grandeur was breathtaking. My favorite afternoon was a hike to the top of Sulphur Mountain with Ken Woodsworth (a lawyer and father of a former student at UBC) and James Barrington (the former Burmese ambassador) ... Martin introduced himself to me after his speech and apologized for missing mine. "I understand you gave a very able presentation."

Bill Holland is inviting me to lunch tomorrow. I have a firm reservation on Air Canada, leaving Vancouver Monday, Sept. 5, but am trying to get something out of here earlier – perhaps Saturday, although chances are not great. Did Chris get off on his trip? I hope he will arrive before I leave ...

HEARTBREAK

The evening of August 31, I was staying with old friends in Vancouver when a phone call came just past midnight from Bellingham, Washington. I heard news that no parent is prepared for: Chris, just twenty-one years old, had died in a car crash. Despite the depths of my grief, I tried to break the tragic news gently to Eileen and Doug by asking my brother David in Montreal to tell them in person.

Doug and I were awakened by banging on our apartment door around 5:00 am. In walked David and his wife Florence. David told me what had happened and I sobbed my heart out: our worst nightmare had turned into a dreadful reality!

The funeral service for our beloved son was held on September 6, 1966, at the William Wray Chapel in Montreal, attended by more than one hundred family, friends, students, and colleagues. I later wrote a tribute to Chris to share with friends not able to be present at his service. It read in part:

We have now laid him to rest at the Mount Royal Cemetery, in a grave on a green hillock, facing east. He is not far from us, so we can visit his resting place to remind us of what he was, what he might have been and what we owe to those who cherished and nourished him ...

Every man is but tissue and bone, but his death can have as little meaning as a feather, be as weighty as a mountain – and the difference lies not so much in fame as in simple integrity of thought and action on the side of justice and the majority of mankind – by which he touches the lives of others ever so lightly, but ever so profoundly. So, I think, was my son.

Father was in Hong Kong at the time of this tragic death. I tried to break the sad news to him gently through our close friends Walter and Junny Chun, who wrote to me on September 9. "Grandpa took the matter with courage and strength despite the great grief. He sighed deeply, kept silent for a while, and then said Chris was a wonderful boy and the tragedy is a great loss to the family, society, and country. He told us that when he first came to Hong Kong, he heard that New China educated young people to be inhuman to parents and old friends. But on seeing Chris, he saw something different, that Chris had all the virtues and good qualities called for in the old Chinese education. He shed tears when we were leaving."

I was deeply moved by their letter. Chris was so much part of us, embodied so many of our ideals and hopes, that the shock of losing him was like tearing something out of our very vitals. It was agonizing to fully accept that our tall, stalwart boy had been taken from us forever – grief filled the rooms he had once walked through, where we still saw his zest for life and heard his gay laughter. In the year of his budding manhood, all the hopes we had had for him, all the promise of his efforts, were now an empty dream. Eileen and I were determined to face this loss squarely, but a recurring flood of memories often came back to overwhelm us like a slowly receding tide. Healing would take time.

I informed Madame Soong Ching Ling of the fatal accident on September 15. "The awful shock of this sudden and irreparable loss, the great void in our little family, has left us weak with grief, for he was more than a beloved son. He carried in him many of the fine qualities of the New China, a strong sense of right and wrong, a vast love of life and of people ... It is an effort to dispel the blackness that has descended on us, but we must and we will – as he would have wanted us to – turn our agony into strength. It deepens our pain to think of what he might have done in his imminent manhood ... but we will try to make up for the loss."

Madame Soong graciously responded: "How I wish I were there to be of some help to you both. My sincere love goes out to you in your hour of sorrow." She was especially concerned about Eileen and advised: "Please keep her busily occupied so she won't have time to mourn over her great loss. Work is the only thing that helps to replace a great loss, I find."

Soon after Chris's death, his grandmother – Choming Chen – established a four-year scholarship at UBC in his memory. The annual $500 scholarship was intended to support talented young persons committed to the study of Chinese, who might one day contribute to the promotion of better understanding between China and the West. Had Chris lived, I believe he would have become a living denial of the cultural Cold War; the scholarship sought to honour this unfulfilled ambition. Dozens of family friends and colleagues contributed and an endowment fund was established in the 1970s, organized by former UBC students Neil Burton and Dick Woodsworth.

LEGAL INQUIRIES

Neither Eileen nor I was prepared to accept Chris's death as simply an accident of his own making. An autopsy demonstrated his system was clean. Soon after he died, we received a call from an old friend who owned a restaurant in Toronto. When Chris and his fellow drivers stopped in for lunch, en route from Montreal, Chris had commented that he thought they were being followed.

Two friends of mine from Vancouver – Andrew Joe, a lawyer, and W.W. Lee – immediately drove down to Bellingham on September 1 to examine the scene of the accident. They told me that Chris's car had struck a light standard in the middle of an intersection in Bellingham, just after midnight on September 1, and that he had been alone at the time. Yet, still we felt that some of the supposed facts from the accident scene did not add up. The following day, I visited the scene with my lawyer, Harold Tupper, and an investigator assigned to the case. We saw that there was a sharp curve to the right at the bottom of the hill, where the crash had occurred. The investigator remarked that it would be easy for drivers to think that the highway went straight on, instead of turning sharply to the right into a two-lane detour road leading onto the freeway. Moreover, highway construction was underway and the contractor had not posted warning signs of the dangerous roadway changes ahead.

I proceeded to track down the two French graduate students who had accompanied Chris from Montreal to Seattle. I wrote, "One thing we would like very much is to have in our memory some idea of how he spent his last few days and you are the only ones who can tell us." Just prior to their return to France on October 1, they replied: "We decided from the beginning, to drive a maximum of three or four hours each, and we went through the States' roads which are better than the Canadian ones. We passed Customs at Sault Ste. Marie and happened to be close to the Yellowstone National Park on Tuesday morning and decided to spend the whole day in the park. Christopher (as well as we) enjoyed a lot that day ... Usually we went to sleep with the darkness and awoke with the sun so that we started early in the morning. On Wednesday, we arrived in Seattle around 8:00 pm and Christopher, who had only been driving in the morning, told us he was not tired and would go to Vancouver. Then we parted with him and he left."

Early on I had contacted Elias H. Jacobs, an old friend and attorney in New York State. He believed that a strong case could be made against the State of Washington and the highway construction company, for negligence in failing to put up adequate warning signs at a dangerous spot where previous accidents had occurred. He then put us in touch with his cousin, a renowned Seattle lawyer and former district attorney, who agreed to investigate the case further. Soon after, the lawyer gave us the disturbing information that when he had tried to get the official police record of Chris's fatal accident, he was told the file was with the FBI and unavailable. The investigation proceeded for several months and then petered out. Without the official police record, there seemed to be no other avenues of legal redress that we could pursue.

⚝ More than forty years after Chris's death, I am still haunted by missing pieces of this puzzle. Chris dropped his travel companions in Seattle around 8:00 pm, saying he planned to drive straight to Vancouver via Bellingham. The distance from Seattle to Bellingham is only eighty-nine miles and would take no more than one and a half hours to drive at normal speed. So where had he been during those four long hours, before his death in Bellingham at 12:06 am on September 1, 1966?⚝

The weeks and months that followed were harrowing, but the loving support of our friends sustained us, as we attempted to rebuild our lives without Chris. In March 1967 we received a most affectionate handwritten letter from Madame Soong, despite her distress over the prevailing turbulence of the Cultural Revolution in China. She signed her letter "Your affectionate Aunty, but not Madame!" Henceforth, she signed all her letters to us "Aunty."

THE REVEREND GEORGE LIM YUEN, 1882–1967

Father and stepmother returned to Vancouver in mid-November, via the US liner *President Cleveland*. In early spring, he suddenly took ill and was taken to Mount St Joseph Hospital, where the the doctors diagnosed cancer. The cancer developed rapidly but, thankfully, under sedation, he passed his last few days without much pain. I managed to fly to his bedside in time to talk with

Christopher, age 21, Vancouver, 1966

Below
Christopher's resting place at Mount
Royal Cemetery in Montreal. The tablet
reads, "Forever Spring."

him and was at his side when he passed away on May 7. My brothers David
and Andy, and my sister Helen, arrived soon after. The Lin Clan Association
arranged for the funeral and reception afterwards in Chinatown. Several hundred attended the funeral at Christ Church Anglican Cathedral in Vancouver;
the Right Rev. Godfrey P. Gower officiated at the service, assisted by the Rev.
K.Y. Kwan. Father had lived to the venerable age of eighty-five.

Chapter Eleven

COLD WAR WARMING

PACEM IN TERRIS II, 1967

In 1967, I was invited by the Center for the Study of Democratic Institutions in Santa Barbara, California to address its second convocation in Geneva based on Pope John XXIII's encyclical, *Pacem in Terris*. Troubled by the threats to peace that persisted in the world since the first *Pacem in Terris* convocation in 1965, more than 300 diplomats, scholars, theologians, journalists, and businesspeople from seventy countries attended.

On May 30, I was the last speaker on a panel titled "Beyond Coexistence." The panellists who spoke before me were distinguished political leaders from Yugoslavia, France, Senegal, and the United States. I was scheduled to speak after US Senator J.W. Fulbright, who left the hall immediately after his address, followed by many journalists in the press gallery. It seems that I offended some of those who remained with my criticism of the United States' foreign policy. "Who is this man?" someone shouted out.

My paper was entitled "Some Reflections on Coexistence" in which I sketched in bold strokes the international structures of power in the 1960s, as I perceived them.

> Let us take the example of the relations between the United States and the various socialist countries. These relations are characterized not by uniformity, but by unprecedented sharp differences of approach, running the gamut of war, violence short of war, and détente ... The government of the United States used to bestow on the Soviet Union a heavy stigma

of evil to be extirpated. More recently, it has turned its demonology on China, which has now been named its arch-foe. Yet in actual practice, it prefers to war on tiny Vietnam, to "contain" China short of overt attack, and to reach an "accommodation" with the Soviet Union – all this without ever, by word or deed, relinquishing any of its long-range worldwide goals couched in the familiar verbiage of "free world defence."

Realistically, however, these policy variants are based on risk calculations. There is, at present, no hot war between the Soviet Union and the United States, and some evidence of détente and even collaboration. This has been dubbed peaceful coexistence. Yet some observers would question whether it is, instead, a mere chimera of suspended annihilation, since it is based on little more than the unnerving assumption that each has offensive and retaliatory weapons to "overkill" the other.

There is yet another assumption underlying these relations, which is perhaps of even more serious import. That assumption is that both superpowers have preponderant power to annihilate all third powers. The predictable corollary is that this calls for shared, or bipolar, policing of the world, according to terms of limited cooperation between the two chief constables, which would leave untouched each other's so-called "core interests."

Understandably, hundreds of millions of people – without doubt the majority of mankind – find little to welcome in this *modus operandi*. These people live mostly in areas of the world where the old colonial empires have been largely destroyed in name, but not entirely in substance, where there are attempts to resurrect empires in a new form. In their own national experience, the Chinese, like other Asians, have had more than a bitter taste of being policed by others. For a whole century after the Opium War, they had the "privilege" of living under "Law and Order" – the "Peace through Law" imposed on her by the Western powers and Japan under the unequal treaty system, which not only robbed her of national dignity and sovereign powers, but also held back her economic, social, and cultural progress. They see little essential difference between this and the "peace through law" that the United States government now seeks to impose by its military presence in the Taiwan area and whole periphery of China in the name of "containment."

Let me cite another example. It is often held that "nuclear nonproliferation" has the aim of stopping the spread of nuclear weapons and that therefore anyone who questions the non-proliferation treaty must be a monster … It turns out that the proposed treaty has nothing to do with the non-proliferation of nuclear weapons. It does not, in fact, prevent the wider and wider deployment by the US and the Soviet Union of more and more nuclear weapons perfected by every means, including underground testing … The substance of the matter is that the non-proliferation treaty is in essence a political rather than a military or scientific proposition, less still a humanitarian one. It has to do with the non-proliferation, not of weapons, but of political control – with maintaining the duality of Soviet and American power to call all the plays in world affairs …

Are the two superpowers to be relied on to be more "rational" and "responsible" than others who now possess, or will possess, nuclear weapons? In fact, once political hegemony as an objective of policy is ruled out, nuclear weapons are useless. They are useful for younger nuclear powers only as bargaining counters – to compel the older nuclear powers to recognize their claims to national security, sovereign equality, and political justice – which are to them, the basic ingredients of peace … There is only one way to stop the nuclear arms race and weapons: their thorough destruction. Anything short of this is a mirage …

People who see themselves as the victims of aggression and intervention can only accept peaceful coexistence if it is linked with the prior withdrawal of aggression and intervention and the true establishment of … the sovereign equality of nations, as envisaged in the UN Charter.

In concluding, I would like to pay tribute to the courageous men and women of America who seek to save the soul of their great nation by crying out, without equivocation, in the name of humanity: My country is wrong.

Following my controversial address, I was pleasantly surprised by a small group of Americans who told me that this was the kind of speech they came to the convocation to hear. Some of them became our good friends for life. *The Nation* magazine carried a supportive comment by a Marshall Windmiller of San Francisco: "One of the few challenging talks of the meeting was by Prof. Paul Lin of McGill University, who argued persuasively that the nuclear non-proliferation treaty negotiations, led by the US and the USSR, are in reality nothing more than an effort by the big two to preserve their monopoly of power. Mrs Borgese (a staff member of the Center for the Study of Democratic Institutions) unfairly dismisses him in her article as a Chinese 'spokesman.' Lin is a Canadian and a professor of history. He spoke as a scholar, although perhaps somewhat out of harmony with those who, like Mrs Borgese, thought that coexistence with China was too remote an issue even to be considered."

MONTREAL HOME SEARCH, 1968

In Canada, the Cold War chill remained. Eileen and I returned home one evening in January 1968 to find two plainclothes men waiting for us at our apartment door. They said they had been sent by the RCMP's Department of Prevention Service to investigate goods brought in from the United States, for which the necessary duties had not been paid. I responded that we had not been to the United States since returning to Canada in 1964, except to investigate the scene of Chris's accident in Washington in September 1966. When they indicated that they wanted to search our apartment, I asked for their identification and search warrant, which they did not have. I told them I first needed to make a few phone calls, but when I unlocked the apartment door, they invited themselves in.

I reached Professor K.A.C. Elliott, chairman of the Chemistry Department and a member of McGill's East Asia Committee, as well as Professor Frank Scott of the Faculty of Law. In front of the RCMP agents, I informed them what was happening and asked for advice. When the two agents heard these distinguished names, one immediately asked the other to return to the office and fetch a warrant, while he stayed in the apartment watching over us. With the warrant eventually in hand, the agents made a thorough search and finally pinpointed three household items that they claimed had been brought into Canada illegally: a radio-record player, an electric knife sharpener, and a combination can opener. I told them that these were gifts from an American friend, but the agents confiscated them. We reported the incident to our friend, who managed to retrieve all the items during his next visit to Montreal. Material things, of course, meant nothing to us, but we felt humiliated by having our home rudely searched by the RCMP, as if we were common criminals. It was discouraging to be three years back in Canada and still under surveillance.

CANADA'S CHINA POLICY

One of the controversial issues of the Spring 1968 federal election campaign was Canada's China policy. Naturally, I took a strong stand in favour of Canada normalizing relations with the People's Republic of China. I saw Canada's helping to open China to the outside world – in the interests of international peace and development – as a key initiative, since Canada was a country the Chinese held in high regard.

My opinions were sought by Thérèse Casgrain, a prominent member of Montreal's intelligentsia, later a senator, who was deeply involved in social justice issues and women's rights, as well as sharply opposed to the United States' military engagement in Vietnam. I had met her shortly after arriving at McGill and we spoke several times about Canada's policy toward China. I expressed to her my concern over recent statements made by Secretary of State for External Affairs Mitchell Sharp calling for recognition of the Beijing Government as the Government of China, while maintaining relations with the Taipei Government as the "Government of Formosa." I thought it would be helpful for the question to be debated more meticulously, before irrevocable statements and actions were made by our leaders. My worry was that instead of improving the international atmosphere, we could start a chain of events that might embitter our relations with China. We had to take a forthright, courageous stand that accorded full dignity and equality to the Chinese people. This meant recognizing the PRC government by normal diplomatic procedures, without the affront of political conditions.

In late spring, Norman Webster, editor of the *Globe and Mail*, asked me to write an analysis of the political parties' stands toward China for the paper. My article, entitled "The Path to Peking Is Littered with Obstacles," was published on June 21, 1968.

In an election campaign full of hazy foreign policy issues, one of the haziest is the question of Canada's policy toward China. Yet if there is one point on which all three major parties seem to be in agreement, it is that Canada must soon establish diplomatic relations with the People's Republic of China.

No doubt, this represents a response to the growing consensus of public opinion on this question. To some Canadians, the quixotism of Canada's refusal to admit officially the legal existence of a country 40 times its population and 40 times its age, is only matched by its inhumanity. To others, non-recognition seems a posture of servility toward Washington or of incredible arrogance toward Peking. To many, it is self-defeating hypocrisy not to seek official relations with a country that purchases such a crucial volume of Canada's wheat.

Informed Canadians have long rejected the puerile claim that recognition is an act of approval of a foreign government's policies. (By this yardstick, few governments would have any relations with each other and, indeed, China would have to refuse to recognize the governments in Washington, Moscow, or even Ottawa.)

Canadians of goodwill are convinced that for world peace, Canada can play a key role in opening new channels of international understanding and human communication, including that between the peoples of China and North America. Whatever the considerations, more and more Canadians have become aware that Canada has an enormous capital of people-to-people goodwill to draw on through the posthumous influence of the Canadian surgeon Dr Norman Bethune, whose exploits for China during the war against Japan have made him a revered model of selfless service and internationalism in the China of today.

Significantly, a Canadian university, McGill, is the only North American university to have an academic exchange with China – the Norman Bethune Medical Exchange.

There seems no longer to be much public doubt about the wisdom of normalizing Canada's relations with this enormous power across the Pacific. It is precisely for this reason, however, that the focus of attention has shifted. It is no longer an issue of whether, but how Canada should recognize Peking. Indeed, whether and how have become one and the same substantive issue, for the choice of method may in fact either bring about recognition or make it impossible.

Each of the major party leaders has actually proposed not a normal procedure, but some form of conditional recognition. This might provoke the query as to whether they really mean business, since the conditions they set pertain to vital sovereign rights, which no government will bargain with.

Unfortunately, the concrete problem is obscured in a miasma of confused ideas. These revolve around what to do with Taiwan, or Formosa as it is called in the West. On this pivotal issue, not all of the campaigners seem to agree with each other or even their own party colleagues.

Among the various formulas, External Affairs Minister Mitchell Sharp has suggested continuing relations with the Government (presumably Chiang Kai-shek's) of a new entity called Formosa, which Chiang Kai-shek himself has steadfastly refused to consider as a separate state with international standing. Yet Mr Sharp insists this is no "two Chinas" formula, but "one China, one Formosa."

NDP leader T.C. Douglas speaks of a "UN referendum" to achieve "self-determination" for a people called the "Formosans." All ignore the overwhelming evidence that neither Peking nor Taipei, with whom dual relations are proposed, is ever likely to accept such a proposal.

The humming and hawing on recognition would no doubt subside if the crucial question were posed and answered unequivocally: Does Taiwan belong to China or not? If the answer is yes, then Canada is perilously close to advocating gross intervention in the internal affairs of another country, in a manner which would make Gabon's little sally ("one Canada, one Quebec?") seem pale by comparison. If Canada maintains that the answer is no, or doubtful, then Canada is questioning the action of scores of countries that have recognized Peking or continue to recognize Chiang's regime, without ever questioning the equally vehement claims of both that Taiwan is only a province of China.

Geographically, Taiwan is an offshore island one hundred miles from the Chinese mainland. Historically, mainland Chinese appeared on the island probably as early as the Third Century AD, and there were successive migrations by Chinese settlers (ancestors of the present-day Hakkas of Fukien [Fujian] Province), starting with the southern Sung period (thirteenth century). The heaviest migrations occurred from the seventeenth century on, after the famous Ming loyalist, Cheng Cheng-kung, made the island a base of resistance to the Manchus. The Chinese made Taiwan a prefecture of Fukien Province soon afterward, and it became a province in its own right in 1886.

In 1895, Japan seized the island after a war with China, but at the end of the Second World War it was compelled to return it to China. This was in accordance with the four-power Cairo and Potsdam declarations, which had stated that "all the territories Japan has stolen from the Chinese, such as Manchuria, Formosa and the Pescadores (Penghus) shall be restored to the Republic of China."

In actual fact, Taiwan was officially recovered by China on Oct. 25, 1945, and later reincorporated as a province by the Chinese Government of that time. Then came the civil war, and Chiang's regime fled to Taiwan and set up a government there under the aegis of the US 7th Fleet, still claiming to be the government of all China.

Juridically, Canada still recognizes that same "Government of the Republic of China" (not some "Government of Formosa"), as all the official communications of the External Affairs Department bear out. Furthermore, Canada entered no caveat in 1945 questioning Taiwan's status as a Chinese province, nor did Canada have a right to do so.

It is thus difficult to understand whence comes Canada's right today to challenge China's territorial claims. Is it merely because Canada is faced with the simple obligation of recognizing its successor government? It is a firmly established principle of international law that a change of government, including a revolutionary one, does not extinguish the international personality nor territorial integrity of the state.

Neither Canada nor any other state in the world has ever recognized the non-existent "state" of Formosa. To have relations with Formosa, Canada would have to create it, unilaterally and against all principles of international law and usage – an enterprise not very likely to enhance Canada's image of a mature power in world affairs.

There may also be political or moral justification for Canada's instigating or abetting "separatist" sentiment in Taiwan, but the reasoning is also dubious. Ninety-eight per cent of the island's 12 million inhabitants are Chinese-speaking Chinese, with indissoluble cultural and political ties with their relatives on the mainland.

True, there have occasionally been independence movements, some indigenous (such as the abortive Taiwan Republic movement of 1895, which defiantly sought to keep the island out of Japanese hands after the Manchu court had capitulated), and others externally abetted (such as the Japanese-sponsored independence intrigues at the end of the Second World War). But the dominant tradition in Taiwan's history, as evidenced in frequent uprisings against alien rule, has been that of a fierce ethnic and cultural loyalty to Mother China.

Of course, in Taiwan today there exists suppressed but widespread discontent among the islanders under the present regime. But whether this is to be equated with anti-China separatist sentiment must be weighed against the historical fact that the islanders danced in the streets of Taipei when China's military and civilian personnel returned to govern Taiwan after Japan's defeat in 1945.

Many observers and scholars have noted that the islanders' mood today is a product of two decades of disillusionment with an oppressive and carpetbagging administration, which would seem to suggest that the true "betrayal" would be to leave them under the rule of the present regime.

But perhaps these observations are superfluous, for Canada apparently is not even instigating some sort of Formosa Libre. Instead, Canada proposes to ask the people of Taiwan to believe that by "deserting" Chiang, Canada is "deserting" them, hence Canada must maintain relations with his regime. It makes strange logic for those who exhort Canada not to "desert" the Formosans, to demand at the same time the perpetuation, by international legal recognition, of the very regime toward which the discontent is directed.

In the absence of a credible historical, legal or moral rationale, Canada's extraordinary posture in favor of a "one China, one Formosa" policy only places Canada under the suspicion of espousing a contrivance whose only purpose is to keep Taiwan out of China's hands. Such a position carries even graver implications than the more shopworn contrivance of "two Chinas," which at least did not exclude Taiwan explicitly from the legal territory of China.

By contrast, Canada's concoction would go the final limit: take Taiwan out of China and congeal this in international law. For Canada, the attempt to turn this trick poses more than the danger of certain failure; Canada would not only be antagonizing a government, but a whole people.

If there are grounds for accusing Canada of again tampering with China's territorial integrity in the 1960s, this would be taken as a hostile and insulting act by all Chinese regardless of political partisanship. It would not only cost Canada its large fund of goodwill in China – which has long memories of a century of depredation and dismemberment at the hands of foreign powers – it would in fact reverse the trend toward improved relations which "recognition" was avowedly intended to launch.

There is no easy opportunism that will enable Canada to place the onus on China if, as we must expect, it rejects such a provocative form of recognition. One need only ask whether Canada would accept the same principle being applied to it by some foreign power. Under such a principle, do not Canada's constitutional and political problems make it even more vulnerable to the proposition of "self-determination" for one part of Canada by benefit of foreign intervention? And would Canada agree to a UN referendum for any Canadian province that emits rumblings of discontent?

Indeed, our own constitutional crises should have led us to a much more delicate sensitivity toward the unquestioned right of the Chinese to settle their domestic problems themselves, without foreign interference. This includes the problem of whether the people of Taiwan should enjoy a degree of self-government that might be called "equal" or "special status," or anything else, a problem that in any case can be settled in the larger context of an overall solution to the "congealed" civil war, and not by foreign interference.

Canada cannot afford risking the accusation of preferring chicanery to statesmanship. Canada must, in straightforward terms, accord China the respect and equality it expects in return. One does not start normal relations with a neighbor by acts of gratuitous insult and injury. If

Canada really means to begin fruitful relations with the People's Republic of China, the only path is the recognition of Peking as the successor government of China, through normal diplomatic procedures, with no strings attached, as other governments have done. If Canada is not yet prepared to take the step, its leaders should say so in so many words.

The article caught the attention of interested parties in Canada, the United States, and even the United Nations. I received an unexpected letter from a French press correspondent, Nelly Marans, in August 1968, telling me that she had found my article in the reading room of the United Nations. She wrote in part: "I was extremely interested and glad to find such good reading ... I share of course your clear-cut viewpoints that are a welcome change from all the muddled nonsense one hears so frequently in the United Nations ... Don't you think that the Western attitude with regard to 'two Chinas' or the nonexistent state of Taiwan is motivated more by a seemingly incurable Western delusion about some self-granted 'right' to interfere in Chinese affairs – as history proves it – than by 'ideological' reasons?"

MEETING CYRUS EATON

Hardly a week had elapsed after the publication of my *Globe and Mail* article when I received a cordial letter from Cyrus S. Eaton – the legendary Canadian-born industrialist and philanthropist. *Time* magazine had labelled Eaton "Krushchev's favorite capitalist" in 1959 for his efforts to further world peace during the Cold War by regularly hosting conferences of distinguished Western and Soviet scientists at his home in Pugwash, Nova Scotia. He wrote on the stationery of the chairman of the board, the Chesapeake and Ohio Railway Company, Cleveland, Ohio.

June 28, 1968

Dear Professor Lin:

I have read with special interest your splendid article in *The Globe and Mail* of June 21 on Canada's policy toward China. Could I persuade you and any of your friends to spend a weekend with me here at my Deep Cove Farm in Nova Scotia? I should be pleased to arrange for your transportation either by one of our planes or Air Canada.

With all good wishes,
Cyrus Eaton

Thanking Mr Eaton for his generous comment, I replied that I would be delighted to accept his kind invitation and would bring my wife and nineteen-year-old son with me. We agreed to the weekend of July 12–14.

What transpired was a most pleasant and interesting weekend, as I expressed in my letter of thanks on 16 July. "We returned Sunday to a Montreal sweltering in 87 degree heat. Hence, all the more vivid was our after-vision of a deep, limpid-blue cove surrounded by idyllic woods and pastures ... The issues we discussed are incomparably far-reaching and I hope that more North American leaders are beginning to approach them with at least some of your deep insight and long vision."

Shortly afterwards, we received a telegram from Mr Eaton expressing his hope that Douglas, Eileen, and I could make a second visit over the weekend of August 9. When we arrived, we were pleased to meet Mrs Eaton, who also participated in the discussion with keen interest. Their other guests at Deep Cove included Ted Sorensen and his family (Ted was former special counsel, adviser, and speechwriter to President John F. Kennedy) and Donald Zagoria and his wife, professors of government at Hunter College in New York. They told us their area of research was world revolutions – both the successful and the failed.

Sharp debates ensued through the weekend on US-China relations, continuing even through meals. Sorenson and Zagoria vehemently defended the US position, while I challenged their arguments. Sorenson declared "Taiwan is non-negotiable [for the United States]." And I countered: "For China as well." I could not help but reflect on the intense atmosphere of those days in a letter to Mr Eaton later that month. "It was perhaps a sharp exchange, but the time would seem to be long past when anything useful could be achieved by gentle circumlocution or by leaving unchallenged the postulates of national arrogance, to which you drew attention on several occasions. I look eagerly forward to the time when Chinese and Americans can speak to one another in the same language of equality, mutual respect and friendship."

Three weeks later, Mr Eaton wrote that the point of view I had presented at Deep Cove had had a constructive effect on both Don Zagoria and Ted Sorensen. He suggested that Eileen and I visit him in Cleveland, because he would like me to meet "some of the men who influence public opinion in academic and editorial circles here." I thanked him for his interest in having me participate in further conversations about US-China relations, but told him that Eileen and I had no plans to visit the United States at the present time. What I did not say was that in addition to the Cold War harassment we continued to experience, I had vowed not to set foot on US soil as long as the Vietnam/Indochina slaughter continued.

Cyrus S. Eaton, Canadian-born industrialist, philanthropist,
and founder of the Pugwash Thinkers' Lodge, Pugwash,
Nova Scotia, 1950 (Photograph by Robert Norwood)

Before Mr Eaton had received my reply, he wrote again on September 12
enclosing an article from the *Cleveland Plain Dealer* by Arthur Goldberg,
former US ambassador to the United Nations and Ted Sorensen's law partner.
"I am sure you will disagree with Goldberg's 'Two-China Policy,'" he wrote,
"I should appreciate having your views in confidence." I responded:

> I can only contend that it is tragic when the spokesman of a big power
> like the United States finds it necessary to descend to subterfuge, instead
> of the courageous correction of its errors, to establish a new foreign pol-
> icy on China. The purpose of Mr Goldberg's "Two Chinas" proposition
> is not, as he admits himself, to bring China into the United Nations in
> the full dignity of equal participation as a founding member, but to satisfy
> US policy needs. Mr Goldberg states that this transparent maneuver
> would "make clear to the world community that it is Peking and not
> Washington that is keeping Mainland China out of the UN."
>
> In my view, this is an unlikely consequence. Many observers are now
> acutely aware that a growing number of military and political leaders in

the United States have been moving towards a "Two Chinas" policy to enable Chiang Kai-shek's regime to retain some kind of "legal" status, which is the sole pivot on which the "legitimacy" of the US military presence in Taiwan is based.

If this is true, then all of Mr Goldberg's efforts, stated in such arrogant terms, become irrelevant except as a study in the pragmatic philosophy of self-aggrandizement. There is no question in my mind that China would likely go on her own way, speared by American hostility, as she has in the past two decades. Ultimately, the problems faced by the United States in dealing with her will be compounded, instead of simplified, and Washington would be the loser.

I am quite convinced that those who propose a "new" policy along these lines will probably contribute more to the further deterioration rather than the improvement of Sino-American relations.

On October 16, Mr Eaton wrote that Professor Donald Zagoria had proposed a two-day conference on Chinese-American relations to be held at McGill University. In addition to my own participation, Zagoria wished to include such people as professors Edwin Reischauer and Jim Thompson of Harvard, Doak Barnett of Columbia, Zbigniew Brzezinski, Ted Sorensen, Senator Fulbright, and others. Zagoria suggested holding two sessions each day devoted to particular aspects of the Chinese-American relationship. Separate sessions would be dedicated to Taiwan, the security interests of the United States in China and Asia, the prospect for economic, cultural, and diplomatic relations, and the obstacles to improving relations. The purpose would be to present a broad spectrum of views to ensure that the conference would not turn into a propaganda forum for either side.

I was open to this idea and believed that McGill University would be glad to host such a conference. I thought our new Centre for East Asian Studies could undertake the organization required. I did, however, note several concerns to Mr Eaton:

Sponsorship: I would prefer that the seminar be under your sponsorship or, if you so choose, under the sponsorship of Pugwash. Although I realize that the initiative comes from American scholars and public figures, it would not seem wise to have an American institution sponsor such a seminar in Canada.
Subject of the Seminar: It would seem to reinstate the old, biased framework to discuss relationships in terms of "the security interest of the

United States in China and Asia," just as it would not do to frame the question in terms of the "security interest of China in the United States and the West." The substantive issue is in reality "the US presence in China (particularly Taiwan) and Asia, and its implications for Sino-American relationships." I have no objection to the other areas of discussion, as suggested in your letter, i.e., "the prospect for economic, cultural, and diplomatic relations, and the obstacles to improving relations."

Participants: Assuming that a broad spectrum of views is desired, I would hope for wider representation than the list of participants suggested by Prof. Zagoria. For example, it would seem particularly significant to include some scholar who could analyze the US self-image and world outlook, from which flows much of the policy-making thinking. I have in mind scholars like William A. Williams or Walter LaFeber. Of course, Chinese images and self-images should also be discussed. Scholars on the "Chinese problem" should probably be balanced by scholars on the "American problem," from the social context of which arise many factors affecting Sino-American relations. What about inviting Professor Douglas Dowd of Cornell? And since political figures are included in Professor Zagoria's list, it may be useful to add a political analyst such as I.F. Stone.

Since the seminar is to be held in Canada and is to seek fresh viewpoints not only from the "other side," but also from non-Chinese and non-American scholars, I would suggest that there be a matching number of Canadian scholars of China and Asia present. I could propose such a list after consulting with my Canadian colleagues.

Among the China scholars in America, I am surprised that an outstanding expert such as Professor Franz Schurmann of the University of California is not included. I would like to see him invited.

Time: In view of the amount of organizing effort that must go into preparing such a seminar, I would suggest a date in either late January or early February [1969]. With your kind offer of assistance, we can provide all the necessary facilities.

A few weeks later, I informed Mr Eaton that Dr Michael Oliver, McGill's academic vice-principal, had expressed warm interest in the prospect of McGill hosting a conference along the lines Eaton had suggested. He agreed with me that the theme of Chinese-American relations should mean all of North America, and that Canadian scholars should be included in significant numbers.

PRIME MINISTER PIERRE ELLIOTT TRUDEAU

On June 25, 1968, Prime Minister Trudeau's Liberal government was elected with a clear majority. Subsequently, I received frequent telephone calls from Ivan Head, senior policy adviser to the prime minister, to discuss China affairs. I noted in a letter of July 8, 1968, to Thérèse Casgrain, that "our new Prime Minister and some of his cabinet colleagues have shown independence and courage on certain issues. I hope they will study the China issue carefully." During the government policy debate on China in 1969, I was asked through Madame Casgrain to submit a position paper to Prime Minister Trudeau.

On November 4, 1968, I received an invitation from the PMO to attend a black tie dinner in honour of Prime Minister Lee Kuan Yew of Singapore. The date was set for the evening of November 12, at 24 Sussex Drive, the official residence of the Canadian prime minister.

✐ Around mid-afternoon on that day, Montreal was suddenly hit with a blizzard, which blanketed the city with heavy drifting snow. I called Paul at his office, urging him to take an early train to Ottawa. But he insisted on finishing his afternoon seminar before taking the five o'clock bus. It took him until midnight to reach Dorion, a suburb of Montreal. Of course he missed the prime minister's formal dinner. ✐

I journeyed overnight in order to be at the Ottawa airport the next morning to see off Prime Minister Lee Kuan Yew. After returning to Montreal, I wrote letters of apology to both prime ministers. I was particularly concerned that Prime Minister Lee Kuan Yew might read my absence as disrespect. I was planning to visit Singapore in 1969 and asked if I might have the honour of calling upon him. Prime Minister Lee graciously replied that he would welcome my visit to Singapore. "Once you have confirmed the dates of your visit," he wrote, "perhaps you may wish to give one or two lectures at the University of Singapore and/or the University of Nanyang."

Years later, when reminiscing with Ivan Head, who had attended this dinner in Ottawa, I learned that Prime Minister Lee had told him: "If I had known Paul Lin was coming tonight, I would have stayed away." His views on China then were very different from his later outlook. But after we met at the Ottawa airport, and later exchanged letters, we became friends and regularly sent each other New Year's greetings.

HONG KONG EXCURSION, JANUARY 1969

Plans for what would be known as McGill's China Consultation, to be held in early February 1969, were well underway when I received a telephone call from Cyrus Eaton on January 3. He suggested that a small number of top US political, academic, and business leaders meet separately in Montreal in late January, to discuss ways of breaking the US-China deadlock. Richard Nixon had just been elected president and Mr Eaton hoped to apply pressure on the Nixon administration before its China policy was set. He was acquainted with Nixon's secretary of state, William Rogers, and congressmen like Senator J.W. Fulbright, and wanted to know whether several top Chinese leaders in business, science, or academics could be included in such a discussion. I counselled that such matters could not be decided on short notice and would be difficult to explain by letter or telephone. I suggested I make a personal trip to Hong Kong to convey the invitation directly to China's representative there. Mr Eaton promptly agreed and offered to cover my costs. He added that the Chinese participants would be his guests in Montreal, all expenses paid, and wanted to assure them that the conference would consist of people generally sympathetic to People's China. The sessions could be open or closed. Late that evening I telephoned Henry Tsoi, head of the China Travel Service in Hong Kong, to confirm that I would arrive in Hong Kong on January 7. Tsoi and his assistant met me at the gate and whisked me off to the Mandarin Hotel.

Contrary to rumours in the Western press, I did not enter China. It was at the height of the Cultural Revolution and my visa application was not approved. This can be verified by my later correspondence with Madame Soong Ching Ling. I wrote to her from Kowloon on January 8, 1969, seeking her assistance in expediting my visa to China, but somehow she did not receive my letter for nine months. She wrote on October 15:

Dear Paul:
Just rec'd yours of [January] 8 from Kowloon. It is a *great* disappointment to me that you did not wire and let me try to request the authorities to invite you! Han Suyin the author is here again, she comes almost every year to see her relatives and get materials for her books. Edgar Snow, an old friend who did so much to make known the reasons of our struggle, was not allowed to come in and he is naturally much disappointed.

I shall try my utmost to make known your desire to visit us, but only Heaven knows what results.

Much love to you and Eileen, meantime, shall try my best for you –
Aunty

SEATTLE CUSTOMS INCIDENT

It was agony to be so close yet so far away from China, but I could not stay in Hong Kong much longer than a week. Unable to get a direct flight back from Hong Kong to Canada, I took the only seat available on a Northwest Airlines flight to Seattle on January 16.

After my plane landed in Seattle at 6:30 am, I was pulled out of a group of in-transit passengers by US Customs officials. They forced me to leave the transit area, demanded my passport, and stamped it with a "Temporary Visit" seal, which gave them the authority to conduct a search. I had to relinquish my suitcase, hand over my briefcase, and empty all my pockets. I was so exhaustively searched in Seattle that I missed my connecting flight to Montreal.

Once home, I reported this outrageous abuse of my rights to my friend and colleague Professor Jerome A. Cohen at the Harvard Law School. He offered to investigate the matter for me, an inquiry that took nearly six months.

PRELUDE TO THE CHINA CONSULTATION

Meanwhile, I still had to line up several Canadian discussants for February's China Consultation at McGill. I phoned Harrison Salisbury, an editor at *The New York Times,* to obtain Chester Ronning's telephone number. Ronning was a former Canadian diplomat who had long supported formal relations with China. Salisbury was shocked to hear of my Seattle experience and told me he would see to it that those in high places were informed. I reached Chester at the home of his brother and informed him of Cyrus Eaton's intention to have a McGill conference on February 8–9. He was scheduled to speak to a Canadian University Service Overseas (CUSO) group at the University of British Columbia on February 8, but promised to hasten to Montreal for the second day of the conference. The next morning I spoke with Alvin Hamilton, former minister of agriculture under the Conservative government. In the early 1960s, he had arranged for the sale of large quantities of Canadian wheat to China. He would definitely accept Mr Eaton's invitation and suggested adding Max Bell, a prominent businessman and newspaper publisher.

I had a letter from Mr Eaton on January 27, enclosing two *New York Times* articles concerning a China conference held at the Center for the Study of Democratic Institutions in California on January 24–26, 1969. The major point of division among the participants was the status to be accorded to Taiwan.

Conservatives with close ties to the China lobby, who had long supported Chiang Kai-shek's Nationalists, resisted any change to the status quo. Even among the liberal-minded participants at the conference, no consensus was reached. The *Times* noted: "The closest thing to a 'solution' was the proposal that the problem be left for Taipei and Peking to work out between themselves in their own way, while outside countries deal with both in deliberate ambiguity." The idea of "Two Chinas" was espoused by senators J.W. Fulbright (Democrat, Arkansas) and John Sherman Cooper (Republican, Kentucky), Justice William O. Douglas of the US Supreme Court, and Professor Edwin Reischauer of Harvard. According to the *Times*, none of the participants at the conference proposed abandoning the Nationalist regime. As Arthur Goldberg insisted, nothing that is being said by the liberals "should lead to the conclusion that the United States in any way should abandon its defense and security commitments relating to Taiwan." Professor Reischauer added: "There is no need to complicate matters further, as we now do, by pretending that Taiwan is the real China. This it most assuredly is not, but what it actually is remains to be defined – a second China, an independent Taiwan, or a part of China that in practice enjoys full autonomy."

Mr Eaton wrote to me a few days later: "It seems to me that the crucial and urgent practical questions to be answered by statesmen in the United States and Canada seeking to establish friendly relations between China and North America are: (1) What are the minimum conditions that China will accept? (2) What are the maximum concessions that the United States and Canada can be persuaded to make? And (3) What is to be the future of Taiwan? If we can reach a consensus on these three points in Montreal, we will make a valuable contribution to the dialogue now under way in California, New York, and elsewhere."

Chapter Twelve

PASSIONATE DIALOGUES

CHINA CONSULTATION AT McGILL

The China Consultation got underway on February 8, 1969. The meeting brought together a small number of academic and public figures concerned with the improvement of Sino-Canadian and Sino-American relations, for the freest possible exchange of views on how such improvement might be achieved. The sessions were off-the-record, informal, round table discussions unencumbered by a fixed agenda. There were two sessions on February 8 and one session on the morning of February 9. Initiated and sponsored by Cyrus Eaton, the consultation was chaired by McGill's vice-principal Michael Oliver; my colleague in the political science department, Professor S.J. Noumoff, recorded the highlights of the exchange.

The substance of discussion was wide-ranging. Professor Donald Zagoria began by suggesting several factors that might lead the United States to change its current posture toward China: disappointment with the Soviet Union; the costs of containing China; pressure from America's allies; shifts in US public opinion; and the openness of the new Nixon administration. Alvin Hamilton, who had been intimately involved in Canada's wheat sales to China, pointed out that it was essential to begin with consideration of the Chinese outlook. Citing his discussions with Premier Zhou Enlai in 1964, he reported Premier Zhou's belief that China's major quarrel was with the Soviet Union – particularly regarding the reclaiming of territories along the Amur and Ussuri rivers presently incorporated into the Soviet Union. According to Hamilton, Premier Zhou had stated China had little quarrel with the Americans, except over the

Taiwan issue. In fact, the premier had been open to a visit from a US delegation – information that Hamilton had relayed to the US Foreign Relations
Committee – but the US Government had hesitated so long in the issuing of
passports that the trip was made impossible by the start of the Cultural Revolution in 1966. (At this point, Ted Sorensen arrived late at the conference.
His first pronouncement was "Taiwan is non-negotiable!" To which I retorted,
"If so, there is not much point in holding this conference!")

Hamilton continued by stressing the importance of mutual respect in relations with China. He shared the fact that, in the late 1950s and early 1960s,
an understanding had been reached between the Canadian Government and
the Eisenhower and Kennedy administrations to inform each other when
wheat was to be sold on the world market. This was clearly in violation of
existing international treaties, but the policy was adhered to by both governments. In March 1961, the Canadian Government proposed to President John
F. Kennedy that the wheat sale that Canada had agreed upon with the People's
Republic of China be split with the Americans – half supplied by the US and
half by Canada. Initially, the United States Government seemed open to the
idea, but the proposal was sabotaged a few months later when Kennedy suggested the United States *give* China grains, *if* China asked for them. This was
viewed as a double insult to Chinese pride: China wanted a commercial relationship of equality and was not prepared to beg for needed resources.

For my part, I stated that I could see no fruitful discussion of issues between
China and the United States unless both parties accepted the principle of equality. Yet US policy seemed to be based on the idea that the world was divided
into satisfied and therefore non-aggressive powers – like the United States and
the Soviet Union – and unsatisfied and hence expansionist, aggressive powers
– like China. This was a false picture strikingly negated by Vietnam and
Czechoslovakia, and indeed much of modern history. Wasn't it symptomatic
that the "satisfied" powers were always on other people's territory in the name
of containment and "defence of freedom"? Furthermore, I asserted that as long
as the basic US policy of containment was not relinquished, it would be difficult for the Chinese to regard US proposals on lesser issues as serving anything
but a hostile policy of containment.

Harrison Salisbury noted that tensions on the Sino-Soviet border had been
increasing; somewhere in the neighbourhood of half a million troops were now
amassed on both sides of the Xinjiang border. This made the Soviet Union
more of a threat to China than the United States. Professor Franz Schurmann
agreed and suggested we were confronted with a triangle of tense relationships
between the United States, the Soviet Union, and China. In his view, the more

American-Soviet relations deteriorated – as evidenced by an increase in the arms race – the better the chances were for improving US-China relations.

The topic of trade and the prospects for reopening trade channels between China and the United States were important points of discussion. Mr Cyrus Eaton observed that China, with a population of some 800 million, constituted an enormous potential market and the Chinese people basically wanted the same good life as people in the West. He thought that President Nixon would pay greater attention to the business community than had previous administrations and this offered an opportunity to exert commercial pressure to change US-China policy. Dr Wilder Penfield, founder of the Montreal Neurological Institute, added that there were important channels of communication other than trade – men talking to their opposite numbers as professionals, scientists, and technicians, making personal visits to China if possible. Canadians were welcome in China not only because of Norman Bethune, but because we talked to Americans; Canada could be a go-between for Sino-American communication. Professor Noumoff suggested that if the United States wanted to begin with small gestures, it could abandon the policy of prohibiting the entry of Chinese goods by sending them through Canada, and then drop restrictions on the export of US components to China. Neither of these moves would be rebuffed by the Chinese.

I interjected that there were also realities involving 800 million people on the other side of the Pacific and that it would be purely academic to discuss any easing of Sino-American relations without involving US withdrawal of her palpable threat to China's security. This was not a nineteenth-century China that could not respond to force. This was a reality of prime importance, with each side measuring the strength and posture of the other. If the United States maintained an intransigent position on Taiwan, China would unquestionably respond with a larger military deployment and buildup.

On the subject of Taiwan, Doak Barnett stated his view that the US military presence in Taiwan was not threatening. In 1962, the United States had informed the Chinese at Warsaw that it would restrain Taiwan from any offensive action against the Mainland. In addition, the United States had dropped its military assistance to the Nationalists from approximately US$250 million per year, to a figure around US$30–40 million. David Hayden, an American lawyer with expertise in Asia, suggested that the operative principle might well be that Taiwan was a matter to be determined by the Chinese people. Zagoria basically agreed, but thought that the United States should issue a statement of principles on the future of Taiwan that was ambiguous enough to satisfy Peking, but not to stir Taiwanese opposition. He proposed the following: (1)

The future of Taiwan should be decided by the Chinese people. It should be understood that there was no desire on the part of the United States to separate Taiwan from the Mainland. (2) A process of demilitarization of Taiwan should continue. (3) Smaller steps should include the lifting of the US trade embargo and the onerous requirement of certificates-of-origin for goods coming from China. For its part, China should be willing to admit US businessmen.

I stated that the first point of his proposal seemed reasonable enough on the surface, but what were the specific implications of the second point, the demilitarization of the Taiwan area? Professor Barnett said that a US commitment to withdraw militarily would have to be accompanied by a "security" commitment, by which the United States would come to the aid of Taiwan if attacked. I replied that such a caveat would destroy the tenability of the first point. How could the Chinese people genuinely decide their own affairs with the continued threat of foreign military intervention? Chinese agreement to any proposal could not be imposed, but must come as a consequence of an absolute recognition of, and respect for, her equal position.

Chester Ronning commented that if the United States demilitarized Okinawa and Thailand, as well as ending the war in Vietnam, China might be reassured. The United States had unilaterally decided to fill the (colonial) vacuum that France and Britain had left in Asia; therefore, the United States should now unilaterally extricate itself from that part of the world. Nothing would persuade the Chinese of US intentions more than concrete actions to drop its armed encirclement of China.

CONFERENCE RESOLUTION

At the close of the discussion, Ted Sorenson introduced the following resolution: "Resolved, that it is the sense of this meeting that early progress toward increased understanding, contact, and dialogue between the governments in Peking and Washington is of utmost importance to world peace. That steps should be explored by which these two powers together formulate a peaceful resolution of their differences over Taiwan, achieve a demilitarization of their present relationship, and initiate an exchange of citizens and goods. And that to further these ends, additional private meetings on this subject should be convened by our hosts with individuals from the People's Republic of China."

The collegiality of the conference was reflected in the letter Harrison Salisbury wrote to me on February 11: "I realize that none of us was talking or could speak for more than ourselves and yet it seemed to me that we did have – in effect – a ventilation of important opinions relative to the future of relations between the United States and China. I think this is a good start and I hope that it can be continued in other forms and by other means. We all learn by this kind of discussion. I know that my understanding of the respective viewpoints, which so condition the complicated problem, was enhanced by listening to the interchanges, particularly those between yourself and Messrs Barnett and Zagoria. One can even imagine that the dialogues to some extent may follow the lines which could (hopefully) emerge in Warsaw [the site of occasional talks between the United States and the People's Republic]."

Professor Franz Schurmann of the University of California, Berkeley, succinctly summarized the conference in a letter to me on February 13: "In the conference I said that there were three subjects discussed: Taiwan, trade, and exchange. The academics among us talked about Taiwan, the businessmen about trade, and all of us want to go to China. The two key issues are Taiwan and trade. I would suggest further that it would be an error to speak of an American position as such on Taiwan, except the aggregate of past policy. I would further guess that the business-oriented people in the Nixon Administration who always look at the world market system, and who listen to the opinions of the other great capitalist nations, are now more favorable to a real change in China policy than they were before. After all, every major capitalist nation (Japan, Germany, France, Britain, Canada) is urging such a change on America. It is the politico-military strategists who keep on insisting that the security criteria must be met. When they demand that America retain some kind of defence assurance for Taiwan, they are essentially saying they want to keep a significant American military establishment in the Far East as a whole."

Incidentally, there was one distinguished delegate in attendance at McGill who made no statement during the conference dialogues, but took copious notes. This was Jacques Hébert, editor and publisher, who visited China with Pierre Trudeau in 1960 and co-authored their book, *Two Innocents in China*.

CONSERVATIVE TEMPEST IN A TEAPOT

Unknown to me, my abortive January trip to China had been bubbling in political circles and was depicted in the Canadian media and the House of Commons as a "secret mission to China." In bold print, the front page headline of the *Montreal Gazette* on February 28, 1969, declared, "McGill Professor Denies Secret Mission to China." The report read:

A McGill University professor last night flatly denied reports that he flew to China early this year as Prime Minister Trudeau's top-secret emissary to Peking. Ottawa sources claimed yesterday that the ten-day mission of Paul T.K. Lin, of the University's East Asian Studies department, led directly to Ottawa's abandonment of earlier pledges to protect the interests of Nationalist China (Taiwan) while dealing with the Mainland. The Vancouver-born China specialist is alleged to have brought back word from Peking that it would veto recognition, as long as Canada maintained relations with the Nationalists. The "undercover" mission was undertaken before formal contact was established. It is claimed that as a result Trudeau has shifted further away from his guarantees to Taiwan. In an interview with *The Gazette*, Prof. Lin insisted he has not been to China since 1964, but said he did go to Hong Kong in January and meet with Communist Chinese officials, "But only on university business and purely for academic reasons" ... Prof. Lin was adamant in denying the role of emissary: "I am an academic and am not involved in political manoeuvres." He stressed his trip ... had nothing to do with conversations with Mr Trudeau.

The Montreal Star reported: "Prime Minister Trudeau has denied that he used Professor Paul T.K. Lin as an emissary to Mainland China in steps being taken to establish diplomatic relations." The question had been raised in the House of Commons the previous day by Opposition MP Angus MacLean, a former Conservative minister of fisheries.

My visit to Hong Kong apparently was considered significant, because of the way in which the Canadian Government soon after abandoned its once-time "Two China" policy, and came around to the open position that establishment of diplomatic relations with Peking would end the existing ones with Taiwan and the Chiang Kai-shek regime.

SEATTLE FOLLOW-UP

Soon after the China Consultation at McGill I heard from Jerome Cohen, the Harvard law professor who had inquired on my behalf regarding the disagreeable treatment I had experienced at the hands of Seattle customs officials in January. "One rumour I've heard from someone in Washington was that the Seattle authorities thought they had intercepted Lin Biao! What a bad joke. We will see what comes of this."

Professor Cohen followed up on March 31, enclosing copies of letters from Senator Fulbright, who was chairman of the US Senate Committee on Foreign Relations, and from the commissioner of customs. Both expressed "regret" over the incident. On April 30, 1969, the *Seattle Post-Intelligencer* ran a front page report entitled "US Apology Follows Seattle Search." The article noted that the State Department had "indirectly apologized" to me for the exhaustive search that had caused me to miss my connecting flight to Montreal. Undersecretary of State Elliot Richardson also sent a letter to Cohen stating that he had been assured that "specific instructions have been issued which should prevent such incidents in the future." The *Post-Intelligencer* claimed that I was "suspected by US Intelligence officials of maintaining links to leading Communist Chinese officials" and may have been "on a mission ... to ease the way for Canada to establish diplomatic relations with the Peking regime (such negotiations are now underway in Sweden)." The newspaper further noted that when Senator Eugene J. McCarthy decided that he would like to visit Peking this summer, "one of the first things he did was to contact Lin, who advised him to write the Chinese Embassy in Paris."

Several weeks later, I wrote to Professor Cohen thanking him for his efforts in investigating the outrageous treatment I had undergone in Seattle. I was, however, still not satisfied and responded: "I think you can understand why I can only react with distaste to the letter which you received from Undersecretary of State Richardson in reply to your queries. It did not convey any official apologies ... I have been told that it is too much to expect any department of the US Government to be honest about such incidents and the facts in this case are an apparent corroboration. The assurance that 'specific instructions have been issued' to prevent such incidents in future, can be of little interest to those who loathe the source of a malignancy that spreads police-state rule at home and abroad. I share the longings of many courageous Americans for a cleansed and healthy America. I am reporting the entire incident to the Canadian Government."

I then wrote to the Honourable Mitchell Sharp, Secretary of State for External Affairs, explaining the incident and enclosing my correspondence with Professor Cohen. "I assume that it is not your policy to allow silence on such incidents to imply tacit tolerance of the maltreatment of Canadian citizens abroad. I request that the Canadian government lodge an official protest with the US Government over this incident. The recurrence of similar cases involving Canadian citizens should be taken as *prima facie* evidence of an official US policy, and it would seem appropriate that the Canadian government should then make clear its right to take reciprocal measures towards US citizens in transit through Canada. I would appreciate your attention to this matter."

FURTHER TEMPEST IN A TEAPOT

Controversy regarding my January 1969 trip to Hong Kong erupted again between former prime minister John Diefenbaker and Prime Minister Trudeau in the House of Commons in November of that year. The Right Honourable Mr Diefenbaker asked the prime minister if there were "any foundation for the generally accredited story that Professor Lin, as a result of his visit to Mao, or at least to Communist China, is to be appointed the first ambassador from Canada to Communist China?" Diefenbaker claimed he was "simply pointing out that Mr Lin was a close friend of the Prime Minister and had reported to him the last time on his visit to Communist China." To this Trudeau replied: "The Right Hon. Member has just stated two new falsehoods. First of all, he said that I was a friend of Professor Lin, a person I have never met and whom I do not know. Second, the Right Hon. Member stated that he had reported to me. That is another falsehood. I have never met him nor read any of his papers. Therefore this is falsehood compounded on the part of the Right Hon. Member."

DR HENRY KISSINGER'S INQUIRY

On January 12, 1970, a gentleman appeared at my front door in Montreal, introducing himself as Ernst Winter. He asked for a safe place to talk, so we went to a nearby restaurant. He confided he was a close Harvard associate of Henry Kissinger, who had sent him to relay a confidential message to Peking – through me – concerning Kissinger's desire to meet Chinese leaders in preparation for a visit by President Nixon to China. I asked if he had brought a letter of introduction and was told, "No, you just have to trust me." He then briefed me that President Nixon had very little confidence in the US State Department and was determined to run foreign policy from the White House through his security adviser, Kissinger.

Winter did not go deeply into the strategic thinking of President Nixon and Kissinger, but it was described in Kissinger's later book *The White House Years*:

Not surprisingly, I was on the side of the Realpolitikers, who argued that the Soviets were more likely to be conciliatory if they feared that we would otherwise seek a rapprochement with Peking. This school of thought urged that we expand our contacts with China as a means of leverage against the Soviet Union ... When the NSC [National Security

Council] meeting discussed these issues on August 14, 1969, little was
decided, but the President startled his Cabinet colleagues by his revolutionary thesis (which I strongly shared) that the Soviet Union was the
more aggressive party and that it was against our interests to let China
be 'smashed' in a Sino-Soviet war. It was a major event in American foreign policy when a President declared that we had a strategic interest in
the survival of a major Communist country, long an enemy, and with
which we had no contact. The reason a Sino-Soviet war was on his mind
was that a new increase of tensions along the border caused us grave concern. It also reinforced our conviction that the need for contact was
becoming urgent (Kissinger, 182).

It seems that immediately after this August meeting, the White House began
to unilaterally sound out the Chinese authorities through various intermedi-
aries, but had received no definite response.

Winter's message struck me as credible, but I was still unclear about his
background. Two days later, Thomas Manton telephoned from New York
to finalize dates for the Montreal seminar of the Committee for a New China
Policy (CNCP). The CNCP had been formed in October 1969, in the wake of
Cyrus Eaton's initiatives to promote US policies of peace and understanding toward China, rather than containment and war. Manton had been
appointed executive secretary and said that he was warmly received by the
Chinese embassy in Paris on December 30, 1969, accompanied by the CNCP's
co-founder – Ernst Winter. He told me that Winter was an Austrian-Ameri-
can who had taught at Yale, been director of the Diplomatic Academy of
Vienna, and currently was director of the Division of Applied Social Sciences
at UNESCO.

It appeared to me that the only person to whom I could convey Winter's
important message was Ambassador Huang Zhen of the PRC embassy in Paris.
As far as I knew, he was the only ambassador who had not been recalled during
the ongoing Cultural Revolution. I had been invited to attend an international
Quaker conference in Vienna at the end of the school term, in mid-April, and
during the summer of 1970 was intending to collect material for a book on
contemporary Chinese history. The most opportune time for me to deliver
Kissinger's message would be immediately after the Vienna conference.

In the meantime, I participated in a leadership seminar for US policy-makers and opinion-shapers organized by the CNCP and held at Hotel La Sapinière in the Laurentian Mountains, about an hour outside of Montreal, from 5–7 March. Congressmen, business, church, and other non-governmental leaders were invited, as well as journalists. The CNCP had hoped for participation by representatives from China and Pu Zhaomin, of the PRC's Xinhua News Agency stationed in Ottawa, was able to attend. I had made clear to Manton beforehand that I had accepted his invitation to be a resource person on the understanding that the meeting would be an exchange of views outside the framework of official policies and polemics. The aim would be to seek an undistorted understanding of revolutionary China, as the basis for reappraising Sino-US relations, and would involve individuals of goodwill responsive to the hopes of ordinary Americans, who saw something tragically wrong with their government's intransigent hostility to the historic transformation of one-fourth of humanity.

Tom Manton sent me a summary of the results of the seminar at the CNCP's national board meeting on June 25: "Because of our deep concern for changing the archaic policies which the United States government has been following in regard to China, we had first to explore a common understanding of what the problem had been for the past two decades. Based on that common understanding, we would then move ahead to add the structure to implement our common purpose. In a large measure, this common understanding came to many of us at a seminar held in Canada in early March, 1970, at which time Professor Paul T.K. Lin helped us break through our traditional American parochialism and provided in a masterful way a Chinese viewpoint of US-Chinese relations. As we recall, he was not suggesting a new policy. He was stating to us the facts of the situation as he saw them, letting us draw the obvious conclusions."

The "new understanding," defining the essentials of a new US policy toward China, was captured on paper by Jerome Cohen. The statement was discussed in depth at the seminar and was taken back to the CNCP's informal working group in New York City. Further opinion was sought, in order to "develop a broadly-based, powerful, citizens' effort to change US policy toward China" and to destroy the old myths of "yellow peril."

The committee adopted the following statement:

The Committee for a New China Policy advocates a new United States' policy toward China, which recognizes that the People's Republic of China is the sole legitimate government of China. We will work for a United States' policy of peace, understanding, and cooperation with the People's Republic of China. We recognize that such a policy must inevitably lead to a new approach by the United States toward Asia as a whole. In order to move toward the new China policy, we advocate our government should: (1) Recognize that Taiwan is Chinese territory (as the United States did prior to the Korean War) and accept the position that whatever the complexities of transition from the present political situation, the United States has no responsibility for determining the future status of Taiwan; (2) Adhere strictly to international law and refrain from intervention in China's internal affairs; withdraw American forces from Taiwan and the Taiwan Straits; and terminate all military, political, and economic aid to Chinese Nationalist authorities; (3) End the current policy of military encirclement and trade embargo of China, and eliminate all punitive and discriminatory trade regulations; (4) Bring the American involvement in the Indochina War to a speedy and unconditional conclusion, since the continuation of that involvement increases the possibility of war with China; (5) Acknowledge that the government of the People's Republic of China is the sole legitimate representative of China in the United Nations and in all other international organizations; and (6) Establish economic, social, cultural, and diplomatic relations with the People's Republic of China on the basis of the principles of equality, mutual respect, and non-intervention in each other's affairs.

FIRST RETURN TRIP TO THE PRC, 1970

At the end of the school term, I flew to Vienna to participate in an international Quaker conference on "China in the Family of Nations." On April 21, I went on to Paris to relay Kissinger's confidential message to Ambassador Huang, who asked me to wait in Paris for word from Beijing. In mid-May, the ambassador informed me that China had extended an invitation to me, Eileen, and Douglas to visit China as soon as possible.

⬔ Doug and I arrived in Paris on May 21, exhilarated to be joining Paul in this exciting adventure. The next morning, we were off to the Chinese em-

bassy to have our visas stamped and to lunch with Song Ziguang, the first
secretary. On May 24, a Sunday, we were luncheon guests of Ambassador
Huang Zhen at his beautiful villa. The following day we headed to the
airport for our flight to Shanghai.

Clearing immigration at the Paris airport should have been a routine
matter, but the French authorities withheld Paul's passport for so long that
we feared the plane would leave without us. Paul finally raised a ruckus,
his passport was returned, and we hurried for our gate. How long would
Cold War suspicions continue to hamper Paul's movements?

Air France's Boeing 707 was fully booked at the Paris terminal. When we
reached Athens, two-thirds of the passengers disembarked. Next was Cairo,
but due to the ongoing Middle East crisis, passengers-in-transit were not allowed off the plane and every window curtain was drawn. When we arrived
in Karachi, Pakistan, everyone disembarked except for the three of us and
an elderly Chinese man, who was returning home to retire. We had the
huge aircraft to ourselves for the last leg of our long journey to China.

As the plane winged its way down for landing, we were surprised to see a
dimly lit Shanghai, with few sparkles of light. It was Tuesday night and Red
Guards were manning customs. We were met by Xiao Luo, a representative
of the Foreign Affairs Office, who checked us into the old Peace Hotel (vin-
tage 1930s) and told us our flight to Beijing was booked for noon the next
day. Exhausted by our journey, we were startled awake early the next morning by the sound of drums and tympani. Peering out the window, I saw the
streets were bedecked with crimson red flags and Cultural Revolution slogans.
Crowds of people were marching, shouting, and waving the "little red book"
of Chairman Mao's quotations. Since we had a few hours before flying to
Beijing, Xiao Luo gave us a tour of the city. Shanghai had lost its former
lustre and appeared very drab. Wherever we went, we were conscious of
being stared at; even in our simple Western clothing we looked very foreign.
During our flight to the capital later that day, the flight attendants entertained us by singing revolutionary songs and reciting revolutionary stories
to the rhythm of bamboo clappers. When the plane touched down in Beijing
we were met by our host Shen Ping, later China's ambassador to Italy, who
took us to the Xinqiao Hotel. 🐿

Over the next several days, two important meetings were held at the hotel,
during which I carefully briefed selected Chinese leaders, policy analysts, and
scholars regarding changes in Canadian and US attitudes toward China. They

were fascinated by my first-hand report about Kissinger's urgent request to meet with Chinese leaders, prior to a visit by President Nixon. I did not recognize anyone in the audience and could only surmise that this secrecy was normal practice during a very abnormal time. Neither did I receive a Chinese reply to Kissinger's query.

⪦ With Paul's mission accomplished, we presented to our host a list of friends and relatives we wished to call on. They included Madame Soong Ching Ling, Liao Chengzhi and his sister Liao Mengxing, Cousin Yao Yilin and Auntie Yao Yimin, and my brother Chen Hui. We were told that they were either "indisposed" or "out of town," standard excuses that meant it would be (politically) inconvenient for us to see them. I persisted and we finally received clearance to see my aunt, a harmless old lady some ninety years of age. She was still living in the large compound the government had assigned to her son, Minister Yao, before the Cultural Revolution. But now the courtyard home appeared sadly neglected, its principal residents gone with the wind. Only a maid remained to look after my aunt.

Auntie Yimin had been frail when we left China in 1964, but now she was totally blind from glaucoma. Hearing our voices, she was stunned but delighted and quickly turned off her radio, which had been playing one of Jiang Qing's model operas. (Jiang Qing was the wife of Mao Zedong.) With contempt in her voice, she commented, "Jiang Qing is very powerful now, but many people don't think much of her." My brother Chen Hui was allowed to come back from Hunan Province to Beijing to see us. He was tanned but gaunt from his time in a May 7th cadre school. The cadre schools were farms where urban bureaucrats and intellectuals were sent to perform manual labour and receive ideological re-education. It was wonderful to see him after so many years, but he was reluctant to tell us much of what had happened to him and his family, and we did not pry. ⪧

Eileen and Doug could only stay in China a few weeks before returning to their jobs in Canada. We were given a bird's-eye view of Beijing since the beginning of the Cultural Revolution and toured new industrial plants, neighbourhood factories, and communes. In the evenings we were treated to model operas and ballets produced under the edict of Jiang Qing.

Accompanied by a guide, we took a circuitous route to Guangzhou and, along the way, visited a number of historical sites pertinent to the early period of the Chinese Communist Revolution. We went to Nanjing, Shanghai, Zhangsha, and Shaoshan (Chairman Mao's village) in Hunan Province. On June 20, Doug and Eileen left China for Hong Kong to catch a plane back to Montreal. I remained in China for three more months, travelled extensively, and did a tour tracing the origin of the Long March to Jinggangshan, the strategic mountain range in western Jiangxi Province where Mao Zedong and General Zhu De had combined their forces in 1928.

I was astonished, however, when I visited the Jinggangshan Museum of Revolution on August 1, 1970, and found that the famous photograph of Mao's meeting with Zhu had been altered: Zhu De's face had been replaced by that of Lin Biao. I immediately raised the issue with the director of the museum, who insisted that Lin Biao had been in charge of the troops and since 1928 had been Chairman Mao's "closest comrade and best disciple." His comments jolted me and I began to question the authenticity of the data I was collecting. When I returned to Montreal in early October, I confided to Eileen that I could not yet write a book – I simply did not know what was fact and what was fiction.

Accompanied by a guide, Paul traces the route of the Red Army's 1934 Long March and collects data for his book, summer 1970.

Paul visits a factory along the route of the Long March, summer 1970.

MEETING PREMIER ZHOU ENLAI

The highlight of my sojourn in China was being received by Premier Zhou Enlai on September 30, 1970. The premier had always been my hero, but I neither expected nor had requested such an honour. He knew I was teaching Chinese history at McGill University and gathering materials for a book on modern Chinese history. Our conversation, therefore, began with a discussion of history. Premier Zhou impressed on me that history should be studied and analyzed from the angles of the forces of production and transformations in the relations of production, which meant that the study of history also required the study of economics. He went on to say that there was an abundance of historical data since the Opium War, but the challenge was finding the "red thread" that would link the numerous facts together. One solution, of course, was to use Chairman Mao's writings as the red thread; his four volumes of *Selected Works* covered the previous thirty years. But other historical materials were still necessary. For a report, it might be sufficient to quote solely from Mao's *Selected Works*, but to teach history, it was important to refer to other sources.

When we said goodbye, I thanked the premier for taking his valuable time to receive me. He asked how old I was and I told him – fifty. He thoughtfully noted, "Then you still have time to do a great deal more work. Come back in two years' time and the situation in China will have changed."

Not once during the evening did Premier Zhou mention Kissinger's request, which had been the raison d'être of my journey to China.

CANADA-CHINA RELATIONS, OCTOBER 1970

On October 13, 1970, Canada and the People's Republic of China established formal relations, with an exchange of ambassadors to occur within six months. It had taken seventeen long months of negotiations in Stockholm before the Canadian side had been able to break the impasse over Taiwan's status. The key that opened the way to agreement was the statement: "The Chinese Government reaffirms that Taiwan is an inalienable part of the territory of the People's Republic of China. The Canadian Government takes note of this position of the Chinese Government ... The Canadian Government recognizes the Government of the People's Republic of China as the sole legal government of China."

Canada had finally shifted from a One China/One Taiwan position to what was essentially the imminent abandonment of Canada's formal relationship with Taiwan. Needless to say, I was delighted that Canada and China would now work with each other on the basis of mutual respect and equality. It was, therefore, most frustrating to find myself once again embroiled in the political games of parliamentarians.

Speaking in the House of Commons on October 20, 1970, John Diefenbaker remarked that the issue of admitting China to the United Nations would shortly arise, and he hoped for assurance from the Government of Canada that such a resolution at the United Nations would "require more than a bare majority for acceptance." Further, he asked the prime minister, "whether there is any basis for the suggestion that the government is giving consideration to or has already decided that Professor Paul Lin will be appointed ambassador to Red China, as he is a Canadian-born Chinese who visits Red China and who, when writing about 'our country,' refers to Communist China?" Trudeau replied, "Mr Speaker, several times in the past year or two the Right Hon. Member has been concerned about this friend of his, Paul Lin." Upon which Diefenbaker interjected, "He is the Prime Minister's friend, not mine." Trudeau responded: "I do not know Paul Lin, I have never met him. I should like the Right Hon. Member to state to me, on my question of privilege, where he got this information and why he thinks Mr Lin is a friend of mine."

When the journalist John R. Walker asked me for an interview, I issued a strong protest at being the subject of controversy again in the House of Commons. I told Walker: "I can only say that I was astounded at the unworthy and childish nature of the exchanges between Mssrs Diefenbaker and Trudeau involving my name. You can understand the distaste with which a private citizen views the use of his name as a political football between partisan contestants in politics. For the record, I have never met and do not know Prime Minister Trudeau. It is true that he did invite me to a dinner at the prime minister's residence on November 12, 1968, but I was not able to attend. I have not been approached to take up any diplomatic post and would not accept even if offered such a post. I am an academic and intend to remain one. Mr Diefenbaker's attempt to identify me as the "Mr Lin" in Mr Trudeau's book is amusing, but false."

≼ Two years later, China sent the spectacular Shenyang Acrobatic Troupe to Canada on a goodwill mission. Paul and I were invited by Chinese Ambassador Yao Guang to attend the troupe's premiere in Montreal at the Place des Arts on November 30, 1972. During intermission, at the VIP reception on the mezzanine floor, I noticed that Paul was standing back-to-back with Prime Minister Trudeau. When I alerted Paul to who was behind him, he instantly turned to face Trudeau. With neither arrogance nor deference, he introduced himself: "Mr Trudeau, my name is Paul Lin." The prime minister was taken by surprise, blushed, and blurted out: "Diefenbaker taunted me …" Paul replied with a smile, "Now you cannot deny that you have met me." ⇉

THE PEOPLE'S REPUBLIC OF CHINA AT THE
UNITED NATIONS, 1971

After more than two years of subtle messaging between the White House and Premier Zhou Enlai's office in Beijing, agreement on Henry Kissinger's visit was finally reached and scheduled for early July 1971. Prior to this, Premier Zhou took the initiative of inviting the US table tennis team (among others) to visit China after the thirty-first World Table Tennis Championship in Nagoya, Japan. This was described in the Western media as China's "ping-pong diplomacy."

Kissinger made a second trip to Beijing from October 20-25 with a large contingent of personnel to prepare for the US presidential visit, scheduled for late February 1972. It was on October 25, just before Kissinger's plane took off from China, that the usual Important Question resolution preventing China from taking its rightful seat at the United Nations was defeated. The Albanian resolution in support of restoring the PRC's rights in the United Nations passed overwhelmingly, much to the delight of many delegates, some of whom danced on the floor of the General Assembly hall, according to US press reports.

On October 29, 1971, at the request of the Fund for Peace, I addressed the opening plenary of "The Convocation on US-China Relations" at the Hotel Americana in New York. The meeting brought together 2,500 scholars and students on China, business people, civic organizations, and church and labour groups to hear wide-ranging opinions on the prospects of normalizing Chinese-American relations and the effect of Beijing's admission to the United Nations. US Senator Edward M. Kennedy and former chief justice Earl Warren were among the distinguished speakers.

I was looking forward to seeing Senator Kennedy again. We had met in Cambridge, Massachusetts, in June, introduced by our mutual friend Professor Jerome Cohen of Harvard. We had then corresponded on subjects of mutual interest and he shared with me his August 2, 1971, Senate Floor statement opposing the Two China Policy announced by the administration, a statement I thought was courageously forthright and unequivocal.

My speech at the October 1971 convocation read in part:

At this moment, we are all acutely conscious of a sense of historic drama in the events of the past few days in the United Nations. The restoration to the People's Republic of China of her rights in the UN has cleared the way for the true voice of one-fourth of humanity to be heard for the first time in that world organization ... For many of the ninety-three states that refused to go along with another round of obstructive gimmicks, it was in the nature of a moral cathartic. This in itself marked the inevitable arrival of a new stage in world affairs. In the sweeping tide of national independence, more and more middle and small powers will no longer tolerate "limited sovereignty" in their foreign relations. The superpower domination of the United Nations is ending.

Some Americans were shocked by the outcome of the UN vote. Why? Such a traumatic effect can, I think, be traced to the long legacy of Cold

War misinformation ... The UN vote was not anti-American but anti-American *policy* ... Americans are, I believe, wearied and appalled by the unspeakable tragedies brought upon other peoples and upon themselves by their government's armed interventions in Asia and elsewhere. These interventions have sapped the body and spirit of America and brought about the massive economic and social problems with which she is plagued today. Many Americans seek to change their government's policy of obdurate hostility to the People's Republic of China. They watched with dismay Washington's calculated attempt to keep Peking out of the UN by keeping Taipei in. Understandably, they wondered what credibility would have been left to President Nixon's declared intention to normalize relations with China, if the US effort in the UN had actually succeeded. Fortunately, by their overwhelming vote in the UN, the great majority of nations in the world has provided the United States, despite itself, with another chance to move toward improved relations with China ... The Chinese and American peoples have no conflicts of basic interest and share common aspirations in their struggles against oppression and for human freedom and progress. In this spirit, let us hope that the friendship between them will grow and flower in the momentous days ahead.

Chapter Thirteen

CULTURAL REVOLUTION
CONUNDRUMS

Less than two years after I arrived back in Canada, the Great Proletariat Cultural Revolution erupted and lasted for a decade. The Cultural Revolution was personally led by Chairman Mao against "revisionism" within the CCP and government leadership, from President Liu Shaoqi down. To do so, he mobilized millions of young people who named themselves the Red Guards. Intellectuals were the next target, which shut down the education system for ten years. During the seizure of power that followed, factional fighting among the Red Guards intensified. Chairman Mao demobilized the Red Guards by sending them down to the countryside and brought in the military. Amidst the turmoil, the Gang of Four led by Mao's wife Jiang Qing emerged as a formidable political force, until Mao's death in 1976.

Today, with more information, I better understand the complexities of the Cultural Revolution. But in 1966, without direct access to information, and believing fervently in the egalitarian principles guiding the leadership, I vigorously defended China against attacks by the Western press. Madame Soong Ching Ling provided us some insight through periodic letters.

October 2, 1966

You must have heard the broadcasts and seen the news of the Red Guard movement that is going on here. It was wrongly reported that I was attacked and beaten up by them as bourgeois and that my house was turned upside down and searched for weapons etc. etc! I was *never* physically attacked altho' the struggle going on in my neighborhood made me nervous for days and nights as I couldn't bear the screaming and noises going on ...

The young Red Guards never studied history, never experienced all the twists and turns of those much older [and] committed some serious actions, such as tearing down Sun's statues in Nanking and Canton, where a big fight took place between the Red Guards and the people of Guangdong, who knew what Dr Sun had done for his people and country. These were unavoidable sacrifices: As Chairman Mao has said, revolution is not inviting guests to dinners, but insurrections!

Yesterday there were a million and a half Red Guards at the Tiananmen and it took five and a half hours [for them] to march by. I am so tired …

November 21, 1966

Peking has three million Red Guards here; therefore, it is *very* crowded. Shanghai, which has a population of over eight million already, also has three million Red Guards, who like it so much that they refuse to budge. Now I hope the new order that [states] whoever stays on, has to pay his or her own way home after this month – instead of a free ride on railways – will cause them to leave soon …

I was taken aback by the excesses Madame Soong described, because the Cultural Revolution seemed violently out of control compared to the political campaigns I had experienced during my fifteen years in China. I replied to Madame Soong, describing the West's reaction to the Cultural Revolution as nothing more than a vicious power struggle and requested that she send me some illustrative materials, which would throw more light on the nature of the movement.

March 10, 1967

I am sending you samples of the recent big-character wall posters which are much more reasonable and restrained than those of the past 8 months. Sorry I can't send you our *China Reconstructs* magazines. During the recent movement several members of the staff were listed as "monsters and demons" and sent to labour reform. The rebels, being new to the required tasks, have not even turned out January and February issues. This happens in many other offices, as you may well imagine. I hope soon normalcy will reign and tensions created [will] relax somewhat.

Cynthia and her brother [Liao Chengzhi] are well, but the latter is almost as busy as our premier [Zhou Enlai], who doesn't get a chance to rest but talks and advises this and that group of the eight millions of Red Guards, who come to link up and exchange experiences. He turned his whole office into dormitories for 5,000 Red Guards and ate millet buns with them at every meal, much to their admiration and astonishment. Being their advisor, he was at their beck and call, even at midnight. His wife, like the rest of us, could not get any sleep, with loudspeakers going on at all hours. No one could concentrate on work!

Now it is verbal struggle instead of resorting to violence and the aim is to grasp production, promote revolution. In this tense class struggle, there's bound to be confusion and blindness. This is because the revolutionaries in general always have to learn what is good and what is bad through their own experiences. Besides, a mob is often easily out of control. In the latter part of the 18th century when the Industrial Revolution just began, the workers in England smashed the machinery they operated with. In the last decade of the 19th century, the anti-foreign movement in our own country destroyed the railway from Shanghai to Wu Song. They could not understand then that rail destruction was not good for them. Now, having learned from experience, such things they will not repeat. People have to learn by themselves. I am afraid that we have to face history, history in its making, and be reconciled to the present situation.

The wind storm is *terrific*. I wish I could return home [to Shanghai] after being here eighteen months already. But there the situation is doubly tense & I'm advised to stay put. My excellent masseuse was sent to labour in the country when it was learned she was a former landlord. She was really a marvelous masseuse; possessing some "secret" methods she had learnt from an old monk in Sichuan Province of pressing on certain nerves to prevent pain. Almost 60 years old but her fingers had wonderful strength; she was a harmless old lady and helped some other colleagues besides myself. We feel lost without her, but could not prevail upon the people in authority to let her remain.

March 12, 1967

I'm rather worried these days over the rapidly spreading encephalitis in several provinces, caused by the Red Guards who were so unsanitary, spitting etc. all over the streets, wherever they link up. More about other troubles later, when I'm less concerned over present trials and tribulations …

October 15, 1969

The Premier is so occupied that he promised to see me within 4–5 days before I return home, after an absence of over four years – up till now he still cannot come. His wife tells me although they live in the same house, yet for days & days she cannot get to see him. Meantime, I have so many important affairs awaiting me at home ... My only girl cousin was so dealt with that she committed suicide by jumping from the fourth floor apartment house opposite my home. She never committed anything to deserve such tortures dealt out to her. My house was not allowed to let her take refuge, when she was driven out of her own house & dispossessed of everything. She haunts me in my dreams – such sufferings that she had to undergo ...

I replied to Madame Soong later that month:

It is difficult to express my feelings to you from this vantage point, observing the world scene. It is unmistakable to me that what is happening in China is one of the great epochs in transition in the history of civilization, dwarfing the imagination of many contemporary historians. Through the Cold War miasma of distortion and half-truth, the outside world is beginning to get here and there the faintest glimmers of an enormous, exciting reality from a few honest but inadequate reports. This has been enough to stir an impatient demand for the whole truth about China, especially among the students and youth of North America. Yet the distortions will remain to plague them if they lack a historical framework of understanding and analysis.

The urgency of this need has persuaded me to take on the awesome task of trying to write a history of the first two decades of People's China focusing on the critical struggle between revolution and reversion, as seen in the light of the Cultural Revolution. I have no illusions of being equal to such a task, but there is the tremendous, objective need here, and it might just as well be done by someone with a little more grasp of both cultures than by snide "China experts" who have never been in the New China. To avoid as many aberrations and errors as I can, however, it is imperative that I come back to spend some time in China in the months ahead during the balance of my sabbatical year. There is so much to learn and relearn before I start teaching others!

It soon became known that I was the only Canadian to have spent fifteen years in China and to have returned with a first-hand understanding of what the people were going through. I was widely sought after as an authority on this new, changing China especially after the announcement of President Richard Nixon's upcoming visit to China in 1972.

Personnel from the Chinese Foreign Ministry arrived in Ottawa in February 1971 to prepare for the establishment of the PRC embassy. Huang Hua was China's first ambassador to Canada. In 1972 he moved to New York as head of the PRC delegation at the United Nations and was replaced in Ottawa by Ambassador Yao Guang and later Zhang Wenjin. During our years in Montreal, Eileen and I extended our hospitality to the Chinese embassy staff to help them settle in and to introduce them to Canadian and American friends.

In 1966, I worked for a year as a library assistant at McGill's undergraduate library. The following year I decided to get a master's degree at McGill's Library School in order to qualify for professional work. Mother encouraged me, even offering to pay my tuition fees out of her pension. It was difficult to return to school at age forty-three, and so soon after Chris's death, but the long hours of hard work helped to numb the stabbing pain. I received my master's in 1969 and was immediately hired by McGill's McLennan Library. I very much enjoyed my new career as a librarian, but in order to help Paul cope with the avalanche of demands on his time, I found it necessary to resign in 1972. This enabled me to travel with Paul and manage his schedule.

CHINA, MAY–SEPTEMBER 1972

In the summer of 1972, Eileen and I made our second visit to China since returning to Canada in 1964. Our son Douglas joined us in the middle of July from England, where he was pursuing a doctorate in astronomy and astrophysics at Cambridge University.

The timing was opportune. Less than a year earlier, on September 13, 1971, Lin Biao – Mao's "close comrade-in-arms" and presumptive successor – had fallen from grace and died in a plane crash at Undur Khan, Mongolia, while fleeing China with his wife and son. This extraordinary turn of events created shock waves throughout the world and posed formidable challenges to Sinologists trying to unlock the mystery of the Great Proletarian Cultural Revolution.

Paul visits the PRC's first ambassador to Canada, Huang Hua, Ottawa, fall 1971.

Below
Paul and Eileen help McGill host Bethune Exchange doctors Chen Wenchieh, deputy director of the Blood Research Institute, and Ha Hsienwen, deputy director of the surgery department, Jih-Tan Hospital, November 1971.

Paul briefs the Kettering Foundation at Dayton, Ohio, April 1972.

To our pleasant surprise, Liao Chengzhi, who had recently been rehabilitated from his ordeals during the Cultural Revolution, was among our hosts
that summer. It was he who, as head of the Committee of Overseas Chinese
Affairs, had facilitated our smooth exit from China to Canada at the request
of Madame Soong in 1964. Without his assistance, I may never have had the
opportunity to build cross-Pacific dialogues between Canada, the United States
and China.

Liao Chengzhi and Madame Liao, with son Liao Hui and daughter-in-law, 1972

❧ For his part, Liao told me how impressed he was by Paul's endeavours in helping to bring about the establishment of diplomatic relations between Canada and China. Despite his heavy responsibilities, Liao spent much time with us while we were in Beijing, helping us to understand the complexity of the political situation at that critical time. ❧

In the wake of President Nixon's February visit to China, Beijing was teeming with Western scholars and journalists. We met and dined with professors John K. Fairbank and Jerome Cohen of Harvard University, the author Han Suyin, and Harrison and Charlotte Salisbury. We even bumped into Roxane Witke, in town to interview Madame Jiang Qing for a controversial biography that would later be published in the United States. We also spent time with Canadian Ambassador Ralph Collins and visited old Xinhua colleagues and foreign experts like Rewi Alley, Ruth Weiss, Eleanor Chaiden, and Sol and Pat Adler. I was especially intent on documenting changes in healthcare and laying the groundwork for future Canada-China medical exchanges. This involved tours of medical supply plants, cancer hospitals, commune clinics and discussions with Dr Zhu Chao of the Ministry of Health. It was also good to touch base with Neil Burton and Paul Brennan, Canadian graduate students on the first Canada-China educational exchange, which I had helped to arrange.

Eileen, Douglas, and I spent most of our time travelling during this visit. We headed first to the industrial cities of the northeast, as far as the Daqing oil field, and then flew to the Xinjiang Uygur Autonomous Region in the northwest.

Paul, Eileen, and Douglas tour Daqing oil field in northeast China, summer 1972.

Along the route, I was busy collecting as much hard data as possible for my book. In retrospect, I realized that although we were given a Grand Tour, we learned little about the intense conflicts that had occurred in these areas at the height of the Cultural Revolution. This was considered classified information, not to be shared with outsiders.

✎ We were the first visitors from abroad given permission to go to Xinjiang. Wang Meng, the author and minister of culture after the Cultural Revolution, told us later that he was then working at a labour camp in Xinjiang and when he heard news of our visit, he predicted that the Cultural Revolution would soon end. ✎

CONVERSATION WITH PREMIER ZHOU ENLAI

Near the end of our sojourn, in late August 1972, we received dinner invitations for the same night from two of our most revered Chinese leaders: Madame Soong Ching Ling and Premier Zhou Enlai. When Premier Zhou heard of Madame Soong's request, he rearranged his schedule to receive us at 9:00 pm that evening.

With great anticipation, we arrived at the Great Hall of the People at the appointed time and were ushered into the Xinjiang Chamber, where Premier Zhou Enlai was waiting. Also present were Madame Zhou (Deng Yingzhao), Guo Moruo, author, poet, and president of the Chinese Academy of Social Sciences, Liao Chengzhi, director of Overseas Chinese Affairs, Madame Liao, and Ambassador Zhang Wenjin.

❧ Premier Zhou greeted Paul like an old friend. I had met the premier once before, back in the mid-1950s, when he gave a reception for Chinese students returned from abroad, to affirm the importance of intellectuals in China's modernization. Now, some twenty years later, at the age of seventy-four and with the heavy burden of a country in turmoil on his shoulders, the premier looked a little frail, but was still as charismatic and sharp as ever. ❧

Premier Zhou touched on many subjects that evening, from the contemporary to the historical, from the domestic to the international. Against the backdrop of the Cultural Revolution, he chose his words with care and expressed his views with subtlety. His aides told us clearly to neither take notes nor publish the contents of our conversation. His thoughts and insights, however, were too important to us to be left forgotten on the dust heap of history. We pieced together our recollections with the official abridged transcript, which was given to us to read afterwards.

After some pleasantries, I commented to Premier Zhou that during my current research trip in China, I had observed the negative impact of Lin Biao's policies everywhere I went. The premier cautioned me not to dwell narrowly on this ultra-leftist trend of thought, but to factor in a population of over 700 million, whose thinking had been shaped by 2,000 years of feudal society and more than a century of semi-colonialism. He described the historical prelude to the Cultural Revolution and twice emphasized the extreme difficulties of transforming the very backward China of 1949 into a socialist society, within a very short period of time.

We had better review a little history. The great French Revolution overthrew the monarchy. That was a relatively thoroughgoing bourgeois revolution, with sweeping land reform. At the time, Napoleon was also

Top: Premier Zhou Enlai greets Paul at the Great Hall of the People, Beijing,
August 1972.

Bottom: Author and poet Guo Moruo greets Eileen at the Great Hall of the People,
Beijing, August 1972.

Portrait taken at the Great Hall of the People, Beijing, August 1972. Centre: Premier Zhou. To the left of the premier (fanning left): Paul, Guo Moruo, Liao Chengzhi, Madame Liao, Pu Zhaomin (Xinhua correspondent to Canada) and wife Song Guiyu. To the right of the premier (fanning right): Eileen, Madame Deng, Douglas Lin, ambassador to Canada Zhang Wenjin, and Fang Xiao of the Friendship Association

a Jacobin, on the same side as Robespierre, but later, he became a dictator ... Thus, the Great French Revolution, which began so spectacularly, was led to failure by a dictator ... It was only after more than eighty years of successes and reversals that the French bourgeois democratic republic was finally founded.

Take the United States as another example – its bourgeois democratic revolution took 200 years to complete. First, there was the War of Independence led by Washington, which in 1776 resulted in a declaration of independence. In 1812, there was a second war with England. Under Lincoln, there was a civil war between the south and the north, which emancipated the slaves in the South. Therefore, the American democratic revolution took three revolutions to complete ...

In Russia, following the 1917 victory of the socialist revolution led by Lenin, there emerged many inner-party struggles and it was not until the end of World War II before the foundation for socialism was finally laid ... There is a big reversal in the Soviet Union now. Western journalists are trying to figure out what was the reason for this change. They said it was due to influences from the United States. But the causes were mainly internal, through which external factors came into play.

If the Soviet Union was like this, then what about China, with its 2,000 years of feudalism and 100 years of semi-colonialism, which now ... is becoming a socialist society, guided by Marxism, Leninism, and Mao Zedong thought? Can we guarantee that our revolution will not be disrupted by revisionism?

In 1949, before entering Beijing, a resolution was adopted at the Second Plenum of the Seventh Central Committee of the Communist Party [March 5], which stated that after we entered the city, the task was no longer to oppose imperialism and feudalism; the struggle would now be between the bourgeoisie and the proletariat, between marching towards capitalism or towards socialism. As soon as we entered Beijing, however, many forgot this teaching of Chairman Mao's ... Why? Because China's revolution began with the villages encircling the cities ... Our cadres were trained in the midst of war and came from all corners of the land with diverse levels in ideological training. It was natural for them to have different understandings and interpretations.

The 1949 resolution recalled by Premier Zhou was extremely significant, especially when one compares it with Chairman Mao's article "On New Democracy" written in January 1940. This article, which was not mentioned by the premier, but can be found in *The Selected Works of Mao Tse-tung, Volume II* declared: "Clearly, it follows from the colonial, semi-colonial, and semi-feudal character of present-day Chinese society that the Chinese revolution must be divided into two stages. The first step is to change the colonial, semi-colonial, and semi-feudal form of society into an independent democratic society. The second is to carry the revolution forward and build a socialist society. At present the Chinese revolution is taking the first step ... [It] cannot avoid taking the two steps, first of New Democracy and then of socialism. Moreover, the first step will need quite a long time and cannot be accomplished overnight."

Was Premier Zhou suggesting that there was a fundamental change in the orientation of policy for China's development after winning the War of Liberation in 1949? In other words, was the first stage described in "On New Democracy" bypassed and never carried out? Was this the root cause of all the problems that followed? His next statements seemed to affirm this interpretation.

Many people were ideologically unprepared for China's change from a democratic revolution to a socialist revolution. At the beginning of the socialist revolution, various trends of thought surfaced. That was why we launched continuous ideological struggles, one after another, soon after we entered the city.

We took less than ten years to move from land reform to mutual aid teams and to the communes. We set up joint public-private ownership after completing three major socialist transformations [of agriculture, handicrafts, and capitalist industry and commerce] in only six years. Chairman Mao did not anticipate [such rapid speed]. The socialist foundation, however, was not solid. It was confusing for the public, which was not ready mentally [for socialism]. We needed more experience to find out how best to proceed. Any mass movement is bound to result in some errors and excesses, either from the ultra-right or from the ultra-left. If we had gone forward step by step, perhaps we would still be at the transitional stage now.

On the immediate cause of the Cultural Revolution Premier Zhou indicated that at the Tenth Plenum of the Eighth Central Committee (1962), there was further emphasis on class contradictions, primarily targeting President Liu Shaoqi. Liu supported Comrade Chen Yi's proposal to set the farm output quotas on the basis of each household, which was equivalent to reverting back to individual farming. Chairman Mao objected and spent the next four years, from the reform of the performing arts in 1962, preparing public opinion politically and ideologically for the Cultural Revolution. The Great Proletarian Cultural Revolution was personally led by Chairman Mao and participated in by the masses (Red Guards) totalling in the hundreds of millions. As to the nature of the Cultural Revolution, Premier Zhou said:

At the beginning, we – the majority of leading cadres – were ideologically unprepared and could not be of much help. Our Great Proletarian Cultural Revolution actually is not a cultural but a political revolution … We launched the Great Proletarian Cultural Revolution even after we had seized political power, and conducted critical evaluations of leaders at every level. This was, of course, unprecedented in history. Therefore, there were side effects each step of the way, and if we were not careful, excesses occurred. The target was Liu Shaoqi and a small group who were influenced by him, but who could have thought that Lin Biao, an ultra-leftist, would appear from the other side?

I asked the premier when Lin Biao's conspiracy to assassinate Mao and seize supreme power had been uncovered, and whether it could have been detected

Premier Zhou's conversation with Paul and Eileen began at 9:00 pm on August 28 and ended at 4:00 am on August 29, 1972.

earlier from his lifestyle, and the dissonance in words and deeds – in short, his political character. He replied:

> We did not know about it until the very end, when we searched his belongings after he had escaped. It takes a process to expose someone ... This is a social problem, prevalent in both bourgeois and proletariat politics. Just like bourgeois democracy, proletarian democracy takes time to develop too. When a person is still needed by society, how is it possible to examine his shortcomings seriously? We cannot be suspicious of every comrade. Those around Lin Biao probably knew a great deal about him, but we did not ...
>
> During the Cultural Revolution, he said many things that were rather absolute, like describing Chairman Mao's thoughts as the "peak" of Marxism and Leninism, or "One sentence by Chairman Mao overrides ten thousand by others." Lin Biao's ambition was inflated after the Ninth Congress of the Chinese Communist Party [1969] when he was designated Chairman Mao's successor. This was at the height of the Red Guards' power ... Now, if he were a genuine Communist, he would not have agreed to such a designation. And if he had declined, it did not have to be written in the Constitution ...

Successors should be nurtured, trained, and tested among many old, middle-aged, and young [cadres]. Only the best and most seasoned will be accepted by the people. They cannot be selected subjectively.

I mentioned that I had heard that Chairman Mao wrote a letter about Lin Biao in the summer of 1966. "Yes," Premier Zhou replied,

The chairman wrote a letter to Jiang Qing in July, 1966. You can read it, but [when you tell people, you] must clarify [certain things]. For example, in the letter [Chairman Mao referred to Lin Biao] as "my friend," which was well intentioned. But the Red Guards claimed that by not addressing [Lin Biao] as a comrade, [Chairman Mao] had negated him. It was not the young people's fault. They were influenced by the rhetoric coined by the conspirators.

At the time Chairman Mao did not wish to make this letter public, because he did not want Lin Biao to know he had used the words "my friend." When Jiang Qing read the letter, Lin had already been promoted to a "close comrade-in-arms," so she burnt it. Fortunately, [Chairman Mao] kept a copy and showed it to me in Wuhan. I proposed, and the chairman agreed, that I visit Lin Biao in Dalian and suggest to him that the word "peak" was inappropriate. Lin Biao agreed, but the word "peak" resurfaced in his introduction to Mao's little red book of quotations.

In his letter to Jiang Qing, Mao expressed his uneasiness over Lin Biao's fascination with coup d'états and his "helplessness" with Lin Biao's idolization of Mao, which was further bolstered by the press. Chairman Mao wrote that he felt he was being used as a tool to combat the rightists, but if he exposed this, the leftists and the masses would not welcome it. Therefore, he could only be resigned to their wishes.

Chairman Mao's personal letter to Jiang Qing was only made public to the Central Committee of the CCP in May 1972, eight months after Lin Biao's demise. The posthumous publication of the letter aroused much curiosity and controversy as to its motive. Was it to vindicate Chairman Mao by revealing that he was aware of Lin Biao's shortcomings back in 1966, before Lin was made his heir apparent in 1969?

Towards the end of our conversation, in the wee hours of the morning, I raised concerns about two old friends who had fared badly during the Cultural Revolution. One was a dear friend from overseas, who committed suicide during the Cultural Revolution. Dr Xiao Quangyan was a chemist, who held a well-paying, senior position at the US Standard Oil Company in Chicago. In 1950, at age thirty, he resigned from his job and returned to China to assist in reconstruction, bringing along his young US-born wife who spoke not a word of Chinese. First assigned to the Chinese Ministry of Petroleum, he was then transferred to the Science Research Centre in Dalian, where he was responsible for a number of important innovations in the petroleum industry.

Unfortunately, after he had been in China for only nine months, a series of political movements occurred which singled him out as a target of attack. Even his motive for coming to China came under suspicion. Xiao was able to withstand the persecution and humiliation through the 1950s, but during the Cultural Revolution, he was repeatedly beaten by propaganda teams and forced to write countless self-criticisms. They finally broke his spirit. He took an overdose of sleeping pills and died.

His wife, who was doing reform-through-labour at a labour farm, was recalled and forced to "confess" about the suicide of her "counter-revolutionary" husband. A few days later, she convinced their sixteen-year-old daughter to commit suicide with her, in order to escape their world of suffering. What a terrible tragedy! After their deaths, the vendetta was extended to other family members, including his sister, Xiao Quangzhen. They were all denounced as "guilty by association."

Premier Zhou acknowledged that it was a "shame" that Xiao was victimized after returning from abroad. "In the case of Xiao Quangyan, his contributions were great, yet his whole family was persecuted. He must have felt deeply hurt, but did not seek revenge. He was a good man. He and his family should all be rehabilitated. In a big revolution, it is unavoidable that prices have to be paid." We learned afterwards that the premier took immediate action to restore Xiao's honour and rehabilitate his family.

Next I raised the case of Madame Dong Zhujun, founder of Shanghai's Jin Jiang Hotel and a member of the Chinese People's Political Consultative Conference (CPPCC) since 1957. In the midst of the Cultural Revolution, in October 1967, she was abducted from her home by rebels of the CPPCC, arrested, and imprisoned. We learned of her frightful experience from her daughter Dong Guoying, who asked if we could help. Premier Zhou acknowledged his acquaintance with Madame Dong and she was released from prison less than two months later.

Towards the end of our conversation, I mentioned that there was a great deal of pressure abroad for me to write a book on China's revolutionary experiences. Premier Zhou cautioned me: "You do not have to rush into writing a comprehensive history of China. That would be very difficult to do and you will have to come back many times. But you can write about some aspects of China, like dissecting a sparrow one bit at a time."

With this helpful advice, our meeting came to a close. It was already 4:00 am. As Premier Zhou shook hands with our son Douglas, he suddenly asked, "Xiao Lin, have you read the classic Chinese novel, *Dream of the Red Chamber*?" Doug replied, "Not yet." Premier Zhou continued, "You should. It is a microcosm of China's social fabric."

GRADUAL AWAKENING TO COMPLEXITIES

With China in such turmoil, I appreciated how difficult it would be to write anything definitive on the contemporary period. Nevertheless my commitment to my students and publisher weighed heavily. I later brought the subject up with Eileen's cousin, Yao Yilin.

Minister Yao was one of China's leading economic planners. As a student at Qinghua University, he had joined the CCP in 1935 and participated in student demonstrations against Japanese aggression. He stayed on in north China to help organize underground CCP activities with Liu Shaoqi and future leaders like Peng Zhen, Bo Yibo, and Liu Lantao. Along with many veteran party members during the Cultural Revolution, he was dismissed from office and sent down to the countryside to do heavy labour.

When I saw him in the summer of 1972, Cousin Yao had just been rehabilitated and was writing a self-criticism to Chairman Mao, before being reinstated to his former position as minister of commerce. I asked him what his thoughts had been when he was doing forced labour; he mused, "I thought *Heaven* had changed."

Regarding my wish to write a book, he confided: "There are three forces in China today. One is represented by Premier Zhou Enlai, another was Lin Biao's, which has just been eliminated. Ideologically, the third force is similar to that of Lin Biao's, but did not play any part in the conspiracy. Under such unsettled circumstances, how is it possible to write the book?" He did not name the third force, but we understood that it was the Gang of Four, headed by Jiang Qing. This cabal effectively controlled the Communist Party during the latter stages of the Cultural Revolution and was only brought down in a coup in October 1976, shortly after the death of Mao Zedong.

"But the pressure abroad is so great for him to write. What will people think?" Eileen chimed in. With a mischievous smile, Cousin Yao replied, "Let them think that Paul Lin cannot write a book!" – and laughed.

MEDICINE AND SOCIETY IN THE PEOPLE'S
REPUBLIC OF CHINA

Despite growing questions about the nature and direction of the Cultural Revolution, I continued to believe that the government's policies were meeting the people's needs, especially with respect to health care. Drawing on my research from the summer of 1972, I gave a lecture to the Annual Meeting of the American Psychiatric Association in Honolulu on May 8, 1973.

I began by placing the development of medical care squarely in the context of the larger processes of fundamental societal change, especially the movement from private to public ownership of factory and farm. This set in motion a profound metamorphosis in human relations, replacing the self-serving values and narrow family loyalties of feudal China with the collective orientation of a cooperative and egalitarian society.

In 1950, Chairman Mao laid out overall guidelines for health policy at the first National Conference on Health. He made clear that: (1) medicine should serve the majority of the population – the workers and peasants; (2) prevention should be given first priority; and (3) traditional Chinese medicine should be integrated with Western medicine. Premier Zhou Enlai later proposed that health work should be integrated into mass movements. These became the generally accepted guiding tenets of the new national health program.

In 1955, Chairman Mao announced it was time for Western medicine to learn from traditional Chinese medicine. This led to the establishment of a research institute of traditional medicine, the introduction of traditional medical practices into major hospitals, the rigorous scientific refinement of traditional medicine, and the publication of journals of traditional medicine. The dramatic improvement in the delivery of health services was inseparable from this policy of integrating the Chinese medical tradition with its modern Western counterpart. Traditional medicine had a rich legacy of several thousand years, including useful techniques of diagnosis and therapy and an enormous pharmacopeia of herbal drugs. The revolutionaries' attitude to this cultural legacy had taken shape as early as 1928, when Mao Zedong and the Red Army were in their mountain bases in the Jinggangshan area. Intellectually, Mao acknowledged the validity of both the indigenous and foreign medical systems, but practically he realized that in the circumstances of continuous enemy blockade and medical shortages, traditional medicine – which was self-reliant in its personnel and pharmaceutical resources – was critical. Subsequently, in 1944, Mao urged the Western-trained doctors working in the border regions to join forces and cooperate with the 1,000 traditional practitioners in the area. This served the people during the war against Japan and built a foundation of cooperation on which to base policies after the founding of the People's Republic.

The merging of the two medical practices was another example of the Chinese developmental strategy known as "walking on two legs," using both imported and indigenous technology so that all resources available for the building of the nation and the nation's health might be fully utilized. Having myself witnessed several major thoracic and cranial operations with acupuncture anaesthesia, I was deeply impressed with the results.

Unfortunately, despite major successes in the initial health campaigns, it soon became apparent that some Western-trained doctors and officials paid only lip service to the guidelines or failed to fully understand them. In June 1965, Chairman Mao made his famous criticisms of the Ministry of Health, labeling it derisively as the "Ministry of Urban Lords." He called for a basic redeployment of health services to place priority on the rural areas. This led to the dramatic development of the para-medical program, which provided over one million paramedics or "barefoot doctors" for China's peasants and rural workers – at least one to every production brigade in a commune. In addition, urban medical personnel and college graduates brought specialist services to the countryside and border regions through mobile medical teams. It is interesting that the paradigm for bringing health care to the people was introduced by Dr Norman Bethune, the Canadian surgeon whose unflagging devotion to the service of Chinese revolutionaries fighting Japanese aggression was immortalized in a short article by Chairman Mao, and became required reading for all medical personnel, indeed for all Chinese.

PRIME MINISTER TRUDEAU'S VISIT TO CHINA

Between August 1973 and August 1974, I took a sabbatical from McGill, determined to write the first draft of a book detailing my experiences of New China. It was for this reason that I was in Beijing when Prime Minister Trudeau made his first official visit to China in October 1973, accompanied by his wife Margaret. It happened that our good friend, architect Arthur Erickson, and his colleagues Francisco Kripacz, and Nina and Moshe Safdie were also in Beijing at the time. All of us joined the Canadian group that went to the airport to welcome Prime Minister Trudeau and his delegation. It was a sunny autumn day with a clear blue sky and crisp air. Hundreds of Chinese

Arthur Erickson's private luncheon for Prime Minister and Mrs Trudeau at Beijing Summer Palace, October 1973. Left to right: Francisco Kripacz, Eileen, Margaret Trudeau, Pierre Trudeau, Mr and Mrs Moshe Safdie, Paul, Arthur Erickson

young people – dressed in festive clothing and waving Chinese and Canadian flags, flowers, balloons, and streamers – chanted in unison, "Huan Ying! Huan Ying!" (Welcome!) for their honoured guests.

Premier Zhou Enlai accompanied Prime Minister Trudeau to greet the crowds. As the dignitaries approached the Canadian contingent, Eileen noticed Tang Wensheng (Nancy Tang), Premier Zhou's interpreter, pointing her finger in our direction and whispering to him. Premier Zhou immediately walked over and shook my hand, saying "Professor Lin, welcome to China." Unexpectedly, Trudeau followed and also shook my hand, saying: "Paul Lin, it is good to see you in China."

Arthur Erickson wanted very much to give the Trudeaus and his friends a private luncheon during the state visit. This was an unprecedented request, but permission was granted by the Chinese premier's office. Arthur decided to hold the luncheon at the Summer Palace and the Chinese Government reserved for him the entire Ting Li Pavilion, alongside Kunming Lake, where the Empress Dowager had listened to the orioles during her reign. Arthur and I worked out a "designer" menu of Trudeau's favourite Chinese foods. Each course was deliciously prepared and exquisitely presented on the Empress Dowager's dishes, much to the delight of the guests of honour. The prime minister and his wife exclaimed with joy that these were the delicacies they had come to China for. Later that evening, I received a phone call from the premier's office, inquiring about the menu that had so impressed the Canadian prime minister that he was almost late for his afternoon meeting with Premier Zhou!

Eileen and I spent the next six weeks in Beijing, before leaving for Sydney, Australia, via Jakarta. I had met Stephen Fitzgerald, Australia's ambassador to China, at a dinner party given by Canadian Ambassador John Small earlier in the fall. This had led to several further meetings and an invitation from the ambassador to speak in Canberra. However, I was shocked to learn that all "Orientals" going to Australia required visas, whereas Caucasians did not. I refused to go on such terms and protested to Ambassador Fitzgerald; after much negotiation, visas for Eileen and me were waived. The trip went well. I gave a lecture in Canberra on "China's Foreign Policy," sponsored by the Australian Institute of International Affairs, and talked at length with graduate students at the Australian National University.

In Sydney, we also had a happy reunion with Ike and Loretta Shulman, old friends from Vancouver. We introduced them to Dick and Lillian Diamond, Australian foreign experts with whom we had worked at Radio Peking and Xinhua during the 1950s. We spent a good day threshing out the contradictions and horrific excesses of the Cultural Revolution.

THE PASSING OF PREMIER ZHOU ENLAI

1976 was a momentous year for China. Premier Zhou Enlai died in January; General Zhu De died in July; the deadly Tangshan earthquake which took more than 250,000 lives occurred in August; Mao Zedong died in September;

and the Gang of Four was arrested in October. The Western world had countless questions about China's next steps, with the result that I gave more than thirty-five interviews and lectures in 1976–77, nearly a dozen of them at memorials for Zhou and Mao in both Canada and the United States.

An immediate, spontaneous outpouring of grief consumed the people of China when they learned of Premier Zhou Enlai's passing in January. The Gang of Four's hatred of the premier continued beyond his death, however. Through their control of the media, they banned most memorial articles on Premier Zhou, halted distribution of a documentary film about his life, and tried to ban all memorial services. Their scheme backfired, however, and instead of erasing his memory and influence, the Gang's actions helped to expose their true character. These efforts to suppress popular expressions of mourning for Zhou earned them the undying hatred of the great masses of the Chinese people.

Chinese abroad were also discouraged from holding memorial services for Premier Zhou. We ignored this unwarranted "advice" and immediately went to the Chinese embassy in Ottawa to express our condolences. I spoke to 1,400 people at a memorial service in New York on January 18, 1976, which had been sponsored by various Chinese organizations in the eastern United States. My address was carried in New York's *Overseas Chinese Daily* on January 21. In it, I reflected:

> With deepest sorrow, we mourn today the loss of Premier Zhou Enlai, a great revolutionary statesman. His passing is a gigantic loss to the people of China and the world. Humanity has been deprived of a rare vanguard of freedom. He served the people with his heart and soul ... Therefore, his death was weightier than the Tai Mountain [in Shandong Province] ...
>
> Premier Zhou's life was a microcosm of China's contemporary history. It spanned nearly eighty years of the twentieth century, which coincided with the era when the people of China shattered the chain of the old order and began the great struggle to build a new society ...
>
> Zhou Enlai was a leader with courage and vision. In struggles, he stood at the forefront, but within the ranks of the people, never allowing them to lag far behind ... Because he tried to shield the revolution from the serious damage inflicted by both ultra-right and ultra-left policies, he was revered and loved by the people. He understood only too well that all humans are prone to errors. With himself, he was very strict through self-criticisms, but patient when helping others to correct their mistakes,

freeing them to renew their service to the people. Once, he said to me: "Just like getting sick, people will always err. The key is prevention. When mistakes occur, the patient should be cured but not killed."

Zhou Enlai was the personification of the couplet authored by Lu Xun: "With leveled brow, I gaze at a thousand accusing fingers. With bowed head, I serve the people like an ox." Sometimes, the second of the two is the hardest to practice, as in the case of the Cultural Revolution.

THE DEATH OF MAO ZEDONG AND THE FALL OF THE GANG OF FOUR

Soon after Chairman Mao Zedong's death on September 9, the "Gang of Four" – Jiang Qing, Zhang Chunqiao, Yao Wenyuan, and Wang Hongwen – were arrested. A few months later, in January 1977, we visited China and spoke with family, old friends, and colleagues to learn more about the struggle against the Gang before their downfall.

In a later interview with the *New China Magazine*, a publication of the US-China People's Friendship Association, I tried to provide some context for the Gang of Four. The reporter noted that "the Western press has characterized the struggle in China as 'moderates' versus 'radicals' ... and what we are seeing now is a rejection of Mao Zedong's emphasis on revolutionary struggle – supposedly represented by the Gang of Four – in favor of a pragmatic emphasis on technology, production, and the building of China's economy – supposedly represented by such leaders as Zhou Enlai, Deng Xiaoping, and Chairman Hua Guofeng."

In my view, the Western interpretation, which identified the Gang of Four with Mao's revolutionary ideas, was wrong. It seemed increasingly clear, I said, "as more of their activities were uncovered, everything they stood for was a gross distortion, almost a caricature of Mao's ideas ... Unlike Mao, who had singled out Dazhai and Daqing ... for praise, because they had made great advances in production, the Gang of Four, on the contrary, labeled as counter-revolutionaries anyone who wanted to discuss technological developments or was concerned with production; at the same time promoting incompetents and politically questionable careerists, whose only virtue was that they echoed the Gang of Four's empty revolutionary rhetoric."

Like Lin Biao before them, the Gang identified Zhou Enlai as their chief target. Not only was he the premier and chief administrator of the far-flung organs of the Chinese Government, but he also enjoyed enormous popularity among the people and had the support of countless officials. The 1974 Pi Lin Pi Kong movement, which supposedly was to criticize the similar ideas of Lin Biao and the ancient Chinese philosopher Confucius, was turned into an attack on a number of recently rehabilitated cadres who had been removed from office during the Cultural Revolution. Although they did not say so openly, the attack was partly directed at Zhou Enlai, who was in charge of the rehabilitation process.

Some of the Gang's most serious disruptions were in the cultural field, in which Jiang Qing had been active since the early days of the Cultural Revolution. Once Jiang Qing became involved in the production and criticism of the performing arts, things changed. She and her allies became self-appointed tyrants of the arts – the sole judges of what was and was not politically correct.

The reporter asked how the Gang of Four had been able to hold such power in China. I replied that China was still only a single generation away from the old exploitative society. Inequalities were still present under socialism – between mental and manual labour, between city and countryside, and between workers and peasants – and these inequalities can lead to the development of new backward forces, who feel they should have special privileges. Despite the fact that the political consciousness of the workers and peasants was much more advanced than it was in 1949, it was still developing. Apparently Mao Zedong recognized the danger inherent in the Gang of Four when in 1974, at a Politburo meeting, he issued an open warning to Jiang Qing and the others: "Take care, don't form yourselves into a faction of four!"

SEARCHING FOR TRUTH

Many questions were directed at me during this period. I based my replies on information available at the time, but a full accounting of the Cultural Revolution was not likely to come anytime soon. Still, the rise of the Gang of Four troubled me.

One of the most complex episodes in the history of human struggle involves strong feudal survivals as well as proto-capitalist elements – hence it is not easy to determine the truth of what we are told. Enemies of socialism in both China and abroad help to falsify and distort the facts, while well-meaning but unsophisticated devotées of both "left" and "right" muddy the analysis.

It is important to wrestle with the Gang of Four, because it bears on whether the great experiments of the Chinese people for human emancipation and development will succeed. It also bears on whether their successes – correct theory and practice – will be useful for other peoples seeking ways out of their historical prisons, and whether they can learn from the errors and shortcomings of China's pioneer experience.

How to separate fact from fiction? Facts are objective and best seen by those wrestling with reality. This reality is not easily apprehended by outside observers, even those who make short trips to China, especially if they rely for their facts on alleged reports sifted through a hostile media or by cynical observers looking through the prisms of class prejudice, aided by cultural chauvinism. Thus the opacity and even the mystique of the China "puzzle."

This is not to say that Chinese official propaganda has helped the search for truth by honest observers abroad. There have been appalling mystifications contributed by the media, and resort has even been made to falsifying the past, in the obliteration of the Gang of Four from official photographs. This is understandable in terms of the sensitivities of an incensed and grieving populace mourning the death of their great leader, who was a target of the Gang's machinations, but such practices have no place in a true record of events.

Chapter Fourteen

CHINA OPENS TO THE WORLD

Canadian interest in trade grew quickly after Ottawa and Beijing established diplomatic relations in 1970. I was approached by individuals in both the United States and Canada who wished to explore business opportunities in China, but it was only after the fall of the Gang of Four and the end of the Cultural Revolution in 1976 that China indicated openness to foreign investment.

Paul Desmarais, Sr., chairman of the Power Corporation of Canada, had approached me about the possibility of a delegation of Canadian businessmen attending China's massive Canton Trade Fair. Initial discussions with the Chinese embassy in Ottawa encouraged us to explore interest among Canadian companies, who responded enthusiastically. Subsequently, I organized a conference in Montreal for senior business executives in early December 1977. McGill's Centre for East Asian Studies and its Faculty of Management hosted the seminar; corporate sponsors included the Royal Bank of Canada, the Bank of Montreal, the Bank of Nova Scotia, the Aluminum Company of Canada, Inco, Canadian Pacific, MacMillan Bloedel, as well as Desmarais's Power Corporation. Approximately sixty participants convened to discuss the Chinese economy and prospects for Sino-Canadian trade.

With the evident success of the conference, the next move was to set up a private organization to help Canadian firms, especially small ones, to tackle the China market. Paul Desmarais and Maurice Strong of Petro-Canada were especially keen to establish a trade presence in China before US recognition opened the country to American competitors. The Canada China Trade Council (later renamed the Canada China Business Council) was established in June

Meeting with Vice-Premier Deng Xiaoping at Xinjiang Chamber, October 1977

Paul Desmarais, chairman of Power Corporation of Canada, leads first major Canadian trade delegation to the PRC, accompanied by Paul as adviser, October 1978. The delegation was received by Chinese Vice-Premier and State Planning Minister Yu Qiuli, along with other senior Chinese trade officials. Vice-Premier Yu stands in the front row (centre), with Paul Desmarais on the left and Canadian Ambassador Arthur Menzies on the right.

1978; in early October, Desmarais led Canada's first high-powered industrial and commercial mission to China. I accompanied the delegation as an adviser.

The mission received extensive press coverage. AFP reported from Beijing that according to mission leader Paul Desmarais, "trade between Canada and China should reach a total value of 10,000 million US dollars over the years up to 1985." The delegation spent a full week talking with senior Chinese economic and trade officials, including Vice-Premier and State Planning Minister Yu Qiuli, a leading economist with extensive experience in the oil industry.

Of course, the full promise of the China market depended upon the liberalization of the Chinese economy itself – a structural change of vast strategic importance. This would begin at the end of 1978, when Deng Xiaoping called on Party and government leaders to emancipate their thinking about China's socialist road of development, moving from self-reliance to interdependence in the global economy.

A TAIL IN LOS ANGELES, 1978

Beginning in June 1977, I took a one-year leave of absence to pursue research into the values behind China's development strategies. Eileen and I spent most of our time in China and southern California; I returned to Montreal only briefly for the December 1977 business seminar. It was during the last few months of my sabbatical leave, as a visiting scholar at the University of California at Los Angeles (UCLA), when I picked up a most peculiar tail.

Long an advocate of improving relations between the United States and China, I had planned a trip to China in late June 1978 to explore opportunities for academic exchange programs between UCLA and Chinese universities. In the course of my visit, I would also meet with Chinese trade officials on behalf of Canadian and American corporations for whom I was consulting. Prior to my departure, however, I became aware that I was being followed and I believed my telephone was tapped. I did not know who was shadowing me. One afternoon, when I spotted an obvious tail, I stopped my car, marched back and demanded that the driver of the trailing car identify himself. He refused. I noticed that he had a camera with a large telescopic lens on the front seat beside him.

When I returned to Los Angeles from China in early July, Eileen met me at the airport accompanied by a lawyer friend and our goddaughter. Straight away, we noticed several men following our movements and decided to turn the tables: we chased them with cameras through the terminal in a vain attempt to find out who they were. "They seemed too blatant, too amateurish to be the FBI," I told the *Los Angeles Times*. Finally I decided to go to the police. As I backed the car out of the driveway of our Santa Monica home to drive to the station, four unknown men jumped into four unmarked cars and fanned out in four directions, in order to keep us covered. They converged when we reached the police station, where (now also tailed by a *Times* reporter) we nearly caused an accident in the parking lot. It was, as the reporter commented, like "a scene from the Keystone Kops." When the license plate numbers of my pursuers were entered into the Department of Motor Vehicles computer system, they returned blank, meaning law enforcement – the FBI. Apparently they suspected me of spying for Beijing.

I was angered by this old accusation and fed up with the FBI's anti-Communist paranoia, which had led to the harassment Eileen and I had experienced intermittently since 1965 in both Canada and the United States.

"There isn't anything secret about what he was doing," UCLA Vice-Chancellor Elwin V. Svenson told the *Times*. "I find it [the FBI investigation] a little bizarre."

Later, I wrote a letter to President Jimmy Carter complaining of the surveillance. Conscious of his concern for human rights and for the furtherance of US-China relations, I simply could not understand how and why such crude government intimidation would be permitted. I never received an official apology, but appreciated that the UCLA chapter of the American Association of University Professors later publicly condemned the FBI for their harassment of me and my family.

THE FOUR MODERNIZATIONS AND SOCIALISM WITH "CHINESE CHARACTERISTICS"

Following the fall of the Gang of Four in 1976, Deng Xiaoping began his third ascendancy to power, having been purged twice by Chairman Mao and the ultra-leftists during the Cultural Revolution. An economic pragmatist famous for the saying "black cat, white cat, whichever catches the rat is the good cat," Deng had worked closely with both Zhou Enlai and Liu Shaoqi to restore the national economy after the Great Leap Forward, only to see this progress destroyed by Mao's utopian visions. Despite having to manoeuvre around Hua Guofeng (Mao's designated successor, who only resigned in late 1980), Deng was determined to redefine the Chinese revolution and to build China into a modern industrial state able to compete in the global economy.

Vice-Premier Deng Xiaoping (right) receives Frank Gibney (centre) of the *Encyclopaedia Britannica* and Paul, in November 1979, announcing for the first time that China can also have a socialist market economy.

The first sign of major institutional change occurred at the Third Plenary session of the Eleventh Chinese Communist Party Central Committee, held in December 1978. Economic development and the Four Modernizations (of industry, agriculture, science and technology, and national defence) were endorsed as government priorities. In 1979 it was announced that four Special Economic Zones would be opened for foreign investment, and that the state would send thousands of students abroad for advanced training in order to catch up with the technically advanced Western nations.

On November 26, 1979, Deng received me and a client – Frank Gibney of the US *Encyclopaedia Britannica* – at the Great Hall of the People. Discussing China's new economic direction and the Four Modernizations, I tactfully asked Deng: "Do you think China made a mistake when it placed restrictions on its non-capitalist market economy too early and too rapidly? Because of this, China needs to make its non-capitalist market economy play a bigger role under the guidance of a planned socialist economy?" His reply startled not only Frank and me, but his entire Chinese entourage as well. Deng pronounced, "We can develop a market economy under socialism!" Such a statement was unprecedented in the history of the CCP. He went on to say: "It is wrong to maintain that a market economy only exists in a capitalist society and that there is only a 'capitalist market economy.' Why can't we develop a market economy under socialism? Developing a market economy does not mean practising capitalism. While maintaining a planned economy as the mainstay of our economic system, we can also introduce a market economy. But it is a socialist market economy ... Market economies emerged in their embryonic stages as early as in the feudalist society. We can surely develop it under social-ism ... in order to release [our] productive forces. So long as learning from capitalism is regarded as no more than a means to an end, it will not change the structure of socialism or bring China back to capitalism."

In addition to reformulating economic thinking to include some capitalistic practices, economic reforms required the "rehabilitation" of thousands of cadres and intellectuals sent to the countryside during the Cultural Revolution. Not only did the state need the technical skills and management expertise of these former "rightists," but the Party had to implicitly admit that errors had been made. This, of course, did not sit well with ultra-leftists elevated to high positions from 1966–76, but Deng and his allies prevailed. The most signif-icant case was that of the late Liu Shaoqi.

Liu Shaoqi had been a Party member since 1921, PRC president in 1958, and Mao's chosen successor in 1961, but had angered Mao by embarking on economic reforms following the Great Leap Forward and became the prime target of Mao's Cultural Revolution. He was subsequently denounced, stripped of Party membership, beaten, and left to die an ignominious death on a prison floor in 1969. In February 1980, the Chinese Communist Party posthumously rehabilitated Liu Shaoqi and on May 17 honoured Liu with a state funeral at which Deng gave the eulogy. I was in Beijing at the time and the collective sense of relief that China was genuinely on a new path was almost palpable. Soon after, Mao's legacy was determined by the Party to have been only sev-enty per cent positive; no longer was he a god, but a human being who could make mistakes.

GLOBAL TRADE

China was now open for business. CEOs from North American and European corporations were eager to establish joint ventures and a number asked for my assistance in navigating the Chinese bureaucracy. I was only interested in help-ing projects that would meet China's urgent needs. Still, I had more business than I could handle in addition to my McGill teaching, involvement in several educational and cultural exchanges, and community work.

In June 1980, I flew to Zurich to address a group of European industrial leaders on China's new economic strategies. I advised them to "make haste slowly": to engage Chinese partners boldly, but to act with caution as China had not yet established a legal framework to deal with Western contractual agreements. Furthermore, there would likely be political ups and downs as the reforms took root.

I began my remarks with a discussion of the Great Leap Forward, which had led to a severe economic slump and massive starvation in the countryside. The disaster was the result of human error, floods, and drought, compounded by the abrupt withdrawal of Soviet experts, which had left key industrial projects in shambles. But from 1962 to 1966, the economy rebounded as a consequence of stringent government measures, which included allowing farmers to till small, private plots. Communes were proving unwieldy in management and were unpopular with the people, who welcomed the reforms. This dissent, especially by Party members, rankled Mao, who perceived a dangerous trend toward "revisionism" and a grave threat to his strategy of development. What ensued was one of the most extraordinary episodes in human history – the Cultural Revolution, launched by the supreme leader of the country calling on his people to rebel!

Originally targeted at bureaucratic power-holders "taking the capitalist road," the attack was spearheaded by young people, dubbed the Red Guards, and quickly took on a momentum of its own. Now positioned to strike at all authority, this exercise in "mass democracy" deteriorated at times into violent anarchy. The havoc that resulted was appalling – in human suffering for millions of pilloried office-holders, in the loss of schooling for a generation of young people, and in economic chaos. A special kind of damage was inflicted on those who fell captive to ultra-left sophistry, in the genuine belief that it was in keeping with the revolutionary spirit of "politics in command."

Aware that my audience could only view Mao's Cultural Revolution as utter madness, I reminded them that since 1949, China had been trying to telescope into a generation or two a modernization process that had taken several turbulent centuries to accomplish in Europe. China was attempting, in one continuous integral process, to transform her low-productivity agrarian economy into a high-productivity industrial society. Burdened by survivals of feudal values and institutions, it was unsurprising that a rapid conversion from old ways to new would be accompanied by sometimes violent swings of policy and personality. And for an extended period, the old and the new, the traditional and the modern, would continue to coexist in China. But because Chinese socialism emerged not out of the highest development of capitalism, but out of a hybrid society of semi-feudalism and stunted capitalism, any regression in the process of socialist development was not likely to assume the form of full-fledged capitalism, but more probably that of a feudal-type reaction in some form or other, mixed with strong small-producer or petit-bourgeois propensities. This would seem to account for some aspects of behavior of the Gang of Four and their adherents.

The most fundamental lesson of the Cultural Revolution was that China had to make a decisive shift and focus on economic development. The central tasks were to raise productivity and the living standards of the people, as quickly as possible. At the same time, stability, a new national unity, and a revitalized democratic system undergirded by law, would be required.

I then touched on the human problem – the discrepancy between the development of human resources and the demands of modernization. The launching of the Four Modernizations had highlighted the continuing paucity of skilled manpower in almost every field. The ten-year interregnum of the ultra-left had aggravated the problem in two ways: an entire generation not only had been deprived of adequate schooling, but had also been exposed to an avalanche of misguided norms of thought and behavior. In a sense, a fifth modernization – the most crucial of all – needed to be added to the four already named: the modernization of the modernizers. I was referring to the upgrading not only of scientific-technical and managerial capacities, but also of qualities of the human spirit. In the socialist perspective, "modernity" included advanced human values. The modernizers themselves must transcend self-serving careerism and embrace attitudes of dedication to the people's interest, to ideals of human equality and cooperation, to the struggle against exploitation, to unyielding intellectual and moral integrity. If the new generation were to scorn these norms, in overreaction to the hollow hypocrisy of the Gang of Four, the great promise of the future would be in danger of vanishing into thin air.

Finally, I left my audience of business executives with a few concrete tips. First, China's long-term goals in engaging with foreign companies were to introduce needed equipment and technologies, to create new industries, and to expand and upgrade current productive capacities. Chinese exports would be aimed primarily at generating foreign exchange to pay for her imports.

Second, although China had begun to accept foreign credit to finance her enormous capital construction program, she was moving cautiously in order to keep the aggregate level of indebtedness to modest levels, preferring "pay-as-you-go" transactions whenever possible. Third, as new patterns of trade evolved, it was increasingly clear that China would be most open to joint ventures which would at once help to solve shortages of funds, generate new export capacity to pay for imports and/or create imports substitution industries.

Paul interviews Premier Zhao Ziyang for the DFS film *The Chinese*, May 1981.

I concluded that the potential of international trade with a market of one billion people was exhilarating. Yet outsiders should know there was little evidence that China would allow the vagaries and uncertainties of the world market to play a disruptive role in her economy or veer her off course. Her first concern had always been to build up her national strength and then work for the most favourable (and peaceful) international environment possible.

CHINA'S OPEN DOOR

In late 1980, a Canadian film company, DFS, based in Toronto, asked me to co-produce a documentary for the Canadian Broadcasting Corporation (CBC) on the Four Modernizations. Through the good offices of my old friend Situ Huimin, the veteran filmmaker whom I had met at a CSCA conference in the United States in the late 1940s, I was able to gain access for DFS to Chinese film authorities. Producing the film meant months of hard work and quite a few unpleasant disagreements with some of my Canadian co-workers over contents that tended to sensationalize the "ugly Chinese," such as a scene that depicted the gory details of how pigs were slaughtered in the countryside. In the end, we managed to gather some superb footage and interviews with the noted author Ding Ling and Premier Zhao Ziyang, among others.

Vice-Premier Yao Yilin receives Paul at the Great Hall of the People and
introduces him to Vice-Premier Gu Mu, 1979.

During this period of reform, Eileen's cousin Yao Yilin was instrumental in
helping me to understand China's current economic needs, direction, and policy. Having held significant financial, trade, and commerce posts since 1949,
he was appointed deputy prime minister in 1978 and became a member of the
CCP Central Financial and Economic Leading Group in 1980. He introduced
me to two of his colleagues in the powerful Leading Group, vice-premiers Gu
Mu and Fang Yi. In addition to their earlier illustrious careers, Vice-Premier
Gu had been chairman of two national commissions since 1975 (Import-
Export Control and Foreign Investment Control) and Vice-Premier Fang had
been president of the Chinese Academy of Science and chairman of the
National Commission on Science and Technology since 1978. Their invaluable
input enabled me to match key foreign corporations with the appropriate Chinese ministries. A few entries from my diary at the time illustrate some of the
insights I was learning from discussions with Yao about China's new economic
and political policies.

January 14, 1981: Discussions touched on Yao's support for the DFS film
and the changes taking place in China. Regarding Hua Guofeng's resignation in December 1980, Yao said that after Mao's death in 1976, Hua
had continued to embrace most of Chairman Mao's ultra-leftist policies.

He was for the glorification of the leader, he resisted the rehabilitation of old cadres, and he was most unhappy with the recent economic reforms. There were concerns among reformers and the military that if he continued to hold power, he might reverse the realignment of the economy, which had begun to take hold by the spring of 1980. Yao, however, was not entirely negative about Hua; he had contributed to the downfall of the Gang of Four and had stepped aside without a struggle.

Yao felt the greatness of Chairman Mao was his solution to China's revolution, which was to surround the city by the countryside. But he never solved the question of socialist construction. He tried his strategy in 1958, but it was proven a failure in practice. He attempted his designs again during the Cultural Revolution and failed again.

He said that after repeated examination, the leadership felt that: "To modernize China will be a relatively long process. It may take sixty to seventy years or even a century or longer. We will have to wait until the third generation before we can enjoy the fruits of our labour. We have to move forward gradually. Haste will result in waste."

And,

March 27, 1981: In answer to my queries about China's economic planning, energy policies (especially oil), and interest in international academic dialogue, Yao said the present economic realignment meant halting some major projects or delaying them for seven to eight years. Priority had to change from chasing after international standards in outputs (oil, steel, coal) to improving the livelihood of the people: food, clothing, and housing. The needs of the people were primary; agriculture and industry could then be adjusted accordingly. [This was in contrast to some economists, who continued to follow the Soviet model and focused on heavy industry and central planning.]

Yao continued that in 1979, there was a debate on the goals of socialist production. Was it to reach one hundred million tons of steel or to raise the living standards of the people and to defend the country? Productivity can be raised by changing the relations of production, which can also help to reform our system of organization. Therefore, we must be determined to stop those projects, which block our progress … We should turn our stockpile of steel into structural steel for people's housing … use World Bank loans for medium size rather than huge hydroelectric power stations. We need to train human resources.

The day after that last entry, I had lunch with Yao's son Ming Wei and son-in-law Wang Qishan [who is currently the vice-premier in charge of the economy and a member of the Politburo]. As I recorded later in my diary, "Wang said it is no longer possible for third-world countries to follow the industrialization path of the developed countries. The new strategy must satisfy the needs of the people. Many young people forget that the West's higher standards were accumulated by the blood and sweat of their domestic workers and colonial slaves. Yao said there would be no possibility of political upheavals. The central issue was economic. Political problems would arise if there were no economic solution."

It was a hectic but enormously exciting time, as China initiated market reforms that would lead to global commerce. I crisscrossed the world in 1981, making four trips to China to discuss potential joint ventures between overseas corporations and the relevant Chinese ministries. This included Canadian companies, whose representatives I had met with in May when the third annual meeting of the Canada China Trade Council convened in Hangzhou.

I concluded the year in Paris, where I again met with Ambassador Yao Guang (PRC ambassador to Canada, 1972–73), and spent time with Wei Buren, deputy general manager of China Offshore Petroleum Corporation, before attending a banquet hosted by him for officials of Elf Aquitaine, France's giant national petroleum company. In his toast, Wei expressed satisfaction that Elf had proven their commitment to China by asking me to be their China consultant. "Professor Lin is highly respected in the PRC," he told his dinner guests. I felt honoured to know that I was making a difference in bringing China to the world and the world to China.

Chapter Fifteen

GENERATIONS

1981 was a busy year. It is only in retrospect that I recognized it as pivotal. Not only did I retire from McGill, after seventeen years of teaching history and directing the Centre for East Asian Studies, but Eileen and I also lost three women who had shaped our lives: Madame Soong Ching Ling, Eileen's mother Choming Tsai Chen, and Madame Marie Thérèse Casgrain, who had welcomed us so warmly to Montreal in 1965. A remarkable generation was moving on.

MADAME SOONG CHING LING, 1893–1981

We travelled to Beijing in early May 1981, for an afternoon ceremony on May 8 at the Great Hall of the People, where Canada's University of Victoria awarded Madame Soong Ching Ling an honorary Doctor of Laws degree. The honorary degree was a tribute to Madame Soong's lifelong contributions as a stateswoman, humanitarian, and social rights activist. It was a moving ceremony. In her acceptance speech, I felt she was delivering her final testament – the human struggles of the twentieth century seemed to resonate through her every word.

After we extended our congratulations, Madame's secretary pulled us aside to tell us she had not been well. The next morning, another secretary called to convey Madame Soong's apology for not having invited us to dinner with her Canadian guests the previous evening, as she had not known we were in Beijing. It was to be her last message to us.

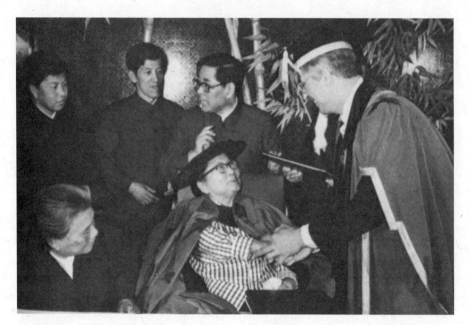

Madame Soong Ching Ling receives an honorary Doctor of Laws degree from
the University of Victoria, Canada, May 1981. (Photograph by Zou Youma)

For the next several weeks we shuttled back and forth between our hotel
and Madame Soong's sickbed. By May 17, it was clear that the end was coming soon. Assisting Deng Yingchao, widow of the late Premier Zhou Enlai,
with Madame Soong's final arrangements was Minister of Overseas Chinese
Affairs Liao Chengzhi. An old friend of the Sun family, he cabled granddaughters Pearl Sun Lin and Rose Sun Tchang in the United States and suggested
they come immediately. I met with a group of Madame Soong's foreign friends,
including Rewi Alley and Israel Epstein, regarding funeral protocols.

Near midnight on May 28, the bedside telephone in our hotel room rang
with ominous urgency. We were asked to come quickly to Soong Ching Ling's
home. We raced to the house. Special white-uniformed traffic officers stood at
frequent intervals along the way, directing a stream of cars that were heading
for her residence through the silent streets. Crowds began lining the road as
we passed the Drum Tower and turned into the lane alongside the lake leading
to her house. Their anxious faces told the story: Soong Ching Ling, one of
China's most beloved contemporary leaders, was dying.

As our car approached the compound, the guards swung open the great red
portals. The mansion and familiar garden, so often graced by her quiet presence, were ablaze with lights. Inside, we were met by the now solemn Liao
Chengzhi, and were briefed by Dr Zhou Shangjue, leader of the team of dis-

tinguished medical specialists who had been attending Madame Soong for the past month. He confided that the inexorable terminal events of lymphatic leukemia were taking their final toll. Despite her remarkable stamina, it was not likely that she would live much longer.

So began our last vigil. Only a week earlier, Pearl Sun Lin, Rose Sun Tchang, and Rose's husband Paul had flown from California in time to tell their still-conscious grandmother: "We love you. The world loves you." She had sighed, tears rolling down her cheeks. By now, other relatives, including Walter and Junny Chun and their daughter Yen, had arrived and, with the doctors' permission, we ascended the broad staircase to her bedroom. Inside, physicians and nurses moved with quiet efficiency around her bed. Soong Ching Ling lay in a deep coma. Her face was flushed with fever but she was otherwise peaceful, and mercifully without any sign of pain.

The doctors' expert interventions had rescued her from death on several occasions during the previous few weeks. Indeed, she had rallied so well that when she awoke on May 20, she had asked the white-clad doctors and nurses: "Why are there so many of you here? I only need Dr Gu and the nurse." A final reprieve, however, was hoping against hope. The rapidly multiplying leucocytes in her body would finally still the heroic heart of Soong Ching Ling.

During one of those hopeful moments, family members had consulted with Mr Liao regarding our wish to send a wire to Soong Mei Ling – Madame Chiang Kai-shek – in New York, to inform her of her sister's serious illness and to express our hope that she might come to Beijing for a final visit. Soong Mei Ling replied a few days later: "Send sister to New York for treatment. Family." She did not even sign the telegram.

Dawn came and we waited through the day, moving between house and garden, overcome by memories. Here was the corner armchair where she always sat when welcoming visitors, the charm and dignity of her personality filling the room. We had often had tea with her around that chair. Soong Ching Ling had never sought wealth or power; her greatest wealth was her friends and her greatest power, the inspiration of her example. She was one of those rare human beings who combined strength with tenderness, militancy with compassion. A redoubtable foe to all human cruelty and oppression, she was to all who needed her a generous and loyal friend.

We went into the garden and crossed the little stone bridge leading to the dovecotes, where the doves would crowd around her gentle presence, offering respite from a busy life. We walked under the familiar willows by the stream, the lilac bushes, the treasured 183-year-old pomegranate tree, the pines, and the magnolia – all subtly suggestive of outer strength and inner beauty.

This had once been the site of a Manchu imperial regent's palace, and briefly the home of the Qing Dynasty's last emperor, Pu Yi. Soong Ching Ling not only outlasted them all, but had lived through three turbulent periods in China's modern history: the extinction of the imperial era, the troubled Republic founded by her husband Sun Yat-sen, and the first thirty-two years of the People's Republic. Never had she flinched from danger or disappointment. Never was she so carried away by triumph as to forget the careful and modest style that was her habit. Never did she label or sit in judgment on comrades who had made mistakes. Above all, never did she go against her own conscience, no matter who was in power.

I remembered from my youth how Chinese communities in Canada had admired Madame Soong as the brave and beautiful comrade-in-arms of their national hero. They mourned with her following Sun's death in 1925, and later came to admire her as a beacon of revolutionary integrity in a regime that had forsaken her husband's ideals. In mid-1927, the Kuomintang led by Chiang Kai-shek betrayed the revolution of 1911 and allied itself with foreign powers and domestic warlords. Chiang ordered the slaughter of workers in Shanghai and the massacre of thousands of Chinese Communists and progressive patriots. In those dark hours, Soong Ching Ling issued numerous articles and statements condemning the KMT's actions and left the country for several years in protest.

Even after Japan annexed Manchuria in 1931, the KMT pursued a policy of passive resistance to Japan, while launching a large-scale civil war against the Chinese Communists and leftists. Along with progressive writers like Lu Xun, Soong Ching Ling sponsored the China League for Civil Rights to provide legal defense for imprisoned revolutionaries. Throughout the 1930s, she continued to write sharp articles exposing the criminal brutality of Chiang's secret service agencies. Her status as Dr Sun's widow protected her from her brother-in-law's tyranny.

With the Japanese invasion of China in 1937, Soong Ching Ling established the China Defence League based in Hong Kong and devoted herself to wartime relief and medical work. Funds raised by her wide network of overseas friends enabled the Defence League to send large quantities of medical supplies to Chinese troops in bases established by the Eighth Route and New Fourth Armies, as well as to the International Peace Hospital set up by Canada's Dr Norman Bethune.

As a college student in the United States, I had seen how student spirits were buoyed by Soong Ching Ling's courageous defiance of both Chiang Kai-shek's repression at home and the invading Japanese. Chinese abroad responded wholeheartedly to the patriotic and humanitarian appeals bearing her name, as the only movements they could trust in Kuomintang-controlled areas. Following Japan's surrender in 1945, Soong Ching Ling continued relief work for her war-devastated people. In 1946, she publicly called for a coalition government between the Nationalists and the Communists, but Chiang, with US backing, resumed fighting the Communists. Soong Ching Ling appealed to the American people to stop their government from aiding the Kuomintang militarily in China's civil war.

Eileen and I continued to pace the garden as we reflected on the arc of Madame Soong's life story. She did not fail the test of integrity after achieving high office in the New China, which she had done so much to bring into existence. She devoted herself to improving the welfare of women and children through her China Welfare Institute in Shanghai, and for many years attended international peace conferences as China's representative. In addition, at the request of Premier Zhou Enlai, she oversaw the publication of a monthly journal for overseas readers, *China Reconstructs*. During the Cultural Revolution, when cruel and corrupt elements took over the government, she used her personal prestige to protect some whom she knew to be falsely accused by fanatic "left" extremists, just as she had done in an earlier era for victims of fanatic "right" extremists. I recalled receiving her courageous letters during the Cultural Revolution, bitterly exposing the criminal suffering wreaked on innocent victims whom she knew well. She herself would have been harmed had she not been protected by Premier Zhou Enlai, who once described her as "an elegant national treasure." Although under attack himself, Zhou still had enough authority left to call in the army to protect this house and this garden from desecration.

Our musings were interrupted in late afternoon, when we were again summoned to Soong Ching Ling's bedside. Entering the room, one felt an overwhelming sense of indelicacy at invading the privacy that she had treasured as much as her public life. There were her books, her writing desk, and photographs. Looking at the photographs of her two foster daughters, in their early twenties, I was acutely aware of the personal deprivations that this great woman had undergone. She had no children of her own, having lost by miscarriage her only child with Sun Yat-sen in the 1920s during the turmoil of battle. Subsequently, she had bestowed her maternal affections on these children of her former secretary.

Had she suffered moments of terrible loneliness since her husband died fifty-six years before? Perhaps, but she never allowed this loss to dampen her spirit, her optimism, her effervescent sense of humor. I marvelled at the many small

222

Top: Paul and Eileen outside the residence of Madame Soong Ching Ling, May 1981

Bottom: Paul confers with Liao Chengzhi and Walter and Junny Chun in Madame Soong's parlour, May 1981.

but significant ways in which she had unfailingly showed her human concern for people, despite the loftiness of her station. I recalled meeting her for the first time at her home in Shanghai in the spring of 1950. She was radiant with joy at China's recent liberation and speculated on the difficult but challenging road ahead to build a new China. At the same time, she took note of my weakness for certain kinds of sweet pastries, and for the next thirty years, never forgot to offer them to me – with that wondrous, indulgent smile of hers – whenever I visited.

In the end, family members were not at her side during her final minutes of life. The doctors felt we all needed a brief rest, and the life-support systems seemed likely to sustain her through the early evening hours. We took their advice and returned to the hotel. The fateful call came the moment we entered our hotel room: Madame Soong Ching Ling had suddenly but peacefully passed away at 8:18 pm on May 29, 1981.

We immediately made the journey back to the house, still struggling to absorb the news. In the hours that followed, I watched the housekeeper, secretaries, and guards as they went about their duties. Grief was etched on their faces. Every one of them had experienced Soong Ching Ling's care and concern in countless small ways, and knew a painful emptiness would soon descend upon their lives. A few days before, they had watched with pride how she had rallied to acknowledge the highest honour the nation could bestow on her, naming her the Honorary President of the People's Republic of China.

With an awful suddenness, the moment had come. Within minutes, official cars bearing the nation's top leaders began to converge on the residence. Throughout the evening they arrived to pay their last respects, while we stood by the bier to receive their condolences. Soon the worst was confirmed to the waiting nation. Soong Ching Ling, one of China's great modern fighters for people's rights and freedom, was dead.

Had it not been for Madame Soong Ching Ling, who gave us her blessing and facilitated our exit from China in 1964, I might never have had the opportunity to fulfill my dream of contributing to the reconciliation of China and the West. I would remain forever in her debt.

The government moved family members from the Peking Hotel to Cambodian Prince Sihanouk's former residence, at 15 Dong Jiao Min Xiang, to give us privacy during the state funeral. We spent most of the next several days greeting mourners at Madame Soong's lying-in-state in the Great Hall of the People. Her ashes were given to us on June 3 and the funeral cortege left for Shanghai the following morning. She had insisted that she be interred alongside her parents at the Wan Guo Public Cemetery, and this was done. The

Madame Soong Ching Ling lies in state with relatives standing by the bier to greet mourners, June 1981. Far right: Madame Soong's granddaughters, Pearl Sun Lin and Rose Sun

Banquet following the interment of Madame Soong Ching Ling in Shanghai, June 1981. Seated: Madame Deng Yingchao flanked by Rewi Alley and Pearl Sun Lin. Standing, left to right: Paul Tchang, Rose Sun Tchang, Eileen, and Paul

interment was followed by a banquet hosted by Deng Yingchao at the Jin Jiang Hotel. On June 5, after revisiting Madame Soong's grave, we drove to Nanjing to pay homage at Sun Yat-sen's mausoleum, as well as the tomb of Liao Zhongkai and He Xiangning, the parents of Liao Chengzhi. They were among several close comrades of Dr Sun who were buried at the Sun Yat-sen Mausoleum.

During the period of mourning after her death, Madame Soong's family issued a press release expressing deep appreciation to the people and government of the People's Republic of China for the meticulous ways in which they had cared for and honoured her; to the distinguished doctors and nurses who had laboured long hours to save her life and relieve her of any pain; to her faithful staff and lifelong companions who had provided so much help and solace during her illness. We were grateful to the thousands of individuals who had sent letters of love and concern. We were overwhelmed by the many moving tributes and condolences we received from people and governments around the world.

Madame Soong had dedicated her life to many noble causes – the liberation of China from internal and external oppression, world peace, and the welfare and education of children. Included in our press release was the announcement that Madame Soong's family planned to set up a foundation in her name to provide educational and cultural opportunities for youth and children – the causes closest to her heart. The foundation would be based in North America, but would seek to further this work in the spirit of international cooperation. Upon our return to Montreal on June 10, we established the Soong Ching Ling Children's Foundation of Canada, in memory of our dear friend and Aunty.

REMEMBERING MOTHER, 1889–1980

My mother, Choming Tsai Chen, passed away in Santa Monica, California, at the age of ninety-one. She outlived my father by twenty-seven years and was alert and lucid to the very end. In early December 1980, she suddenly asked my sister Mary to take her to the hospital, not because she was ill but because, she said, "It is time for me to go." The hospital transferred her to a hospice, where she left us three days after Christmas.

A memorial service was held on December 31 at St Augustine-by-the-Sea Episcopal Church. My sisters and I attended, as well as dozens of grandchildren, nieces, nephews, and close friends. Unfortunately, her two sons were unable to come. Paul and my younger brother George Chen, then in Washington, DC, working for China at the World Bank, had managed to have one last visit with her in hospital.

I still feel some guilt that I could not be there for Mother more often as she aged. Throughout her own turbulent life, she had supported us through thick and thin. Choming was not only a kind and wise mother to her children and a devoted companion to my father, but was a generous citizen,

who had helped to build two schools in China. One was in my father's village of Diankou, Zhejiang Province, where she shepherded us to safety after
the 1937 Japanese invasion of Shanghai. The village had only one tiny primary school, built in 1904 after the Boxer Rebellion. My mother made a
substantial donation and raised 20,000 yuan from Father's connections in
banking, political, and military circles, to build extensions for the village
school. When she visited in 1945, she was gratified to find it thriving, with
an enrollment of over 1,000 students. In October 2008, I went to Diankou
for the first time since 1937 and was pleasantly surprised that the village
elders still held my parents in great respect. The little village school, which
Mother had helped to expand during the war years, has now become a well-
endowed public school, providing education for children and teenagers at
kindergarten, primary, and secondary school levels.

   The success of Diankou inspired Choming to build another school in
Shanghai in 1946, which provided free education for poor children in her
neighbourhood. The school was erected on the empty lot next to our home,
which Mother had bought before the war. For building funds, she sold her
jewellery and valuables. This moved her Chinese and Western friends at the
International Church to pitch in with donations for the children. She was
elated when one day Madame Soong Ching Ling visited the school and
helped her to apply for surplus food – milk powder, cod liver oil, vitamins,
and cereals – from the United Nations Rehabilitation and Relief Administration. Although she moved to Hong Kong with Father in 1949, these small
schools remain her legacy to the New China.

AN INTERNATIONAL DIALOGUE WITH THE
CHINESE CHURCHES, 1981

Although the son of a clergyman, I had not been a regular churchgoer since
leaving the University of Michigan in 1943. However, I never repudiated the
social gospel values of my generation, and my ongoing involvement in the Chinese Students' Christian Association (CSCA) in the 1940s brought me many
lifelong Christian friends. I was therefore very interested to learn that, in the
wake of Deng Xiaoping's reforms, the churches in China had begun to reopen
their doors in 1979. Furthermore, discussions were underway for a 1981 conference to be held in Montreal, which would include Chinese Protestants and
Catholics. This would be the first time in thirty years that Chinese Christians

Choming's school in Shanghai, which provided free education, food, and medical care for poor children, 1946

Choming's last portrait at age 85, taken in Santa Barbara, California, spring 1974

Zhao Fusan, director of the
Institute of World Religions,
Chinese Academy of Social
Sciences, Montreal, 1981
(Photograph by
Wolf Kutnahorsky)

had joined fellow believers from around the world in theological discussion.
Zhao Fusan, formerly with the Chinese YMCA and now deputy director of the
Institute for the Study of World Religions at the Chinese Academy of Social
Sciences, had contacted me in the spring of 1980 about funds held for China
by the United Board for Christian Higher Education in Asia since 1951. Several months later, Ray Whitehead, director of the Canada China Program with
the Canadian Council of Churches, asked if I would open their Montreal
China conference – "God's Call to a New Beginning" – with remarks about
the Four Modernizations and China's reforms. I happily agreed.

On the evening of October 2, when I took the podium and looked out over
my audience, I could not help but smile. I felt a strong sense of *déjà vu* – so
many *lao pengyou* (old friends) from the springtime of my life! In the front sat
Bishop K.H. Ting, whose wife, Kuo Siu May, had followed me as general secretary of the CSCA in 1949. A few rows back were Cyril and Marjorie Powles,
whom I had met at Harvard through the ethicist Joseph Fletcher and who had
been present when I translated for the "Christian General" Feng Yuxiang in
1948, during his anti-KMT speaking tour. Katharine Hockin, a Student Christian Movement stalwart and China-born educator with the United Church of
Canada, had been at Columbia University when Eileen and I lived in New
York. I recognized Jiang Wenhan, who had been in charge of the Student Divi-

sion of the Chinese YMCA when he came to New York to complete his doctorate on patriotic student activism. (I later learned from Eileen that he was actually related to her mother). Zhao Fusan sat near the back of the audience, a few chairs down from James Endicott, who had been a plenary speaker at a CSCA conference alongside Owen Lattimore and Israel Epstein. Born in China, an ordained minister in the United Church of Canada, Endicott had once worked with Madame Chiang Kai-shek in her New Life Movement, but after two years had quit in disgust at KMT corruption. He later became a staunch supporter of New China and Mao's socialist revolution, which made him *persona non grata* in the United Church during the 1950s.

Feeling at home, I spoke briefly about the changes afoot in China since 1978 and the inauguration of economic reforms. My central point was that the Chinese leadership was not taking the "capitalist road," but was seeking to raise the living standards of the people through a mixed market economy, after more than a decade of ultra-leftist policies. The egalitarian goals of the 1949 revolution remained paramount. It was the strategy – seeking truth from facts – that had changed. I counselled patience and expressed hope that outsiders would not rush to judgment concerning China's reforms.

It has struck me in the past thirty years, and particularly in the sixteen or so years since I have returned to Canada, that there is something about China which inspires possessive instincts in the observer. There are those of the left who, when China is militant, will defend her to the very end, regardless of the realities. And there are those of the right who will disapprove of anything that has the label of the Chinese Communist movement on it. Neither of these categories of people regards China as belonging to the Chinese themselves, first and foremost; yet it is the Chinese people's aspirations, hopes, and concerns that must be the basic thrust of China's process of transformation today ...

This conference is a new beginning. It is new because we are now ready to communicate with China on an equal basis of mutual respect. It is this mutual respect, this equality of status, this concern for and sharing of enormously difficult human problems, which will make possible a new beginning. The Chinese are attempting to telescope into one or two generations the two or three hundred years of human trauma and suffering that Europe and the West experienced. That process is bound to be difficult, complex, and full of ups and downs. But in God's name, it is working.

MADAME MARIE THÉRÈSE CASGRAIN, 1896–1981

We received the sad news in early November 1981 that our dear friend the Hon. Marie Thérèse Casgrain, had died. We paid our last respects at her service at St Leon's Church in Montreal.

It was our privilege to have met Madame Casgrain soon after our arrival at McGill, through Jean Louis and Hélène Gagnon. All three were prominent French Canadians who had long been actively involved in Canada's political, social, and cultural circles. Madame Casgrain was an early campaigner for women's suffrage in Quebec. In 1946 she joined the Co-operative Commonwealth Federation (CCF), which later became the NDP, to promote labour and social welfare policies centred on the common good. In 1961 she founded the Quebec branch of the Voice of Women, a movement dedicated to world peace. She opposed the US war in Vietnam and was very open to New China. Over the years we shared many China-related occasions with her, especially following the establishment of Canada-China relations in 1970. She had also introduced us to her circle of progressive friends, whose warm welcome was a blessing after the chilly reception we had received in British Columbia when we first arrived in 1964. Her death was a great loss for us and marked an end to our seventeen-year sojourn in French Canada.

RETIREMENT FROM McGILL

By September 1981, I had decided to request early retirement from McGill. As much as I enjoyed teaching and working with graduate students, the university had not made the Centre for East Asian Studies a priority, with the result that we were always scrambling for funds. Moreover, my own intellectual concerns and fields of research (development strategies of the People's Republic of China and China's relations with the West) significantly diverged from the academic and organizational priorities of the History department, in which I was paid to teach. My colleagues had displayed little interest in the work of the Centre for East Asian Studies, which I believed was of strategic importance to McGill's future as a university of international standing.

I made the decision with some reluctance, because I derived considerable satisfaction from teaching, but decided I would rather devote my time to research, writing, and consulting. In addition, I had undertaken tasks outside my teaching duties, which had become more onerous. Some were directly related to the university (the establishment of academic exchange programs with China), others only indirectly (my activities as senior adviser to the Canada China Trade Council). And after Madame Soong's death, I was involved in building cross-cultural educational programs on behalf of the Soong Ching Ling Children's Foundation of Canada.

Above all, I wanted to finally write a book on contemporary China, which had not been brought to fruition due to the unreliability of earlier data I had collected. I believed it essential to continue my efforts to bring China and the West into dialogue about issues critical to world peace. Considerations of health also played a role in my decision to apply for retirement. In truth, I was exhausted by my constant travel and multiple consulting projects.

McGill's principal, Dr David Johnston, graciously hosted a farewell party for me at the Faculty Club in December 1981, attended by many colleagues, students, and friends. Dr Johnston noted that when I arrived at McGill in 1965, after fifteen years in Beijing, "the People's Republic of China, the new China, was virtually a complete mystery in the West." He spoke about my creation of the Department of East Asian Languages and Literatures, which had introduced the first Chinese (and later Japanese) language and literature courses to a student body in Eastern Canada. And he had warm words for the Centre for East Asian Studies, which now offered a multi-disciplinary degree program, was instrumental in bringing to the university visiting professors from both China and Japan, and had established an exchange program between McGill and Peking University. These activities had drawn students from across the world "who knew him to have an 'open-door' policy and to be a professor who gets deeply involved with his students."

He mentioned my role in the founding of the Canada China Business Council and my involvement in many organizations that furthered understanding between East and West. "Paul has worked unceasingly to clarify the position of China at a time when that was neither popular nor academically rewarding. He has been instrumental in creating literally thousands of opportunities for people to visit China and to get to know the new Republic."

In closing, Dr Johnston honoured me with these words: "For McGill, Paul Lin leaves behind a tradition of understanding, teaching, and involvement with East Asian countries. And well beyond McGill's hallowed halls, where historians will no doubt work out the great imponderable forces that changed the international configuration of the powers in the 1970s, it must be recognized that, in human terms, it was Paul Lin who has so often been at the heart of the process that has led to a greater understanding between the great number of people who are represented by the People's Republic of China and the people of Canada."

In response, I expressed my heartfelt appreciation for the good wishes expressed by Principal Johnston and my other colleagues. "Your gift – the magnificent silhouette painting of the great writer Lu Xun – hangs in my study, and will always evoke warm feelings of my association with you," I said.

I left the farewell party with mixed feelings. I knew my decision to retire was timely, but my experience at McGill had been intellectually enriching and I would miss my many friends in the university community. In the years that followed I was proud that many of my students took up China-related posts in government, the media, higher education, and international trade. What more could a teacher ask for?

Part Four

1982–2004

Chapter Sixteen

UNIVERSITY OF EAST ASIA, MACAU

In the swift flow of political and economic events, I remained essentially an academic. I retired from McGill in 1982 to move to Vancouver, intending to do some long-delayed writing. But a few years later, I was offered the post of rector of the University of East Asia (UEA) in Macau, a Portuguese colony in southeast China. I could not resist the challenge of building a university that would play a key role in training students from Macau to run their own Special Administrative Zone, when the territory reverted to Chinese sovereignty in 1999.

UEA embraced five colleges: the University College, Junior College, and Polytechnic College were situated in Macau; the Graduate College and Open College were in Hong Kong.

The Macau campus was situated on Taipa, a picturesque island linked to Macau City by a bridge. It had been founded in 1981 by a Hong Kong company, Ricci Island West (RIW), on land provided by the Portuguese colonial government of Macau. In the spring of 1986, RIW's president, Peter Eng, came to Vancouver to offer me the new position of rector. After one of my frequent trips to China in late June, I toured UEA with Eng and his managing director K.K. Wong. I later met their third partner, Edward Woo, a lawyer. They told me, "The mandate of the rector is to establish an academic reputation and to make the university a world-renowned institution."

I was installed as rector at the university's fourth congregation on October 25, 1986. In my opening remarks I reflected upon the importance of education, and how my experiences in Canada, the United States, and China had deepened my belief that education was the key to the modernization of the entire East Asia region. The University of East Asia, Macau, had an exciting

View of the University of East Asia on Taipa Island, Macau, from the banks of the Pearl River

opportunity to bridge the psychological and intellectual distances of the Pacific Ocean, leading to deeper mutual understanding between the peoples on both sides.

The topic of my inaugural address was "Holistic Education," wherein I urged young people not to pursue simply technical know-how, which would be a grave misinterpretation of modernization. "A university should not deal with just the practicality of the day," I said. "It should provide students with opportunities during their few years of study, to consider the meaning of their life and work, the role they wish to play in their historical era. In addition to their chosen fields of specialization, they should also learn more about culture, history, and subjects which will enrich their spiritual lives and expand their intellectual horizons."

✒ While Paul was immersed in his mandate to revamp UEA into a "world-renowned academic institution," I remained in Canada for several months. Packing up again, so soon after moving to Vancouver from Montreal, was daunting – but I did not begrudge Paul this opportunity. Cousin Yao Yilin, with whom Paul had consulted so often in Beijing, agreed with me that being a university president was a most fitting career for him.

I joined Paul on November 4, 1986. Over the years I had passed through Macau several times, but had never stopped to explore the island. This time, however, I discovered its unique character. The main street was like a little Hong Kong – crowded and chaotic with pedestrians and traffic jams, lined with small shops selling curios, antiques, and daily necessities. Yet meandering away from the downtown and following narrow side streets, I found the remains of grand Mediterranean architecture, European churches, old Chinese temples, museums, and gardens. In the residential area, all government mansions were painted pink. Of course, garish casinos were part of the landscape too. A dozen were operating by the late 1980s, including a floating casino and one located in the lavish Hotel Lisboa.

CONFERRING HONORARY DOCTORATES ON TWO WORLD STATESMEN

A highlight of my tenure as rector of UEA was conferring honorary doctorates on two world statesmen – Henry Kissinger in March and Pierre Trudeau in October of 1987. The degrees were awarded in recognition of their historic roles in facilitating the resumption of relations between China and the West. I often reminded people that China had experienced two "open door" policies – one at the end of the nineteenth century when China's door was kicked open by uninvited marauders, and the other near the end of the twentieth century when she opened her door with dignity, in response to a respectful knock.

I conferred an honorary Doctor of Law degree on the former US secretary of state on March 5, 1987. Kissinger spoke on the topic of "America and East Asia, a Partnership for World Growth and Stability." His acceptance of an honorary degree from an unknown, private university in Macau stirred much curiosity and interest in the Hong Kong press. Years later, a Chinese friend told me that before making his decision on UEA's invitation, Kissinger had sought advice from the Chinese ambassador in Washington DC, who had diplomatically recommended he accept the honour.

Upon Kissinger's arrival in Macau, while riding alone with him by limousine into town, I asked if he recalled sending Ernst Winter to Montreal in 1970 to see me about President Nixon's desire to visit China. Kissinger replied, "Yes, of course, but why did the Chinese take so long to respond?" It was a question for which I had no answer.

As rector of the University of East Asia, Paul (centre) conferred honorary doctorates on (left to right) British historian Lord Briggs, Governor Michado de Macau, Henry Kissinger, and Lord Kadoorie, March 1987.

VISIT TO PORTUGAL, APRIL 1987

At the invitation of the Portuguese Ministry of Education, I attended a meeting of the Council of Portuguese Rectors in Lisbon on April 6, 1987. Eileen and I arrived in Portugal on March 31, stopping first in Porto, home of the famous "port" wine. Porto is the second-largest city in Portugal, unique for its thriving industry and commerce, as well as its magnificent baroque monuments and colourful medieval quarter. From Porto we went to Portugal's capital of Lisbon for my meeting. Afterward, we visited half a dozen universities in Lisbon and then traveled to the University of Coimbra, dating back to the year 1290. We completed our tour in the intriguing city of Braga, home to the University of Minho.

The visit gave Eileen and me significant insight into the makeup and worldview of the Portuguese people – their long history, rich culture, scenic landscape, warm hospitality, and pride in their institutions of higher learning. We could not tarry, however, because I was due in Beijing on April 12 to attend Premier Zhao Ziyang's state banquet for the Portuguese prime minister, Anibal Cavaco Silva. The two formally signed the Joint Declaration on the Question of Macau on April 13, 1987. Under the terms of the Sino-Portuguese agreement, sovereignty over Macau would be restored to China on December 20, 1999. I was among the guests from Macau invited to witness the signing ceremony.

MY VISION AS RECTOR

In June 1987, at UEA's eighth congregation, I restated my understanding of the major challenges faced by the university: "A shortage of local professionals at all levels, and especially in the higher echelons of government and management, is the most serious problem in Macau's twelve-year lead-up to the Chinese takeover in 1999," I said. I then announced that to help increase the number of professionals, the first teacher-training program at the university would be launched in the next academic year. Furthermore, ambitious new proposals were under review to establish a law school, a language centre for translation and interpretation, a centre for Portuguese language and culture, a centre for design and industrial innovation, and a medical advisory services program, and to expand open education and extension programs.

To ensure a smooth transition after 1999, I believed it was vitally important to conduct studies of various sectors of Macau society. On June 1, 1987, the Institute of Macau Studies was founded at the University of East Asia. The Institute's primary objective was the scientific analysis of Macau society, from the standpoint of Macau's people in broad historical and geographical context. The Institute's new publication, *The Journal of Macau Studies*, was designed to serve the same purpose. I wrote in my foreword to the first issue of the journal:

Macau is an extraordinary historical anomaly. Though part of Chinese territory, it has been administered by Portugal for over four centuries. It has a remarkable history as an international entrepôt of trade and was an early crossroads of culture and thought between China and the West. Today it flourishes as a free port on the fringe of the burgeoning economy of China. On December 20, 1999, Macau will become a Special Administrative Region of China, preserving its own socio-economic system within the broad design of China's "one country, two systems" policy. The transition is to be a unique, peaceful twelve-year changeover from the old order to the new, and the process has already begun ...

Although the focus is on Macau, it would be self-defeating to narrow this focus into an isolated view of the territory. Because of its historical role, Macau has built up a vast web of relationships ... These relationships are with Guangzhou and the Pearl River Delta, with the other "open" special regions of Zhuhai, Shengzhen, and of course Hong Kong, but they also extend to the rest of China, the Pacific region, and beyond – to the countries of the world, which are its economic lifeline and enrich its intellectual and cultural heritage. To understand the nature of these relationships is to begin to find new, creative ways of enhancing Macau's future role in the world.

After a year as rector, I began the fall term full of enthusiasm and with further plans for the university. Former Canadian prime minister Pierre Elliott Trudeau received an honorary Doctor of Law degree from the University of East Asia on October 6, 1987. Trudeau had just completed an arduous journey from Pakistan through the Karakoram Pass into China's most western Xinjiang Province. He had then flown east to Beijing and had cruised the Three Gorges of the Yangtze River, before arriving in Macau. Although his visit was brief, Eileen and I thoroughly enjoyed seeing the former prime minister again and received a warm letter from him several months later. "I cannot tell you enough how grateful I am. In offering me a doctorate from the UEA you were doing more than honouring me, you were associating me with an event of historical significance: The establishment of firm and friendly relations between Canada and China ... And, of course, getting there was half the fun! ... A thousand thanks for the arrangements, which not only made dreams come true, but uncovered a reality which surpassed even the dreams."

The visit from Trudeau also gave me the opportunity to reflect upon my Canadian and Chinese commitments, which had so shaped my life. James Rusk, senior correspondent of Canada's *Globe and Mail* who accompanied Trudeau on his trip, wrote an article about me and the sense of mistrust with which I was perceived in Canada. He referred to me as a "firebrand Chinese nationalist" in my youth and as "one of the most controversial figures in Chinese-Canadian affairs." He reminded readers that in 1950 I had marched on Beijing's Tiananmen Square in China's National Day parade and, when I returned to Canada in 1964 and advocated the establishment of Canada-China relations, I had drawn "the fire of supporters of Taiwan's Kuomintang Government, including the late Tory leader John Diefenbaker, who attacked Mr Trudeau in the Commons for his relationship" with me. Rusk continued: "Ideal as his background may be for an intellectual bridging between East and West – ethnically Chinese, schooled in Chinese values by his family, but academically trained in the West – Prof. Lin's position as a man caught between two cultures and two modes of involvement, study, and activism has left him open to criticism from all directions."

He was right. In an interview I had told Rusk: "This business of being a sort of amphibious character between two worlds is part and parcel of my life. I don't think there has been one moment when I felt, however, that I lost my

Top: Paul welcomes former Canadian prime minister Pierre Trudeau, October 1987.

Bottom: Paul confers an honorary Doctor of Law degree on former Canadian prime minister Pierre Trudeau, October 1987.

integrity. One could easily have bent with the wind. I think my wife will tell you that, in my whole life, it is precisely because I have not bent with the wind that has landed me in controversy."

I told him that I had never joined the Communist or any other party, adding: "I think I would be the worst party member possible, just because I have no respect for dogma or even for a show of feeling for any institution."

PORTUGUESE INTERESTS IN MACAU

In contrast to his predecessor, who reportedly had no interest in UEA because its teaching language was English, the newly minted governor of Macau, Carlos Melancia, suggested that he could play a more effective role if he were given an academic post. The university responded by installing him as chancellor in October 1987, at the same convocation at which Trudeau accepted an honorary degree. In his address, Governor Melancia said that the existence of a university like the UEA was an "absolute necessity" for Macau, but as the sole property of a private enterprise, he believed its development would be hindered. The solution, he declared, would be to place the university under the control of a public non-profit foundation, with its main centre of operations based in Macau. The participants of the foundation would include the local government, philanthropists, and academic institutions, which would guarantee the university's educational quality and ensure its degrees were recognized. In his view, the professional training of local technical personnel was the government's foremost concern and "as the only institution of higher learning in Macau, the UEA can assume a most important role." He added, "Since most courses are now taught in English, there will be an increase in subjects to be taught in the Portuguese and Chinese languages."

Without fully grasping the ramifications of Governor Melancia's new policy, I responded enthusiastically and applauded his installation as chancellor. I thought it was positive that the Macau Government was willing to put significant resources into UEA, with the commitment of developing Macau's human resources for the twenty-first century.

Two weeks later, the full extent of the government's plans became clear. The Macau Government Information Service issued a press release stating that the Council of Portuguese Rectors in Lisbon had formed a team to work out a Portuguese-language curriculum for the University of East Asia in Macau. It also stated that negotiations were underway for the government's purchase of UEA. Agreement was imminent.

I was dumbfounded. I had been kept in the dark regarding the details of these negotiations and had just told the *Macau Daily News* that UEA was not being sold, but that the government was planning to set up a foundation to help the university solve its financial problems and participate in its development. This was based on my discussions with Governor Melancia a few days before, in which he assured me that the academic and administrative independence of the university would be preserved.

A seeming urgency to popularize Portuguese language and culture in the waning years of colonial rule had recently surfaced in the local press. At the invitation of Governor Melancia, the wife of President Mario Soares of Portugal arrived to attend Macau's first International Music Festival. Well-known for her interest in Portuguese education, she toured a number of Macau's Chinese and Portuguese schools. She seemed perplexed to discover how few educators or students spoke Portuguese and declared that, in light of Macau's return to China in 1999, the teaching of Portuguese should be vigorously promoted.

When Madame Soares visited the University of East Asia, Eileen and I were on hand to greet her and her party. I briefed her on the educational goals and curriculum of the university. Madame Soares responded that she hoped UEA would train more students in the Portuguese language and strengthen the cultural ties between Macau and Portugal. "Even after sovereignty is transferred back to China," she said, "I trust that Macau will preserve its Portuguese cultural identity." She asked Eileen, "Why is it that so few people in Macau speak Portuguese?" Eileen replied diplomatically that for centuries Chinese in Macau were not encouraged to learn Portuguese, and this seemed to be the official policy of the Portuguese Government. Madame Soares responded, "This was a wrong policy and I will report it back to the president."

THE PURCHASE OF UEA

Dr Jorge Rangel, the Macau Government's UEA representative, officially announced the purchase of the University of East Asia by the Macau Government on December 7, 1987. He noted pointedly in his remarks that "the Administrative Committee, under the Macau Foundation's Board of Trustees, will be in charge of the administration and policies of the UEA. The Rector will be responsible only for academic work."

On December 19, a declaration was signed by Governor Carlos Melancia, in his capacity as the president of the Macau Foundation, with the founders of Ricci Island West, Peter Eng, Edward Woo, and K.K. Wong, to buy UEA and take over its finances. The local press commented on the exceptionally good deal Ricci Island West had made. Not only did RIW realize five times its original investment, but the original owners were also able to retain the university's two money-making colleges in Hong Kong – the Graduate College and the Open College.

The purchase of the University of East Asia by the Portuguese colonial government of Macau created major dilemmas for me as rector. Governor Melancia immediately appointed a Board of Trustees with indefinite terms of office. Under this Board were three committees (administrative, advisory, and supervisory), which replaced the previous structure. Before the Macau Foundation took control, the rector of the university had been a full member of all the committees and the Board. Under the new system the rector would be permitted to attend the Board's meetings, but would have no voice. Furthermore, Dr Rangel – the Macau Government's representative at UEA – was appointed chairman of the administrative committee, which meant that he held the highest administrative position in the university. This contravened the University Charter prohibiting any member of the foundation from holding high office and violated Article 76 of Portugal's Constitution guaranteeing university independence. In countries with academic freedom throughout the world, those who are responsible for funding do not assume academic posts, to prevent them from controlling the university's direction of development.

A second concern for me was that the Portuguese Government had begun to assert their language and culture only now, twelve years before their departure from Macau. It looked like a policy drawn up in panic, when they suddenly realized that they would leave without a legacy. The Macau Government was now allocating 70% of its education budget to a small number of schools that used Portuguese as the teaching medium, with only 30% going to Chinese schools, of which there were many more. Primary schools had a choice to teach or not to teach Portuguese, but those that did not would be denied government subsidies. While I did not oppose the teaching of Portuguese, I felt that education should meet the needs of the people of Macau first, and that the government should give them the right to choose the kind of language education they desired.

Just before Christmas 1987, I sent a lengthy memo to K.K. Wong with copies to his RIW partners, Peter Eng and Edward Woo, who had originally recruited me for the position of rector. I had met with Wong and Eng earlier in the month, but my request to examine the exact proposals governing the university's new structure was rebuffed and I was accused of displaying a "lack of trust." As rector, I had the right and the need to examine what those proposals were in order to carry out my mandate. I reminded Wong that when I accepted the post, my mandate was to discharge my duties as the "principal administrative and academic officer of the university" and that from my long academic experience, I could not conceive of any university president being willing to accept the consequences of a major university decision on which he was not even consulted.

I went on to assert that the university, including the academic staff that is its vital core, was a vibrant intellectual community with its own goals and interests, and not a mere "possession" of its "owners" or "managers" to be bought or sold like chattel. I felt that the university's own needs and objectives had not been given the careful consideration they deserved. I also failed to comprehend why it took so much effort on my part to gain the inclusion of even a simple clause to ensure the autonomy of the university, in the joint sales agreement signed on December 20 between Ricci Island West and the Portuguese colonial government of Macau.

I concluded that the University of East Asia, as I had envisioned it and as it had been presented to me, had changed fundamentally with the university's sale to the Macau Government. The notion of government control (veiled or otherwise), which had been introduced into the university, manifest in the emasculation of the Board of Trustees, did not sit easily with me. The new situation was not conducive to the hopes and plans that had attracted me to UEA and I knew that I could not remain in my role as rector. With great regret I announced my intention to resign within six months.

MY RESIGNATION AS RECTOR

Peter Eng, chairman of the UEA Executive Committee, announced my resignation publicly in January 1988. While expressing profound regrets, Eng explained, "the Rector's resignation was purely for personal reasons. Professor Lin firmly believes that since he has accomplished most of the major projects he set out to do, it is time for a younger person to administer the UEA."

My own announcement followed the next day and provided a different explanation. I straightforwardly told reporters that my resignation was due to differences in academic policy with the Macau Government. The catalyst was the Macau Foundation, which had moved to take complete control of UEA, deliberately undermining the authority of the rector's office. I understood that this had been done in order to prevent the university from being under

Director Ji Pengfei of the Hong Kong and Macau Affairs Office receives Paul, 1987.

"Beijing's direct influence," as Macau moved toward its 1999 return to China. On the same day that I announced my resignation, the *Macau Tribune* reported that during negotiations between China and Portugal in 1986–87, I had often been received in Beijing and Guangzhou by Ji Pengfei of the Hong Kong and Macau Affairs Office. At these meetings, Director Ji had expressed his desire that UEA would train Macau personnel who would be able to run Macau after the handover, and I had agreed. According to the *Tribune*, however, "these views aroused the Macau Portuguese government's suspicion and misgivings. They are concerned that large numbers of 'Chinese-style' human resources will be trained by UEA under Beijing's influence. Such a scenario would be detrimental to their strategic goal of preserving Portuguese cultural traditions in Macau after 1999. To ensure that UEA train 'Portuguese-style' human resources, the Macau government, through the purchase of UEA, diminished the Rector's power and took control of the university in order to minimize China's influence."

On February 11, 1988, the Macau *Tai Chung Po* published an open statement issued by UEA's Faculty Association, urging me to remain as rector. "In the one year since Professor Lin Ta Kuang became UEA's Rector, the University's development has been accelerated. Academic research has received unprecedented importance. The University's goal to serve Macau is clearer than ever before. We members of the Faculty Association are fully convinced

Top: Banner hung by UEA students urging "Rector, Please Stay with Us," February 1988

Bottom: UEA students present Paul with a large fan with hundreds of signatures expressing their appreciation, March 1988.

of Rector Lin's charismatic leadership, and are deeply impressed by his work ethic – his willingness to bear the burden of his office, his impartiality, and his perseverance in times of adversity. It is very necessary to have Rector Lin continue administering the affairs of the University, after its transfer to the Macau Foundation, so that he could lay a sound base for its future development."

Following the faculty association's public statement, the student unions of three colleges hung long strips of yellow cloth on college buildings with the message, in both English and Chinese: "Rector, Please Stay with Us." They also launched a signature drive protesting my departure and on March 2 presented me with a list of some 700 students who hoped I would change my mind. I responded that I was deeply moved by their appeals and hoped they would understand my decision to step down. At my farewell luncheon, the students gave me a huge fan covered with hundreds of signatures, expressing appreciation of their "good teacher and helpful friend." UEA faculty and staff hosted a banquet for me that evening, where they presented me with a majestic painting of a large old pine on top of a mountain, inscribed with a Chinese poem. The English translation read: "Upon a high mount, stands a giant tree. The harder the wind blows, the firmer it grows."

Several factors had contributed to my decision to resign at this time. Of central importance was that by resigning first, I would have six months when I could still work for UEA, free from the stigma of personal interest. My major aims were, first, that the university acquire some form of administrative independence, outside the jurisdiction of ownership; second, that UEA would become an academic institution that could study Macau issues without reference to politics; and third, that a Senate be established within the university to exercise democratic management.

CHINA'S INTERESTS IN MACAU AFFAIRS

The question of China's relationship with Macau was a sensitive one, on both sides. In an interview a few months after my resignation from UEA, Shi Hua of the *Hong Kong Nineties Monthly* asked me directly: "What is the attitude of the Chinese side, in regard to obtaining the administrative rights, autonomy, and self-determination from the Portuguese authorities, in order for Macau to be run by the Macau people in 1999?" I answered that China seemed to fear that interfering in the affairs of Macau might cause repercussions in Hong Kong. In fact, before the signing of the Sino-Portuguese Joint Declaration, Chinese interventions were routine, but after the signing they became cautious because of Hong Kong's scheduled return to China in 1997. Yet Macau was quite different from Hong Kong. Portugal never regarded Macau as an independent entity to be developed on its own, and both the personnel and policies of the Macau Government were very much affected by domestic political changes in Portugal. Each governor came with his entourage with the primary goal of working, some might say "grabbing," for a few years before returning home. Unlike the British, who had a long-term strategy for their colony, Portugal had done little for Macau in terms of education and the training of human resources. Localization of civil servants existed only at the lowest rank, with none at the managerial level. The upper and lower echelons of the government literally spoke different languages. The majority Chinese population and the tiny community of Portuguese lived separate lives, with little interchange or communication. In Hong Kong, the localization of personnel by the British Government had a long history, so there was no real need for China to worry about "the running of Hong Kong by the Hong Kong people." But in Macau, there were many problems of capacity and the Portuguese seemed to want to train Macau personnel, Portuguese-style. If China was to be concerned about how to build a solid administration in Macau – run by the local people trained to be civil servants, professionals, and even political leaders with real power – who could blame them for that? It would only create a sense of stability among the people.

But as I said to Shi Hua, "the Chinese side seems hesitant to voice their opinion on this matter." On March 14, 1988, I had received a warm letter from Lu Ping, an old friend currently serving as Beijing's deputy director of the Hong Kong and Macau Affairs Office. He wrote, "Respected Rector: With profound regrets, I learnt recently of Your Excellency's decision to resign as Rector of the University of East Asia. Your Excellency's wholehearted devotion to develop UEA, and nurture and train qualified personnel, is deeply appreciated by compatriots in Hong Kong, Macau, China and abroad ... With sincere hope and in great anticipation for your reconsideration." I appreciated Lu Ping's sincere sentiments, but knew this was the extent to which the Chinese Government was willing to intervene in the University of East Asia's affairs.

MY FINAL CONGREGATION AND DEPARTURE

My last congregation as rector was held on March 26, 1988 – the seventh anniversary of UEA's founding. In my farewell remarks, I addressed the tensions that had arisen over language requirements and the vital question of freedom within the university. I said: "Freedom refers to academic freedom. A true university must fulfill its most basic role, which is leading the quest for truth without fear or favour. That is why it must jealously safeguard its academic freedom, with sufficient administrative and financial autonomy to support it. The debate on academic freedom has been going on for years, and in some places for centuries, all over the world. In Portugal, this debate resulted in the autonomy of universities being guaranteed in Article 76 of the Constitution of the Republic." I also spoke at some length about specific initiatives that I thought would strengthen the university and concluded with high hopes for UEA's future.

Paul, pictured here with Governor Melancia of Macau, attends his last convocation at UEA, 1988.

The *Wah Kiu Po* reported the next day: "Both Governor Melancia and Rector Lin addressed the event, each enunciating his own views. As Governor of Macau and Chancellor of the University, Mr Melancia emphasized that a century ago, the Portuguese were able to build the first lighthouse along the shores of South China to serve coastal navigation and that they are definitely capable today of turning the University of East Asia into a cultural lighthouse for the twenty-first century. Lin Ta Kuang stressed that Macau is part of China and its population is 97 per cent Chinese. The Portuguese administration is a heritage left by history and UEA is now working for the future and not the past of Macau." I appreciated the reporter's insight and knew that most of his readers would agree.

Stepping down as rector of the University of East Asia in Macau was a wrenching disappointment for me, but politics, greed, and colonial arrogance had conspired to cut the ground from beneath my feet. I felt certain both the university and Macau would flourish in the future, but I would follow their progress from the other side of the Pacific.

Chapter Seventeen

FROM IDEALISM TO IDEALISTIC
PRAGMATISM

We left Hong Kong on June 18, 1988. After a reunion with our son Douglas and his family in Santa Cruz, California, we re-established our residence in Vancouver in early July. I resumed my research and writing, consulting, public speaking, and community activities. The Soong Ching Ling Children's Foundation claimed more of my time, and soon I was involved as a research associate and later honorary professor in the Institute of Asian Research at the University of British Columbia. How times had changed since my return to Canada in 1964!

STUDENT PROTESTS, SPRING 1989

On April 15, 1989, Hu Yaobang, former general secretary of the Chinese Communist Party, passed away. He had been forced to resign in 1987 for being too tolerant of intellectuals' calls for political reform, which the Old Guard dubbed "bourgeois liberalization." Similar to the outpouring of grief for Premier Zhou Enlai in the spring of 1976, students flocked to Tiananmen Square to honour Hu. Despite being told to go home, more than 30,000 students marched to the square the night before his funeral and refused to leave. On April 26, the *People's Daily* condemned the demonstrations as "counter-revolutionary." This enraged the students, who considered themselves patriotic. On May 13, some students began a hunger strike and increasingly the world press broadcast their demands. The government declared martial law on May 20.

Bishop K.H. Ting and Kuo Siu
May visit Canada, April 1989.

At the same time that tensions were building in Beijing, I was occupied with
the Vancouver Board of Trade, the Dr Sun Yat-sen Classical Chinese Garden,
and meeting with visiting Chinese dignitaries. Li Dan, one of the first Chinese
students at McGill in the 1970s, brought over a delegation from Radio Peking
and I was delighted to welcome my old colleague Li De Lun, a renowned conductor from China, who performed as guest conductor one evening for the
Vancouver Symphony Orchestra. Our good friends Bishop K.H. Ting and his
wife, Kuo Siu May, were also in town in early May before flying to Toronto,
where both received honorary doctorates from Victoria College at the University of Toronto. Siu May had taught in the Foreign Languages department of
the University of Nanjing since the 1950s and was being especially honoured
for her book *Venturing into the Bible*, a text for Chinese university students
that explains the many biblical references found in English literature and
speech. Harsh work conditions during the Cultural Revolution had exacer-
bated her rheumatoid arthritis, and Siu May was now in a wheelchair, but her
keen intellect and quick wit were untarnished. After their return to Nanjing in
late May, she wrote to thank us for our hospitality, adding: "Because of difficulty in securing train tickets, we spent one extra day in Shanghai, staying
at the YMCA guesthouse. We saw much of the student demonstrations. I bet
you've never seen anything like it: so orderly, so well-organized, and such a

rapport between them and the on-lookers! The placards showing their demands express the opinions of the general public. No wonder they were greeted by clapping and laughter. Things have taken a drastic turn, of late, we don't quite know how matters will develop, but I am sure in the long run, God is on the side of the people."

I was following events in China closely and on May 28 I sent warm greetings to be read at a rally in Toronto in support of the students at Tiananmen Square. "This movement will go down in history as a landmark in China's struggle for democracy," I wrote. "The students have won a preliminary victory in their fight against official corruption, arbitrary rule, and abuses of privilege which endanger the people's rights, economic reform, and China's modernization. The success of their non-violent, orderly demonstrations has given them new confidence to defend themselves against intimidation and outright suppression. In the short term, we should not be surprised that there will be some setbacks and suffering. But martial law and the use of armed force against the people is the last resort of those who have lost their legitimacy as leaders of the nation. We call on them not to take reprisals against students, intellectuals, and others who truly express the soul of the nation. If this happens, it will be a dark day for them and for China. But the only enduring result will be a further reawakening of the people."

Students from Beijing's Central Academy of Arts sculpted a Goddess of Democracy, an iconic "sister" to the American Statue of Liberty. When they rolled the statue into Tiananmen Square on May 30, however, I worried that the students had gone too far. At least symbolically, the demonstrations seemed to have moved from demands for democratic reform to calls for an American-style political system. The legitimacy of the Chinese Communist Party was now at stake. Less than a week later, on June 4, violence exploded in and around Tiananmen Square.

Although I had lived in Canada since 1964, I was not considered a foreigner in China and the Chinese leadership had generally been very friendly to me. When I had criticisms, I shared them first in Beijing before raising them in Western circles. The Western press continued to be generally hostile to the People's Republic and I had no desire to help them further bash China. After June 4, however, my posture changed. By opening fire on and slaughtering its own citizens, I believed the Chinese Government had committed a crime against the people. The regime had made a qualitative change and I had to speak out in condemnation. I also felt it was my duty to "speak truth to power" on behalf of friends and colleagues in China who had been silenced by the government's violence.

"Goddess of Democracy" replica statue at the
University of British Columbia, Vancouver

The media had pestered me all spring for comment on the student demonstrations and an avalanche of requests followed after the tanks rolled into
Beijing. I wrote a commentary for CBC Radio which aired on June 8. I will
reproduce my exact words here, for they reflect so well the outrage I felt at
that time.

The Tiananmen massacre will be recorded as a day of infamy in the
annals of human experience. The world has reacted with deep shock. The
Chinese army had previously been widely seen as a people-oriented,
people-supported, people's army. Perhaps the trigger-happy 27th Army
running amok in Tiananmen Square was an anomaly. Yet its character
had been in the making for years. Despite the Chinese Communist Party's
dictum that "the Party controls the gun, the gun shall not control the
Party," the 27th was in fact for years personally loyal to General Yang

Shangkun, who is now President of China. This is reminiscent of the dreaded tradition of the warlords. Hardened by its role in the Vietnam War and equipped with modern firepower, this army was accustomed to mindless obedience to superior orders. Its commanding officers undoubtedly were trained not to question punitive slaughter. This was, as the old adage goes, killing chickens to scare the monkeys – a way of keeping control over an intimidated population ...

It is certain that once military force has been used against the people, any such regime cannot sustain itself without continued use of force. We can, therefore, expect a period of military or military-backed rule. But in the long perspective of history, the Chinese people have learned a costly lesson: democracy and people's rights cannot be bestowed from above. They must be won by popular initiative and hard struggle. They must then be institutionalized permanently into the fabric of political life and made immune from the vagaries of leadership. Especially in China, this means overcoming the feudal culture of patriarchal and nepotistic relations that frustrate people's power.

On June 20, I addressed a memorial meeting held at the Plaza of Nations in Vancouver. In struggling to understand the reasons behind the massacre, I reflected briefly on the decade since Deng Xiaoping had initiated economic reforms and opened China to the world. The grievances of the Chinese people had been mounting for years. Absolute power was held by an entrenched and increasingly corrupt elite, who had largely funnelled the fruits of economic reform into their own pockets. While they paid lip service to socialist ideals, the common people had become the victims of their corruption. This had resulted in the polarization of wealth, spiralling inflation, shortages of food and raw materials, unemployment, and the degradation of unpaid workers and professionals seeking to survive by every means available.

"June 4, 1989, will go down in history as a day of infamy," I said, "but also as a turning point in China's continuing revolution. A regime that has lost all human feeling has committed a massacre of its own people on a scale beyond belief. History has shown that a regime that turns its guns on its own people begins the process of its own downfall – and thereby also starts a new, deeper, and broader stage in the struggle for democracy." The ideals of the student patriots cut down at Tiananmen could be enshrined in the following words, I told the crowd: "All power in the People's Republic of China belongs to the people. No organization or individual may enjoy the privilege of being above the Constitution and the law. The armed forces belong to the people and serve the people. Citizens should enjoy freedom of speech, of the press, of assembly, of association, of procession, and of demonstration. Only the Standing Committee of the National People's Congress may decide on the enforcement of martial law throughout the country or in particular provinces, autonomous regions, or municipalities directly under the Central Government."

I had quoted, word for word, from key articles of the Constitution of the People's Republic of China, as promulgated on December 4, 1982. "Will the regime now pronounce that the Constitution itself is 'counter-revolutionary'?" I asked. "Or will it ever ask the people's forgiveness for the most counter-revolutionary of all crimes – the mass murder of unarmed civilians demanding good, honest government?" And to the young martyrs of Tiananmen, I spoke from the heart: "Your indomitable courage, your great vision of China's future will live on, in the hearts, the minds, the actions of the Chinese people and their friends around the world."

NATIONAL DAY, OCTOBER 1, 1989

As the fortieth anniversary of the People's Republic of China approached, I wrote an article for the Hong Kong *Ming Pao Daily News*, entitled "China Belongs to the Chinese People," which ran on September 16, 1989. I remarked that many of us who had supported the Beijing Government for the previous forty years, applauding its successes and sadly indulging its mistakes, never lost hope because we believed that basically it was sincere in its attempts to "serve the people." Tragedies like the Cultural Revolution shook our faith, but did not destroy this hope. Indeed, the reform program that began in 1979 seemed to promise the invigoration of the economic and political life of the nation, despite some errors of policy. I wrote:

But there is a world of difference between "errors" and "crimes" and the June 4 massacre belongs in the latter category. Can we be sure of the facts on which to base such a grave allegation? We need only answer two questions: First, did government troops shoot and kill peacefully demonstrating students and civilians? This is an indisputable fact. Not even the government disputes this, although it tries to reduce a grave matter of principle to a technical matter of numbers. And second, is the government engaged today in the massive use of force to suppress dissent among the people? The regime continues to arrest, imprison, and even put to death large numbers of student leaders and intellectuals, labeled "counter-revolutionaries," who disagree with the present regime. For many of us who have deep affection for the long-suffering people, the answer is unequivocal. For our own integrity and the integrity of the Chinese people; for our own dignity and the dignity of the Chinese people; for our own rights and responsibilities and the rights and responsibilities of the Chinese people; we stand firmly on the side of truth and justice. Only in this sense can we – with honour – "celebrate" China's National Day.

In late September I was interviewed by James Rusk of the *Globe and Mail*. He began by asking me whether the events of the spring and summer in China were a betrayal of the promise of 1949. "Absolutely," I replied. "Today the party leaders' ideas and ideology are just a method of controlling the populace and maintaining their own hegemony ... They fear pluralism because of the old political culture of China. There can be only one sun in the sky and there can be only one orthodoxy – that has been the case all the way from the Han dynasty until today. We Chinese must make a really painful reassessment of ourselves and our cultural tradition."

"Perhaps no other Canadian knows just how painful the self-analysis will be," Rusk wrote. "Although his background ... would seem to fit him ideally for bridging the gap between Canada and China, he has always been a man of controversy in Chinese-Canadian affairs. Too intellectual for the activists and too activist for the intellectuals, he has not always been trusted on either side of the Pacific. Some Canadian China hands, diplomats particularly, wonder about the loyalties of a man who would work in Beijing for the Communist regime for fifteen years. Yet, in China his fealty is also questioned, as he neither stayed on to become a lackey of the regime, nor became the sort of foreign supporter who backed the regime no matter what."

PAINFUL SOUL-SEARCHING

As I had been dubbed in the West as a "loyal friend" if not an "apologist" for New China, my fierce public criticisms of the crackdown by the Chinese Government surprised my foes and shocked some of my friends. Cousin Yao Yilin, a member of the Standing Committee of the CCP Central Committee's Political Bureau – which had ordered the troops to fire on protesters – lamented that I had stayed abroad too long. My old friend Walter Chun criticized me for "opening up my big mouth." I felt I had become *persona non grata* to the Chinese Government. Just prior to China's National Day, October 1, a staff member from the office of Consul General Duan Jin called to cancel my invitation to their annual reception. "Fine! You can label me a counter-revolutionary too if you wish!" I retorted.

&After his initial outrage Paul became painfully depressed. He had dedicated his life to helping build a strong, democratic, and prosperous China, so that its people might live in dignity and with pride. Despite his doubts over the excesses and mistakes made by the Beijing authorities since 1949, he had never lost faith. But he could not rationalize their brutality and disdain toward the defenseless youth. Fortunately, he did not become a bitter soul, but focused his energies on probing Chinese history to answer the question: How had a tragedy like June 4 been possible in a "People's China"?&

My harsh words about the Tiananmen tragedy were not sudden outbursts of emotional indignation, but the result of a final rude awakening to the reality of China and its governance. I grew up in the West, received a Western education, and identified with many Western values. But as a Canadian of Chinese descent, my father's teachings of Confucianism and cultural nationalism nurtured in me a passionate attachment to the values of my Chinese ancestry. I also experienced racial discrimination in "British" Columbia. My feelings, therefore, were quite mixed. During the 1940s, I had come to strongly believe that the China led by Chiang Kai-shek was too weak. Even after the end of World War II and the defeat of Japan, China remained beholden to foreign powers – especially the United States – which had provided her with both troops and armaments. It was not until 1949, when Mao proclaimed atop the Gate of Heavenly Peace that "the Chinese people have stood up," that I felt I had finally found an ideal with which to identify completely. I had enormous expectations for democracy in China and believed it could be carried out on the basis of Marxist and Leninist principles. As to whether modern democracy could emerge from the philosophies of Confucius and Mencius, my thinking was vague, but I thought that it must be possible to root democratic practices in the rich soil of Chinese humanism.

Reviewing my ideological odyssey from student days to my twilight years, I found myself worrying with increasing pain. Why had China's civilization been unable to match the political, social, economic, and technological progress made elsewhere in the world and evolve wholesomely? A sense of guilt later replaced the pain. I had always hoped the day would come when as a Chinese, at least in the cultural sense, I could be completely proud of my civilized motherland. But now I saw that I had grossly underestimated the ingrained nature of China's authoritarian feudal values and autocratic politics. In retrospect, I realized that to seek to be always proud is but a form of self-indulgence.

When I first went to China in 1950, my intention was to learn from and to serve the people. I tried to be objective about the enormity of China's challenges and to ground facts in historical perspective. Although mentally prepared to endure the physical hardships of China's massive poverty, I was not prepared for the incessant, all-pervading ideological struggles that Mao's revolution involved. By the early 1960s, I had become more sensitive to the nuances in political discourse around Chairman Mao and sensed another major movement was in the making – one that could potentially have a major impact on the future of China and the world. It was then that I decided to return to Canada with my family. I felt it was critical that ways be found to bridge the chasm of misunderstanding between East and West, to encourage dialogue and cooperation.

Arriving back in Canada in 1964, however, I found the West still heavily shrouded in Cold War smog, blocking communications within a divided world. The US escalation of the Vietnam War was justified in part to "contain China." I tried to describe New China to my Western audiences as I had experienced it. And despite personal doubts about extreme policies like the Great Leap Forward, I believed the Chinese people were pushing back the very frontiers of social change, with an emphasis on egalitarian political and economic policies that genuinely served the people.

A small group of progressive Canadians and Americans in the 1960s and 1970s shared my views. This was an era of high idealism, growing opposition to the US war in Vietnam, and a surge of "people's movements" advocating the rights of women, racial minorities, and other marginalized groups. Building on the work of political leader Tommy Douglas, universal health care became a reality across Canada. In Latin America, Catholic priests were writing theologies of liberation intended to empower the poor. The Western press and powers-that-be, however, continued to malign China.

As I reflected on the Cultural Revolution that Chairman Mao launched in 1966, I reread the series of letters Madame Soong Ching Ling had written, trying to alert us to the growing turmoil in China. She cited specific and vivid cases of horrific excesses that had been committed by Red Guards. Although

I completely trusted her integrity, my naive idealism, subjective loyalty, and limited access to unbiased information from China prevented me from grasping the true essence of the Cultural Revolution. As I pored over my old speeches from that period, I realized that my blind spot had not been due merely to naiveté, but to a mistaken assumption about the purity of the Party's motives – an assumption shattered by events around June 4, 1989.

For example, in a presentation I made in the spring of 1968 entitled "The Change of Values in Contemporary China," I was extremely supportive of what I understood to be Chairman Mao's reasons for calling on the people to rebel. I acknowledged mistakes, but severely criticized Western press reports which depicted the Cultural Revolution as utter chaos. I wrote:

> There is something profound at stake in the Cultural Revolution ... nothing less than democracy itself. Some years ago, in an address that has not been published, Mao said that the question of democracy is crucial because without it Party Centralism could become fascist ...The only real insurance against this is for the Party to remain close to the masses and to preserve for the masses the right, in fact the responsibility, to "rebel." Indeed, the awakened masses must be regarded with genuine faith and deference. Members of the Party and bureaucracy cannot be seen as the sole custodians of truth and value ... This is an especially crucial experience for the young who did not experience pre-Liberation China. Hence the spectacular flowering of wall posters, criticism/self-criticism meetings, and other methods of direct, mass democracy.

Only now, in the wake of June 4, did I understand that Mao's call for "democracy" in 1966 had little to do with democracy and everything to do with using the Red Guards to destroy his opponents in the CCP, comrades like Liu Shaoqi and Deng Xiaoping. I had always accepted the necessity of the Party's leadership in guiding the country forward, but had assumed there were mechanisms within the Party itself to ensure the leaders would remain accountable first to the people, not to their hold on power. It struck me that the Party had, in effect, claimed for itself the role of dynastic emperors whose rule was justified by holding "the Mandate of Heaven."

I recalled doubts I had had about the Party's integrity as early as 1970, when I travelled to the Jinggang Mountains, in Jiangxi Province, where Chairman Mao and General Zhu De had converged with their forces in 1928. The legendary photograph of that meeting had been altered – General Zhu's face had been replaced with that of Lin Biao. This was repeated after 1976 when the faces of the Gang of Four were airbrushed out of official photographs. This insistence by the government on rewriting history to serve its present agenda was a feudal remnant that deeply compromised the idea of a leadership account-able to the people. I was beginning to better understand what Premier Zhou Enlai had hinted at during our long conversation in 1972, when he suggested Doug read *The Dream of the Red Chamber*. The dead weight of China's long feudal past still shaped the psyches of most Chinese leaders and was preventing the realization of a true people's democracy.

RECONCILIATION

I began to receive friendly signals from various quarters in China as early as 1990. Vancouver's former consul general Duan Jin contacted me in the spring and the new consul general, An Wenbin, invited us to a reception at the consulate that summer. In 1991, I received a request from the Chinese Academy of Social Sciences (CASS) inviting me to Beijing to speak on Canadian values and institutions. This coincided with an invitation from the Soong Ching Ling Foundation of Shanghai for us to attend its board meeting as honorary members. We were also present at the opening of the Soong Ching Ling Kindergarten, a model school that aimed to adapt the best of Chinese and Western teaching pedagogies for early childhood education.

Eileen and I arrived in Beijing in October, not at all sure about the reception we would receive. Our CASS colleagues could not have been more welcoming, but avoided the sensitive topic of June 4, 1989, as did other friends, old and new, whom we met on this visit.

Following my lectures, we were called upon by Yao Guang, an old friend who had been China's ambassador to Canada in 1972–73. He was cordial, but tried to convince us of the official line on the Tiananmen crackdown. However, because it was a matter of principle for us, rather than a political stand, we did not agree. He appeared disappointed in us when we parted.

We asked to see Cousin Yao Yilin, who was now officially retired. We had heard he was convalescing in hospital and sent word we would like to visit. His aide relayed Cousin Yao's message that a visit was "inconvenient." We never saw him again, and when he died in 1994, we learned through a family member that our mourning wreath was not displayed at his memorial service. I am saddened that our decades-long warm relationship ended in estrange-

Paul in conversation with Dr Zhou Peiyuan, noted scholar and retired president
of Peking University, Shanghai, 1991

ment. Despite my utter disagreement with him over June 4, I never doubted
his integrity as an upright official who sincerely wanted the best for the
Chinese people. Happily, we later reconciled with his children.

The tenor of our visit in Shanghai, as guests of the China Welfare Institute,
was more relaxed. Without saying so directly, it seemed that many of our
friends shared our views about June 4. There were a few who tried to persuade
us otherwise, but failing, advised us to at least dilute our position. We returned
to Canada encouraged that China's political situation was more fluid than we
had anticipated.

The Chinese community in Vancouver is very diverse – linguistically, politically and socially. After the June 4 crackdown, however, a strong desire to
dialogue across our many differences emerged. This resulted in a China Forum
Society (CFS) that hosted a series of public lectures on the Chinese democracy
movement and cultural topics, in both English and Chinese. Beginning in 1992,
the CFS coordinated its activities with the China Program for Integrative
Research and Development (CPIRD), which I established at UBC under the
auspices of the Institute of Asian Research. Funding came from my registered
retirement investment fund, with a matching grant from the university.

CPIRD was intended to encourage Canada-China collaborative research on
the major issues in China's transformation. The initiative arose from the need

to monitor and holistically understand the nature of China's sudden conversion into a rapidly growing economic giant that would change the lives of its own people, as well as play a pivotal role in the global economy. In the 1980s, China had created a hybrid system called "market socialism" and linked it to the global market. Soon the economy had reached the highest growth rate in the world. Despite its astonishing success, China was still in a complex transition whose future path was in many ways uncharted. If all the economic fundamentals were there for sustained rapid growth, what about non-economic fundamentals? How would the factors influencing stability be identified and weighed in both the medium and the long term?

CPIRD's first partner was the Institute of World History at CASS, which had invited me to Beijing to speak about Canadian governance in October 1991. A delegation of five scholars came to Vancouver in 1992 to participate in a seminar on "Democratic Values and Institutions – Chinese and Canadian Perspectives." Over the course of the next several years, CPIRD sponsored a series of lectures on controversial subjects by well-known Chinese intellectuals. Zhao Fusan, China's former representative to UNESCO, discussed "Modernization and Cultural Change." The literary critic, Liu Zaifu, spoke on "Fin-de-Siècle Chinese Literature – New Perspectives on Culture." Sociologist Chen Yiyun addressed "The Family and Social Change in China Today." Deng Shoupeng, a computer specialist, presented a paper on "Restructuring China's Information Superhighway and its Impact on China's Development." In a special seminar on "The Taiwan Crisis and US-China Relations," Li Shunzhi, a CASS scholar then in residence at Harvard University, engaged in a lively dialogue with Professor Greg Guldin of Pacific Lutheran University and Earl Drake, former Canadian ambassador to China. Wang Meng, the novelist and former PRC minister of culture, and the film critic Shao Mujun, reviewed recent trends in literary and cinematic circles.

In November 1992, I flew to Hong Kong to accept the nomination by the Hong Kong Society of Chinese Scholars as a "most distinguished Chinese scholar." In addition to presiding over its symposium, I gave a public address on "Hong Kong's Future – A View from the Chinese Diaspora." The following year, I was pleasantly surprised to receive an official invitation to visit China by Lu Ping, Director of the Hong Kong and Macau Affairs Office of the State Council of the People's Republic of China. He requested the honour of my presence and received me on November 11, 1993, at the Diao Yu Tai State Guest House for prominent dignitaries. This was followed by a sumptuous banquet. When he asked whom I would like to see, I named Vice-Premier Li Lanqing, who was in charge of education.

A delegation from the Institute of World History of the Chinese Academy of Social Sciences visits the University of British Columbia in Vancouver, September 1992.

Paul visits his father's village in Xinhui County, Guangdong Province, and meets the village cadres, November 1993.

In addition to my gradual reconciliation with China, some of my old critics in Canada seemed to have adjusted their opinions of me. Trevor Lautens, a columnist for the *Vancouver Sun*, wrote in early 1993:

Paul Lin wouldn't toe the line under either communism or democracy. So both put the boots to him. Only metaphorically, that is. In fact it could be said equally that Lin, a player in some of the most significant events of this century – confidant of Chinese Premier Chou Enlai in the Mao Zedong regime, a scholar suspected of subversion in the West during the Cold War – has been wooed by both. His approval counts. [Lin] strongly rebuked and thus angered the Chinese Government for the Tiananmen Square massacre of 1989 – yet was invited back to speak on Canadian constitutional matters in 1991. He was long blacklisted in Taiwan, but last year was granted entry and given "almost red-carpet" treatment there ... I'll add that during the Cold War I intensely disliked his reported opinions. When we met for the first time last week, I found him humanistic, sensitive, open – and felt something like old combatants do when they meet after their war is history.

GAINING CLARITY ON CHINA'S TRANSFORMATION

The results of my quest for clarity on the dynamics and trends in China's transformation were reflected in a speech I gave at the Imperial College, London on September 17, 1994. It began:

China is at a critical juncture in its history. Future historians may record that when the Chinese Communist Party under the leadership of Deng Xiaoping made a dramatic decision to change course in December 1979, it plunged China into a profound stage of socioeconomic transformation. The previous three decades had been marked by self-reliant efforts to achieve forced economic growth under centralized state planning led by Mao Zedong. By boldly casting off the shackles of "ultra-left" baggage, Deng launched a fresh two-pronged approach to China's development through internal economic reforms and by opening China to participation in world markets.

If Mao Zedong's economic development strategy was a counter-paradigm to both the Western capitalist and the Stalinist paradigms, Deng's appeared to be a counter-paradigm to the counter-paradigm. The spectacular pace of economic growth after 1979 was seen as proof of the effectiveness of the new paradigm. Yet there were some who questioned the "newness" of the "counter-paradigm." Simply put, how different was it economically from the capitalist mode or politically from the Stalinist mode? The official Chinese answer was equally simplistic: the counter-paradigm was "Socialism with Chinese Characteristics" – a universal category with a particular stamp, neither of which was clearly defined during the uncertain stage of transition between the old and new systems. Instead, the transition was a matter of "feeling one's way stone by stone across the stream," meaning trial and error.

In 1979 Deng Xiaoping and the Communist Party set forth the "Four Cardinal Principles": adherence to the ideological heritage of Marx, Lenin and Mao; proletarian rule; socialism; and the leadership of the Chinese Communist Party – [which were] intended to protect the continuity and orthodoxy of the Party. In fact only the last principle, the Party's leadership, carried any weight. The others had lost all practical meaning. It was clear that de-ideologizing would be necessary in order to emancipate the minds of the people and permit wholehearted pursuit of the new economic policies, which were only concerned with the bottom line. Given the Party's connection with the abuses and failures of the past, there were compelling political reasons against articulating new social goals and guiding values too soon. At the same time, articulating shared goals and values is the responsibility of a nation's leadership, and the longer responsibility was evaded, the deeper the crisis might become. Left to itself, the market would create its own goals, values, and culture and, in the process, could alienate broad sectors of the population who aspired to different goals and values.

For Deng to call for the casting aside of the old, sterile dogmas and empty slogans was to release millions of entrepreneurial minds from the guilt of participating in the long-stigmatized market. But to cast aside old dogmas and slogans without rallying the people around revitalized goals and values that they could identify with, was to invite serious consequences. Such consequences could appear in many forms: rampant official corruption, widening disparities between city and countryside and between wage-earners and the "nouveau riche," poor and unsafe working conditions, environmental pollution, and an erosion of noble social values in favour of a crass "me-first" attitude.

I elaborated on these ideas in an interview with Andrew Yang, Vancouver correspondent of *Chinese World Journal*, on May 21, 1995. "Under Mao Zedong's era, the paradigm was to value nobility of spirit rather than self-interest. This was distorted to mean loyalty to Mao alone. There was also talk about democracy, but in practice it was class struggle that was used to settle domestic social issues. Unnecessary and man-made contradictions were created … and were dealt with by brute force. Deng Xiaoping, on the other hand, promoted material gratification rather than the nobility of spirit, totally ignoring politics and human relations. I believe that economics is but a tool. The ultimate goal is to improve the quality of human experience. Now is the time to gradually build up a new political culture. It needs time, because its prerequisite is changes in values."

After the London speech, Eileen and I joined a Mediterranean cruise to belatedly mark our fiftieth wedding anniversary of June 24, 1944. We returned to Canada in early October. A few weeks later I had a fax from Jia Qinglin, secretary of the CPC Fujian Provincial Committee and governor of Fujian Province, inviting us to visit in November. I had first met Governor Jia in the early 1980s, when he was general manager of the China National Machinery and Equipment Import and Export Corporation, and I was acting as a consultant for a Canadian company. He generously hosted us for a week and offered to arrange side trips to tourist destinations. I told him we were much more interested in learning about the progress of the economic reforms in Fujian and how academic institutions were preparing students for work in this new era. In addition to visiting universities in Fuzhou and Xiamen, we had fruitful discussions with cadres at the Fujian Economic Research Centre, the Fujian Planning Commission, and the Huli Development Zone. I asked them about their needs and told them about the work of CPIRD in Vancouver. I was not entirely surprised, therefore, when Jia Qinglin contacted me in early 1995, regarding training in public policy and business management for Fujian cadres in mid-career. A delegation of scholars from UBC visited Fujian in April 1995 to hammer out a proposal with the participating institutions; Governor Jia and his entourage made a return visit to Vancouver that summer to consolidate the partnership. Together we decided that the cadres would spend time in Canada, where they would be exposed to Canadian practices in government and corporate management, as well as taking academic courses tailored to their level of professional training and linguistic capabilities. We expected that CPIRD's participation would yield mutual benefits by providing UBC researchers with opportunities to examine comparative leadership cultures. The first group of trainees arrived at UBC in January 1997.

Paul and Eileen celebrate their fiftieth wedding anniversary in Vancouver, June 24, 1994.

1997 — CANADA'S YEAR OF ASIA PACIFIC

The Standing Senate Committee on Foreign Affairs and International Trade met on the morning of February 7, 1997, to examine the growing importance of the Asia-Pacific region for Canada, with emphasis on the upcoming Asia-Pacific Economic Cooperation (APEC) forum, which would take place in the fall. The meeting was held in Vancouver and I was invited to speak on the China panel. My colleagues were Professor Pitman Potter from the UBC Faculty of Law, Patrick Brown from the Canadian Broadcasting Corporation, and Senator Jack Austin from the Canada China Business Council.

I began my remarks with a reference to China's economy, which with an eight per cent growth rate, a healthy debt-service ratio, and a rate of savings in the thirty per cent range, seemed to indicate that 1997 would be another bullish year for business in China. But I soon shifted to the question of China's relations with the Western world, which in some quarters had been reduced to a simplistic trade versus human rights debate that argued "democracies" should either boycott China entirely, or coddle the "butchers of Beijing" by continuing to do business with them.

This dichotomy struck me as arrogant and lacking in historical perspective beyond the events of June 4, 1989. I reminded the senators that the economic reforms initiated by Deng Xiaoping at the Fourteenth Congress of the Communist Party at the end of 1978 were revolutionary. Establishing and institutionalizing a market economy required the jettisoning of not only Marxist but also Confucian values, which had governed the behaviour of the Chinese people for more than 2,000 years. The Confucian ethic had placed economic activity, over and above what is necessary to sustain life, at the bottom of its priorities. Where there was a conflict between *yi* and *li* – *yi* meaning integrity and loyalty, and *li* meaning profit – Confucian teaching endorsed the values of loyalty, service, and responsibility, and viewed the chasing of profit as a lowly approach to life. Although noble, this was not an ethos that would spur a system of rapid economic growth. (Indeed to a certain extent, Mao Zedong had continued to hold this anti-commerce Confucian attitude.) It was essential for the West to understand these roots of Chinese thought and to appreciate how they continued to influence Chinese actions in the present. China was a civilization in abrupt transition, I argued, and its traditional authoritarian governance was not likely to instantly resemble democratic systems in the West, centred upon private property and individual rights, which had taken centuries to develop.

Later in the conversation, a senator asked about American academic Samuel P. Huntington's thesis of the inevitability of a "clash of civilizations" between China and the West. I told him that the idea of a "clash of cultures" was, in my view, a dangerous intellectual position, because it might prove to be a self-fulfilling prophecy. The Chinese intellectuals with whom I had been in touch over the last few years, felt that what we needed was exactly the opposite. They were calling for the revival of the Silk Road: a new corridor between the East and the West that could serve as a land bridge between China and Europe. The idea was not simply a ribbon of land, like a transcontinental railway, but a ribbon of development, which would include both economic exchange and the exchange of cultures. This was based on the hope that we were now at a stage where a partial symbiosis of cultures was possible and that people from different historical backgrounds could learn from one another.

I thoroughly enjoyed this exchange with the senators and my colleagues on the panel. Professor Potter gave a masterful presentation on China's legal reforms and the collabourative research being done at UBC's Centre for Chinese Legal Studies. Patrick Brown, a journalist fluent in Mandarin Chinese, provided balanced anecdotes from his long experience on the ground in China. My old friend and colleague Jack Austin straightforwardly raised the concerns of the Canadian business sector. We did not reach any grand conclusions, but the dialogue was rich and will continue long after I am gone.

A CURIOUS ENCOUNTER

On March 3, 1997, I received a phone call from a stranger who said he had heard me lecture at the Canadian National Defence College in the early 1990s. He introduced himself as a teacher of Asian Studies at Columbia College in Vancouver and hoped to discuss China's current situation with me. Intrigued, I agreed.

A few days later, a middle-aged, well-built Caucasian gentleman showed up at my home office. To my great surprise, he said he worked for CSIS (Canadian Security Intelligence Service) and was about to retire. He had brought along his successor, who was waiting in the car park, and asked if I would like to meet him. I told him honestly I would rather not and commented quietly, "You people were not very nice to me." He nodded, "Yes, I know, but that was the RCMP. I apologize for what happened. Is there any way we can make amends?" I shook my head and said, "No."

He then asked if I would give a lecture to his students at Columbia College. I did and later, over lunch, he mentioned that after retirement he hoped to teach in China. He wound up teaching at a police academy in Beijing. Amazing!

HONG KONG'S RETURN TO CHINA

The highlight of 1997 for me was witnessing the return of Hong Kong to Chinese sovereignty, more than 150 years after the Opium Wars. Lu Ping arranged for me to be a guest of both the Government of the United Kingdom of Great Britain and Northern Ireland and the Government of the People's Republic of China. I attended the British handover ceremony at 11:30 pm in the Great Hall of the Hong Kong Convention and Exhibition Centre on Monday, June 30, 1997. At 1:30 am on Tuesday, July 1, at the invitation of the State Council of the PRC, I attended the Chinese ceremony for the establishment of the Hong Kong Special Administrative Region (SAR) of the People's Republic of China and the inauguration of the Government of the Hong Kong SAR.

The one person I truly missed at this historical event was Liao Chengzhi, founding director of the Hong Kong and Macau Affairs Office. It was his intimate knowledge of Hong Kong, and the bold plans and proposals he initiated, which played a pivotal role in the negotiations between China and Britain. Unfortunately, he passed away in 1983. What had always impressed me about Liao was his firm belief that a modern China should stand proudly in the forest of the world's nations.

After the ceremonies, I wrote the following impressions in my diary:

On July 1, 1997, with proper pomp and circumstance, Britain returned its colony of Hong Kong to the sovereignty of China. Although this was seen to be an unprecedented act of dignity and equality on both sides, there were, inevitably, widely divergent views of the meaning of this historic turning point. For the average Chinese, it was an emotional vindication of their deep sense of foreign-inflicted injustice inherited through five or six generations, and a final reassertion of their dignity as a nation. This effect will undoubtedly lead to a healthy change in the Chinese psyche in a way favorable to internal reform and external openness.

The simultaneous creation of the Special Administrative Region with considerable autonomy given to Hong Kongers to handle their own affairs, will bolster confidence in terms of both economic and political stability with healthy dynamism. The innovative concept of "one country, two systems" is enigmatic, only because its main intent is to protect the "system" in Hong Kong while the "system" on the mainland is still to be further defined, tested, and refined over an extended period of time. Conceivably, there will be a quiet merging of the two systems, with more to be gained in the learning process by the Mainland in transition.

I could not help but muse that Father, who had arrived in Canada in 1897 from a China being devoured by the colonial powers, would have been gratified.

Chapter Eighteen

AN ENIGMA RECONSIDERED

I have never sought after honours, but would be less than honest if I pretended that recognition of my endeavours meant nothing to me. So when the Right Honourable Roméo LeBlanc, Governor General of Canada, pinned the medal of the Order of Canada to my lapel on October 22, 1998, I was deeply moved. Having been labelled an "enigma" (not to be trusted) when I returned to Canada from China in 1964, I never expected the country of my birth to bestow on me the nation's most prestigious award. "At last my Canadianism has been vindicated!" I told Eileen with a broad smile.

⁂ Paul's eyes twinkled mischievously when he said this – of course he needed no vindication! His dedicated life and work spoke for themselves, despite the suspicions of some Cold War bureaucrats and pundits who hounded him for decades. Only ever responding with courage and dignity, he continued his quest to build stronger ties between the Chinese and North American peoples. Paul was a principled man with a big heart and held no grudges. He was genuinely delighted to receive the Order of Canada. ⁂

This honour was bestowed on me as "a leading figure in the development of Chinese-Canadian ties in the field of international relations ... [who]

Paul receives the Order of Canada from Governor General Roméo LeBlanc, Ottawa, October 22, 1998.

encouraged East-West cooperation, believing that it must be built on the basis of equality and mutual respect." According to the official citation, my "unique experiences in China" had given me "insights and knowledge which helped bring about exploratory diplomatic trips by North American leaders to China in the 1970s" and had "contributed to strengthening the diplomatic and commercial relationships between Canada and China."

The investiture was held at Rideau Hall in Ottawa, the residence of the Governor General. Both Eileen and Douglas were present – the final touch that brought my joy to its fullness. Due to space limitations, recipients were allowed only one guest at the investiture. Douglas, who was then teaching at the University of California, was able to attend owing to the kindness of a former member of Parliament, Sophia Leung, who invited him as her guest.

I received numerous letters of congratulations from friends, colleagues, and government officials, including Prime Minister Jean Chrétien. Thanking him warmly, I wrote: "As a citizen in the land of my birth, I accept this honour

Paul and Eileen after the investiture ceremony, October 22, 1998

with both pride and humility – with pride, because I have made a contribution to Canada's international role, and with humility, because my contribution was a modest one ... In this spirit, may I congratulate you in turn, Mr Prime Minister, for your farsighted and important decisions over the years in international affairs. I take this opportunity to wish you Bon Voyage and every success in your imminent trip to China."

ASIA PACIFIC FOUNDATION OF CANADA

In 2000, in light of the approaching millennium, the Asia Pacific Foundation (APF) of Canada produced an essay reviewing Canada-Asia ties during the twentieth century. Created by an Act of Parliament in 1984, the APF is an independent think-tank devoted to research, analysis, and information-gathering on Canada's transpacific relations. In addition to noting important historic events, the essay named ten Canadians who had contributed significantly to the building of relationships with Asia. I was surprised and humbled to find myself on the list in the company of Norman Bethune and Chester Ronning.

THE SOONG CHING LING CHILDREN'S FOUNDATION OF CANADA

A few months after the death of Madame Soong in May 1981, Eileen and I established the Soong Ching Ling Children's Foundation of Canada: a non-profit foundation devoted to improving the education, health, and welfare of children in China and Canada. We did this in the spirit of international co-operation, which Soong Ching Ling's life had personified.

Since its inception, the SCLCFC has carried out several dozen small but significant projects. One of the earliest was a documentary entitled *The Children of Soong Ching Ling*, which explored the lives of youths who had grown up in New China since 1949. In 1983 I met with Satish Prabasi, the United Nations Children's Fund (UNICEF) representative in China, who agreed that UNICEF would co-sponsor the film. I then enlisted the support of the Soong Ching Ling Foundation in Beijing, which assisted with the logistics of the production, including recruitment of the actors. Canadian Gary Bush directed the film, while I served as producer and narrator. It was a very satisfying Sino-Canadian collaboration and I was proud of our final product. Nevertheless, I was astonished when it was nominated for an Academy Award in 1985, in the category of "Best Documentary Short Subject." Although the documentary did not win an Oscar, the National Educational Film and Video Festival in Oakland, California, awarded it first place in its 1985 competition. Later that year the National Council of Family Relations gave it an "Honorable Mention" in its Family Film Award category.

During the past thirty years, the SCLCFC has built two schools and a community library in poor, rural areas of China, fostered early childhood education through international symposia and teacher exchanges, provided learning opportunities for teachers at the Beijing Stars and Rain Institute for children with autism, and granted annual scholarships to students in need. On this side of the Pacific, the SCLCFC has provided funds for a multilingual family support worker to assist immigrant children – primarily Chinese – in an after-school program at the Hastings Community School in Vancouver. All of these projects have been accomplished with a limited budget raised by a dedicated board of volunteers, who generously donate their time to the children. They share Madame Soong Ching Ling's faith that "work for the children is always work to mold the future, for it is to the young that the future belongs."

Filming *The Children of Soong Ching Ling* in a national minorities area in southwest China, 1983

Certificate showing the nomination of *The Children of Soong Ching Ling* for an Academy Award, 1985

Board members of The Soong Ching Ling Children's Foundation of Canada attend a retreat on the University of British Columbia campus, May 2001.

THE SOONG CHING LING CAMPHOR TREE AWARD

Of the awards I have received in my lifetime, the Soong Ching Ling Camphor Tree Award touched my heart most profoundly. Due to ill health, I was unable to attend the December 2002 ceremony, hosted by the China Welfare Institute (CWI) in Shanghai, but the following October Lu Ping, the vice-chairman of CWI, came to Vancouver to present the award to me in person. In China, the camphor tree is known as the "fragrant tree" and was Madame Soong's favourite. The citation, signed by Hu Qi Li, chairman of the CWI Executive Committee, stated: "The Soong Ching Ling Camphor Tree Honorary Award is bestowed upon you for your outstanding contributions over a long period of time, in promoting education of children and youth in China and Canada, as well as cultural exchange between the two countries."

Lu Ping hosted a banquet for our friends and colleagues. In his speech he said, "Professor Lin has been a long-time supporter of the work and development of the China Welfare Institute, which was founded by Soong Ching Ling

Vice-Chairman Lu Ping of the China Welfare Institute

[in 1950] ... In 1996, thanks to his initiative, the SCLCFC and the CWI together founded the China-Canada Children's Development Research Center in Shanghai. To support the preschool education of the CWI, Professor Lin introduced us to Dr Glen Dixon of the Department of Preschool Education of UBC, thus paving the road for our preschool teachers to take lessons at UBC ... By introducing the advanced education theory and methods of Montessori and ECE of North America, we have opened up a new horizon in international exchange and cooperation in the field of preschool education." Lu Ping concluded: "I have known Paul since the 1950s. Through our long friendship, I am deeply impressed by his integrity, selflessness, and his love for China ... He well deserves to receive this honour."

In accepting the award, I reflected on the remarkable life of its namesake – Soong Ching Ling – who throughout her life had defended and carried forward Sun Yat-sen's vision of a China free of foreign oppression, where the livelihood of the people, especially the masses of workers and peasants, would be the priority. I concluded my remarks at the Camphor Tree Award ceremony by saying: "This award does not belong to me alone, but to all of you and the countless others who share Soong Ching Ling's vision and work to carry out her legacy to better the life of humanity."

FINAL THOUGHTS

Growing up in the 1930s, I fervently hoped that China would become strong one day, so that Chinese everywhere could regain their dignity. More than a hope, this intention became a central mission in my life.

In university and graduate school I studied international law, which I believed could be used to defend China's interests in the international arena. I assumed I would become a diplomat. As it turned out, I never had an opportunity to work formally in the foreign service of either Canada or China, but informally found ways to bring leaders of the two nations into constructive dialogue.

My life's journey has been unconventional, and not without profound sorrows and disappointments, but I have been extraordinarily fortunate in having family and friends – comrades and companions – who supported me always in my endeavours. Together we have made a difference.

✍ Although Paul was considered too "Western" in China and too "Chinese" in the West, he did succeed in his mission. Success is only possible, according to a Chinese proverb, when there is a union of three elements – 天时 (heavenly timing), 地利 (earthly benefitting), and 人和 (humanly sustaining). Close friends and former colleagues at McGill University – Margot Becklake and her husband Maurice McGregor – also touched on this when they congratulated Paul on his Order of Canada in 1998: "There are times when the right person in the right place and at the right time, can influence the thinking and attitudes of individuals and countries. We think that is what you did in the 1970s by describing, explaining, and interpreting China to those of us – individuals and countries – who had not been there, and this you did with clarity, gentleness, and perspective."

Today, as we enter the second decade of the twenty-first century, China has emerged as a major player whose cooperation in resolving global challenges – financial stability, war and peace, climate change, and human suffering – is critical. In the last forty years, countless educational, cultural, and scientific exchanges, in addition to joint commercial ventures, have led the peoples of Canada and China to much greater mutual understanding and respect. But more work needs to be done.

Paul determined to write his memoirs not to justify himself, but in the belief that by telling his life story he might spark the curiosity of Canadians to further explore the tumultuous history of twentieth-century China. Paul was an historian and was disturbed that after the Chinese government's violent suppression of student protests on June 4, 1989, Western political

Paul Lin, 1987

scientists and journalists tended to focus almost exclusively on ideological debates about human rights, from a Eurocentric perspective. As a humanist, he felt that arguments about supposed "universal rights" – without reference to culture and history – were futile and divisive. Biography, on the other hand – where the personal is political – might lead Western readers to deeper empathy and insight into the choices that the Chinese people have made in the past, and illuminate the decisions they are making in the present.

For the sake of brevity, *In the Eye of the China Storm* could provide only a schematic account of Chinese history and the history of Canada-China relations. Both Paul and I hope that future students and scholars will pluck threads from his story and weave new interpretations of the times and places in which he lived. There are three areas of research that I believe would help to expand Canadians' appreciation of China and the Chinese people.

First, it is time to integrate the role of Chinese Canadians into Canada's national history. Inasmuch as Chinese were marginalized in Chinatowns prior to the lifting of the Exclusion Act in 1947, the history of Chinese Canadians has tended to be marginalized as "immigrant history," set apart from the national stories of both Canada and China. Paul's roots were in the Vancouver Chinese community and when he returned to Canada in 1964, and later retired to Vancouver in 1982, he always participated in the community where his father had long been a prominent leader. Paul's support for the PRC was problematic for many Chinese Canadians; an examination of the coverage of him by the Vancouver Chinese press would open an aspect of Canada-China history that has not yet been studied. Regarding the history of Canada-China relations, the current literature is thin and omits mention of Paul's role in shaping public opinion to accept the formal establishment of relations in 1970. Other Canadians of Chinese descent have also made significant contributions, but remain unacknowledged by the majority.

Second, as Canadian as Paul was, he was a Chinese intellectual who supported Mao Zedong's Communist revolution, although he was never a Party member. Western scholars have written some excellent studies of a few famous Chinese writers and intellectuals of this period, but the broader generation has remained largely invisible. A particularly important group of intellectuals were those who studied in Europe and the United States between the two world wars, before returning to China in 1949. Paul and I knew these "returned students" well from our involvement with the Chinese Students' Christian Association during the 1940s. Some of these returned students also served the PRC as envoys and ambassadors, due to their superior language skills and acquaintance with diverse foreign cultures. A study of the life stories of China's ambassadors to Canada after 1970 would be one small avenue for furthering Canadian understanding of China during the twentieth century.

The third topic that Paul would wish to highlight is the importance of non-governmental organizations (NGOs) in the history of Canada-China relations. This began with the churches and their missions in China and Chinatowns from the late nineteenth century, but continued after 1949 when some churches advocated strongly for recognition of the People's Republic. Canada-China Friendship Societies were established in the 1970s to educate Canadians about New China through tours, public events, and publications, while other organizations were formed to promote cultural and artistic collaborations. Canadian cities came to be twinned with Chinese cities, universities from both countries established joint programs, and hospitals and medical personnel exchanged experiences. In the early 1980s, CIDA (Canadian International Development Agency) began to assist Canadian NGOs to work with partner agencies in China. The true story of Canada-China relations is not primarily an account of the diplomats in Ottawa and the businessmen who flocked to China after 1978, when Deng Xiaoping opened China's doors to the world, but the cumulative effect of all these people-to-people activities.

One generation can only sow seeds for the next to nurture and make fruitful. I hope that – in a small way – the life of Paul T.K. Lin will provide the seeds for the further flowering of mutually beneficial relationships between the Canadian and Chinese peoples.

THE PACIFIC CHARTER

The full text of the winning speech delivered by Paul Lim-Yuen at the Northern Oratorical League contest in May 1942.

Perhaps I have no right to say the things I shall say to you tonight. I have frequently imposed upon myself the obligation not to criticize the faults of America. I have rather, in the past, undertaken to examine the faults of my own people, the Chinese, and to ask your aid for them.

But today, I am wearied, and confused, and pained. For three years now, I have lived in America, privileged to pursue my studies in one of her greatest institutions of learning. For three crucial years, I have witnessed every step this great nation has taken inevitably toward war. During these years, I have talked intimately with American students, American businessmen, and American factory workers. And in nine cases out of ten I was disappointed, until I began to believe that what they said represented widespread confused thinking in the great masses of the American people. They extolled my people's fight; they made much of fine phrases about international bills of rights and Atlantic Charters, but they seemed addicted to circumlocution whenever challenged to take their clear and realistic role in defense of right throughout the world. I had expected the deep, clear faith that America had brought into the world in the Declaration of Independence, but it was not there.

That is why I must speak frankly to you today, not in bitterness, but because, having lived in America, I love America. And loving America, and hoping for the common salvation of both America and China, at this dark hour I must speak of you as I would of my own people, without reserve. If

I offend, I shall ask your forgiveness. But I shall also be gratified that the offense will have attested to a truth sent home.

I want first to tell you that my people have been fighting this war not for five months, but for ten years. For them, Pearl Harbor was not enacted on December 7, 1941. It was enacted on September 18, 1931, at Mukden, in Manchuria. It was enacted again for 88 bloody days in Shanghai, the following year. It was enacted again at Lukouchiaou, in North China, on July 7, 1937. Pearl Harbor has been enacted ever since in every unholy act of drug distribution, incendiarism, outrage, and murder in 800,000 square miles of Japanese-penetrated territory. How I could tell you the whole ghoulish tale of those ten years of agony – of the rape of Nanking, the sack of Hankow, the bombings of Canton and Chungking, where the casualty lists alone would dwarf the total of all the other bombed cities of the world put together. Imagine this great university bombed from the air, invaded by foreign troops, these great halls converted into military headquarters and torture chambers and enemy barracks. Imagine yourselves, together with students from your sister universities in the East and Midwest, trekking on foot for over 1,000 miles to establish yourselves again in universities dug in the hillsides of Nevada. You can then appreciate what has happened to over 90% of China's universities and colleges since the Japanese descended upon them. Imagine fifty million starving refugees, over one-third of your total population, driven by war from the Atlantic and Pacific seaboards, into interior states like Utah, Colorado, Wyoming, and Nevada, there to find their only subsistence. You can then approach a correct view of the colossal migration into Free China.

This is the picture you must have of fighting China before you can talk about her courageous resistance. Surely to my people who have braved ten years of these conditions, freedom and democracy and justice cannot be mere catch phrases to win the war. They are as real and virile and vibrant as life itself.

Are they as real – as virile – as vibrant – to Americans? Are they truly alive at all in Western democracy? Have the British, and the Americans, shown any imaginative desire to break the sad precedents of history in making this a revolutionary war? Do they know and believe what they are fighting for? Or have they come to cherish liberty and democracy as they cherish automobile tires, and unrationed sugar, and two-piece pantsuits, and sheer silk stockings?

I cannot doubt that deep in the heart of the American people there burns a fierce love for the highest of principles. But can it be that in their desire to do fullest honour to these principles, they have enshrined them in a great national temple so encrusted with gold and other glittering symbols of material civilization that this inheriting generation has come to worship the whole fetish of wealth and luxury and has forgotten the shrine within the temple? I fear that they must have come to identify a high standard of national living with a high standard of national morality. That is their false icon.

Ten years ago, in Manchuria, the Chinese nation filed into the front-line trenches of democracy. At first, they too knew little what they were fighting for in terms of principles. To most Chinese, these principles were identified with the great art treasures of Peiping, the modern brilliance of Shanghai, or the vast rice fields of Kwangtung. Even to the humblest peasant, these principles were identified with the little thatched hut that was his home, and the tiny plot of land that was his subsistence. But when the Japanese bombers came and blasted the cities out of existence, when the Japanese tanks came and drove the peasant from the land that he tilled, the Chinese people suddenly found *their* false icon destroyed. And they hastily helped to destroy it in their moral emancipation. Then they knew that if they were to fight on, it would not be for the destructible institutions their hands had raised, not for an earth that could be rendered sterile, but for the deeper, elemental things of the spirit, indestructible and creative – freedom, democracy, equality and tolerance, truth and morality for *all* men – the final principles that must never be violated by the invaders.

They turned hopefully to the Western democracies, which they had always deemed to be the stronghold of these principles of faith. They appealed for aid to save their idealism by stopping the Japanese. But the great Western powers literally rejected the appeal, and in effect helped turn the articles of the League Covenant, the Kellogg Peace Pact, the Nine-Power Washington Treaty, into waste paper in which was destined to be wrapped and discarded nearly every international code set up by the nations. In the tragic years that followed 1931, while China pleaded for Western recognition of the global implications of Japan's expansion, America and the British Empire supplied on the one hand nearly 100% of Japan's war needs, while on the other, nearly 100% of China's medical supplies. It was as if the West were enjoying a sadistic drama in which the victim needed to be given new leases on life that the drama could go on. And to obtain places as spectators in the gallery of nations, they paid exorbitant prices in ideals.

Germany and Italy viewed Japan with admiration and America and Britain with satisfaction. They took Japan's cue, and the stream of events since 1931 has grown into a turbulent flood of world disaster. Manchuria in 1931, the so-called "Chinese problem," was the broken dike democracy itself helped to breach. Ethiopia, Austria, Munich, Czechoslovakia, Poland – every point along the banks of the flood marked a shipwreck of democratic conviction as much as an advance of aggression.

But why disinter the past? The present is more important. The Japanese have been winning. The whole Allied cause is in grave danger. It is time we took inventory, and investigated the causes of our defeats.

The reason for the losses we have suffered so far does not lie ultimately in disunified military strategy, in lack of military decision, in lack of planes and ships. The trouble lies ultimately in disunified democratic thinking, in lack of moral decision, in namby-pamby dereliction of democratic faith. It lies in the kind of British Tory dereliction of faith that could afford to be mealy-mouthed about inequality and injustice to half a billion colonial Asiatics, that could prevent the British prime minister himself, indomitable war leader though he be, from applying, with a sweep of noble boldness, the towering principles of the Atlantic Charter to 390 million Indians. It lies further, in the kind of "America First" dereliction of faith that for ten years, while world civilization tottered, could see only isolation as a national policy – a policy which has, for five months of war, persisted in appealing not to the highest of international ideals, but to the narrowest of national passions. No, my friends, it is not the planes and the guns and the tanks that are at fault. It is the state of mind – a state of mind far out of consonance with the true spirit of this revolutionary, global war, which we hope to win.

I know these are bold utterances. Forgive me if they pain you. But my people have a right to speak – however unworthily I represent them. Before any Atlantic Charter was set up to marshal the scattered moral forces of Atlantic nations (for such indeed had come to be its purpose), my people had written a *Pacific* Charter for their nation and *all* democratic nations without exclusion. It is a Charter, not a facsimile of the Atlantic Charter, not written in ink, but written in the blood of five millions of China's manhood. And the parchment is her scorched earth, the pen the indomitable will of her people. That Charter is not set up in eight meticulously worded points. It is etched deep into the daily thinking of her people, from the humblest peasant to Generalissimo Chiang Kai-shek himself. And the clear, unfettered terms of this Pacific Charter might well have said: "We hold these truths to be self-evident, that *all* men are created equal; and that they are endowed by their Creator with certain inalienable rights, and among these are Life, Liberty, and the Pursuit of Happiness."

These words flame today in China's battle skies. These words declare a glowing faith in the universal meaning of the revolutionary struggle in which they are engaged – "inalienable rights" not alone for Americans and Chinese and British – not for individual nations and races – but for common humanity. These words declare that China is fighting for the expansion of an ideal long cherished in her own philosophy, an ideal for which America, over a century and a half ago, struck the first revolutionary blow.

China is at her Valley Forge. She is confident of final victory for this ideal, because she is confident of America, the America from whence came the re-emphasized, dynamic philosophy for the moral resurgence of her people. If only America could see – could see herself as the Chinese people have seen her in the past one hundred years – the true America, in the role of mighty champion, towering among the nations, with justice and liberty and equality and democracy emblazoned on her escutcheon – names that spell neither national nor racial creed, but the creed of mankind.

Not only China, but all Asia, is looking toward America. Let there be a definite assurance of her spiritual return to the dynamic, unalloyed idealism that we believe to represent the real America, and a thousand Asian armies would move with her and China to fight for a world empire of freedom. I adjure you to believe me, a continent and a billion men and women have cast you in the greatest role in the most soul-stirring drama of all times, O America! We are, in the words of Matthew Arnold, "Wandering between two worlds, one dead / The other powerless to be born." The world of yesterday is dead indeed – cremated in the consuming fires of great-bombed cities. At this hour, reaffirm your faith, O America! Upon you depend the light and the life of the coming world! This is the message, and this is the exhortation, of the Pacific Charter!

Appendix 2

PAUL LIN'S INFLUENCE
ON A GENERATION

Paul Brennan, vice-president of international partnerships for the Association of Canadian Community Colleges, was a graduate student of Paul Lin at McGill University in the early 1970s. In 2008, he recorded his memories of his former professor and the influence that Paul Lin had on a generation of students.

In 1970 I was taking an East Asian history course at Loyola College (now Concordia) in west-end Montreal, when a young faculty member told me about a new professor at McGill University who had lived through the recent, turbulent transformations in China and who was teaching in an informed and inspiring way. His name was Paul Lin. With that encouragement I signed on for one of Paul Lin's courses on modern Chinese history, and my life changed direction.

Listening to Paul lecture about China at McGill in 1971, to packed classrooms full of attentive students, was a mixture of history lesson, personal témoignage, and inspirational speaker session. China was very little known in the West at that time and was painted either diabolically black or idealistically white. For a group of young idealists looking for something to believe in and fight for, the attraction was great.

Paul's gift as a teacher was to respond to that growing interest with a mixture of essential historical context and personal interpretation on the relevance of the past to the present realities of a rapidly changing China. For the restless student crowd, studying the Opium Wars was sometimes a bit of a bore, but Paul managed to make the link between China's colonial history and evolving contemporary realities. Abstract notions of dialectics were linked to the Taoist *yin-yang* analysis of the world and illustrated by the ebb and flow of political movements and counter-movements in China at the time. Paul opened China's heavy, imperial-like doors to his students, inspiring many of us to continue studying the language and history of that great civilization in transition. I applied for the master's degree in East Asian Studies at McGill under Paul and became one of his teaching assistants.

Because of this, I had the privilege to watch and learn from Paul at close range, preparing myself for the weeks when his trips to China would leave me in front of a class of his students. He was a natural-born teacher and I learned a lot from him about the art of teaching and inspiring students. I would later initiate the teaching of East Asian history at l'Université du Québec à Montréal and at Collège de Rosemont, and can trace my high evaluations as a teacher to the lessons I learned by observing Paul in the early seventies.

In time, my desire grew to see China for myself and, together with one of Paul's other graduate students, Neil Burton, we organized the first Canadian student tour of China since well before the beginning of the Cultural Revolution in 1965. Paul encouraged and supported us through his contacts in China and in other East Asian Studies departments across Canada. With his backing, we recruited thirty Canadian students from Victoria to Halifax who began fundraising for the trip, while Neil and I sought sponsors at the national level. The Canadian departments of Foreign Affairs and Secretary of State put in some money that reduced the individual costs and allowed us to hold a pre-departure orientation session in Vancouver, with Paul as an expert resource.

Our group of thirty students toured China for a full month. It was another world entirely and a transformative experience, as Paul had predicted. For most of us it was our first encounter with China, with Asian culture, with stark poverty, with the challenges of rural areas emerging from feudalism, with a political structure and movements that we had no way of fully understanding. Most of us came home even more dedicated to learn and to do more to change our own world, which is the ultimate objective of learning.

Paul's background as an historian was critical to our understanding why China was going through so many convulsions, convulsions that had even forced him to leave the country in the early 1960s. I remember him saying, "the weight of 2,000 years of well-maintained tradition combined with the brutal awakening by the violent incursion of most of the Western powers who carved China up, had unleashed powerful popular resentment and forces that would be difficult to quell and would take a long time to play out." He reminded us that moving from a consolidated, bureaucratic, feudalist system to a more modern, socialist society was not going to happen smoothly or be without regular setbacks.

And this is what critics of Paul, who viewed him as a propagandist for China and for socialism in China, did not take time to understand. Yes, he was enthusiastic about the necessary revolution in China and would encourage us to understand it through studies and visits, as he had done himself in his early years, but his lessons never failed to place the changes there within their specific historical context. That some of us got overly enthusiastic and unilateral about what the Chinese were trying to achieve, and did not pick up on the undercurrents of repression and excess that were also present, is not attributable to Paul so much, but more to the lessons we did not learn well from Paul. Processes move forward, as he explained, when there is the right balance of revolutionary push forward and consolidation of the transformations. Unfortunately, that balance was often either not sought or was blown aside by those with their own personal and political agendas. We were not always subtle enough to apprehend the distortions and oppression that resulted.

Paul's work also contributed to the Canadian Government recognizing China diplomatically during those years and doing so ahead of the American government. When Zhou Enlai and Pierre Elliott Trudeau signed the mutual recognition and diplomatic relations agreements in October 1970, they also agreed to begin a student exchange program that would allow students of both countries to learn about the other and, hopefully, to play key roles in facilitating Sino-Canadian relations.

During our first China trip, Paul told Neil and me about this new scholarship program offered by the Canadian and Chinese governments. The time frame was very short (a month only), so we had to decide immediately if we were interested and make our application from China. McGill was to have five of the twenty spots, which was good for us, and a sign of the role Paul had played in negotiating the exchanges.

The few of us who did apply from China to Canada via Paul were selected for the first student scholarships. I still remember arriving at the Dorval airport upon our return from the study tour. My parents were crying for joy that I had survived a month in Communist China and was back in Montréal alive. They did not yet know that I had applied to go back for two years. Then Paul came up and, in front of them, enthusiastically congratulated me on being selected to return to China to study, the very next month! My parents and the rest of the family were dumbfounded. Paul realized that I had not yet told them the news and began to apologize profusely. It was a great moment, mixed with excitement, adventure, apprehension, and, yes, fear. Yet Paul was able to reassure my parents that I would be very well taken care of and that he would make sure of it.

And so five of us from McGill University, and fifteen from elsewhere in Canada, departed in November 1973 to live and learn in the PRC for two full years. The first year was dedicated to the study of language at the Beijing Languages Institute, while the second year was comprised of studies in a number of disciplines at Beijing University. I chose modern Chinese history and wrote my master's research paper, in Chinese, on the historic railway workers' strike of February 1923. In researching the paper I interviewed five retired railway workers around Beijing who had actively taken part in the strike. It was oral history at its most fascinating, based on the lessons I had learned from Paul.

Upon my return to Canada, I taught modern Chinese history in universities and colleges in Montreal, helped to set up the Canada-China Society of Montreal and the Federation of Canada-China Friendship Associations, worked as an English-French-Chinese interpreter for Hydro-Québec and various levels of government, and even set up a company for tourism and interpreting called Sinocom.

In 1983 I was hired to help launch the first large CIDA-funded program with China. This was the Canada-China Human Development Training Program (CCHDTP). We brought over one hundred "middle-level cadres," or managers, for part-study/part-work placements in a variety of Canadian government agencies, companies, and research agencies. Today many of these Chinese are senior level managers and leaders in their respective fields and are helping to drive China's new revolution.

An agent from the Canadian Security Intelligence Service (CSIS) once visited me at work to chat about the danger of industrial espionage with all these Chinese being placed with Canadian companies. I sympathized and told him that, as in all endeavours, there surely were some who would get into that, but that the majority sincerely wanted to learn another way of working, not to spy and steal. I explained that the CCHDTP was a bilateral program negotiated by the Government of Canada to help China modernize and to establish strong personal relationships with the leaders of tomorrow. I wished him well in preventing espionage and thought that the interview was finished, but no.

He suddenly asked me why I had decided to go to China in 1973 for two years and how had it changed me? He had obviously studied my "file" and knew my history. I told him that I had been inspired by a great Canadian, Paul Lin, to want to learn about one of the world's great civilizations, which would soon rejoin the global community as a full and respected player. I thought later that I had perhaps gotten Paul into trouble, but reassured myself that he also surely had a "file" and that they knew a lot about him, for he was the ultimate teacher: one who not only inspires one to learn, but who also inspires one to act in accordance with what one has learned – the truly "radical" idea.

I smiled and thought of all those lectures, chats, debates, and jokes that I had the privilege of sharing with Paul Lin over the years. He would be proud to see what had grown from the seeds that he had sown amongst many of us who needed someone to open the doors to the world, with a bit of historical guidance. I hope that you are still teaching, wherever you happen to be now, Paul!

ACKNOWLEDGMENTS

Many family, friends, and colleagues contributed to the telling of Paul's story. I am extremely grateful for their ideas and insights, all of which have strengthened the book, while I accept full responsibility for any errors or weakness of analysis.

Douglas Lin proposed my completion of his father's memoir from the beginning and read a few of my drafts. He could be counted upon to verify the accuracy of Paul's voice.

Professor Zhao Fusan, formerly of the Chinese Academy of Social Sciences, shared his insightful analysis of Paul's spiritual endeavour to build bridges between East and West. This became a major theme in the book.

Harry Chao Wang and Dick Woodsworth have been simply indispensable friends who, in countless ways, enabled me to undertake the many tasks involved in bringing this project to fruition. Harry Lam kindly led me to Johanna Li of Simon & Schuster in New York in 2007. While pointing out the shortcomings of my first draft manuscript, she offered many positive suggestions for improvement.

Hong Kong University of Science & Technology has brilliantly organized the Paul T.K. Lin archives and made them available to the public on their web site. I especially want to thank the university's vice-president Yuk-Shan Wong, librarian Samson Soong, and former librarian Josephine Tsui for their generous assistance.

Jennifer and Sam Tan never failed to revive my lagging spirits when I was faced with yet another revision by their regular long distance calls through the years. Dasan, Jiguang, and Tianhao Luo, Yeh Lihong, Pierre Dansereux, and

Cecilia Leung always responded to my calls for technical support when my computer or printer went on the blink. Solina and Alan Sze lent a helping hand with digitizing the many photographs. Edward and Theresa Odishaw helped me to navigate the legalities of my book agreement.

Naomi Pauls helped me to focus and better organize the second draft of my manuscript, as well as to prepare an excellent index. Kyla Madden, my editor at McGill-Queen's University Press, responded to Paul's story immediately, deftly wielded her red pen, and raised exceptionally good questions about China. In addition, I have deeply appreciated her constant encouragement and cheerful willingness to answer questions throughout the editorial and publishing process. The entire team at McGill-Queen's University Press has been a joy to work with. Thank you! I would also like to express my appreciation to Barry Weldon at McGill who took the initiative to interest the Press in Paul's memoir. The book has also benefited from several practical suggestions made by the two reviewers assigned by McGill-Queen's University Press.

Paul Brennan eloquently summarized Paul's teaching career and role as a mentor to so many students. I very much appreciate his generosity in allowing me to include his tribute as an appendix.

My greatest debt of gratitude is owed to my narrative editor, Cynthia McLean. Shoulder to shoulder, we carved out the storyline through the forest of treasured documents Paul left behind. She brought to the task a deep knowledge of twentieth-century Chinese, Canadian, and American history, as well as an intuitive understanding of Paul's quest to reconcile the values of his Chinese ancestry and his Canadian upbringing. It was a long march and hard work, but we laughed often – I could not have asked for a better comrade and companion on such a journey.

Eileen Chen Lin

BIBLIOGRAPHY

Brady, Anne-Marie. *Making the Foreign Serve China: Managing Foreigners in the People's Republic*. Lanham: Rowman & Littlefield 2003

Cheek, Timothy. *Propaganda and Culture in Mao's China: Deng Tuo and the Intelligentsia*. Oxford: Clarendon Press 1997

Chen, Yuan-tsung. *Return to the Middle Kingdom: One Family, Three Revolutionaries, and the Birth of Modern China*. New York: Union Square Press 2008

Chu, Theresa and Christopher Lind. *A New Beginning: An International Dialogue with the Chinese Church*. Toronto: Canada China Programme 1983

Chung, Arthur W. *Of Rats, Sparrows & Flies: A Lifetime in China*. Stockton, CA: Heritage West Books 1995

Dikotter, Frank. *The Age of Openness: China Before Mao*. Berkeley: University of California Press 2008

Endicott, Stephen. *James G. Endicott: Rebel Out of China*. Toronto: University of Toronto Press 1980

Evans, Paul M. and B. Michael Frolic, eds. *Reluctant Adversaries: Canada and the People's Republic of China, 1949–1970*. Toronto: University of Toronto Press 1991

Fairbank, John K. *The Great Chinese Revolution, 1800–1985*. New York: Harper & Row 1986

Grove, Lyndon. *Pacific Pilgrims*. Vancouver: Synod of the Diocese of New Westminster 1979

Hahn, Emily. *The Soong Sisters*. New York: Doubleday, Doran & Co. 1941

Han Suyin. *Birdless Summer*. London: Jonathan Cape 1968

– *My House Has Two Doors*. London: Jonathan Cape 1980

– *Phoenix Harvest*. London: Jonathan Cape 1980

Hayhoe, Ruth, ed. *Knowledge Across Cultures: Universities East and West.* Toronto: Hubei Education Press; OISE Press 1993

Hooper, Paul F., ed. *Remembering the Institute of Pacific Relations: The Memoirs of William L. Holland.* Tokyo: Ryukei Shysha Publishing Co. 1995

Ji, Chaozhu. *The Man on Mao's Right: From Harvard Yard to Tiananmen Square, My Life Inside China's Foreign Ministry.* New York: Random House 2008

Kissinger, Henry A. *White House Years.* Boston: Little, Brown & Co. 1979

Lai, Him Mark. "The Chinese-Marxist Left: Chinese Students and Scholars in America and the New China, Mid-1940s to Mid-1950s." *Chinese America: History and Perspectives* 18 (January 2004)

Lu, Ping. *The Return of Hong Kong.* Shanghai: China Welfare Institute 2009

Mar, Lisa Rose. *Brokering Belonging: Chinese in Canada's Exclusion Era 1885–1945.* Toronto: University of Toronto Press 2010

McLean, Cynthia. "The Canada China Programme." In Christopher Lind and Joe Mihevc, eds. *Coalitions for Justice: The Story of Canada's Interchurch Coalitions.* Ottawa: Novalis 1994

Ng, Wing Chung. *The Chinese in Vancouver, 1945–80: The Pursuit of Identity and Power.* Vancouver: University of British Columbia Press 1999

Pu, Bao, Renee Chang and Adi Ignatius, eds. *Prisoner of the State: The Secret Journal of Zhao Ziyang.* New York: Simon & Schuster 2009

Rittenberg, Sidney and Amanda Bennett. *The Man who Stayed Behind.* New York: Simon & Schuster 1993

Shephard, David A.E. and Andrée Lévesque, eds. *Norman Bethune: His Times and His Legacy.* Ottawa: Canadian Public Health Association 1982

Snow, Edgar. *Red Star over China.* New York: Grove Press 1968

Soong, Ching Ling. *The Struggle for New China.* Peking: Foreign Languages Press 1953

Soong Ching Ling Foundation. *The Great Life of Soong Ching Ling.* Beijing 1987

Spence, Jonathan D. *The Search for Modern China.* New York: W.W. Norton & Co. 1990

Tseng, Timothy. "Religious Liberalism, International Politics, and Diasporic Realities: The Chinese Students' Christian Association of North America, 1909–1951." *Journal of American-East Asian Relations* 5 (1996): 305–30

Wickeri, Philip L. *Reconstructing Christianity in China: K.H. Ting and the Chinese Church.* Maryknoll, NY: Orbis Books 2007

Worrall, Brandy Lien, ed. *Finding Memories, Tracing Routes: Chinese Canadian Family Stories.* Vancouver: Historical Society of British Columbia 2006

Yee, Paul. *Saltwater City: An Illustrated History of the Chinese in Vancouver.* Vancouver and Toronto: Douglas & McIntyre 1988

INDEX

United States: China policy, 153–4,
157, 159, 177, 259; China relations, 161–2, 258; foreign relations, 142–4; KMT and, 53; Korean
War and, 86–7; Taiwan and, 152,
154, 155, 158–9, 161–4, 170; USSR
and, 142, 143, 167–8; Vietnam
War and, 134–5; World War II and,
42–3
University of British Columbia:
Paul's lectures and dismissal
(1964), 124–9; meetings, 158, 277;
return to (1988), 251, 262; scholarship established, 138–9; studies at
(1938–39), 13–16; teaching at,
106, 114, 122–4; visiting scholars,
264, 267. See also Institute of
Asian Research
University of California, Los Angeles, 207
University of East Asia (UEA): about,
235, 236; Paul's vision for, 235–6,
239, 248; purchase by Macau,
242–5; rectorship, 235–40, 241,
246; resignation, 245–8, 247, 249–
50, 250
University of Michigan, Ann Arbor,
16–25, 17, 43
University of Victoria, 217, 218

values: Christian, 10, 89; Confucian,
7–8, 44, 125, 269; democratic
ideals, 19, 21, 22, 55, 263; feudal,
211, 259; humanism, 8, 258, 280;
idealism, 44, 84, 102, 259; individ-
ualism, 71, 73, 127; justice, 54, 69,
137, 144, 257; of New China, 73–
5, 88–9, 127; "serve the people,"
86, 88, 202, 256; and transforma-

tion of China, 266–7; truth, 71,
182, 203–4, 249. See also respect
Vancouver Chinatown, 4, 9, 15,
116, 141
Vancouver Province, 23, 128
Vancouver Sun, 265
Vernon, BC, 6–7, 8, 9
Vietnam War, 134–5, 143, 152, 163,
170, 229, 259

Wang Jingwei, 34
Wang Meng, 187, 263
Wang Qishan, 216
War of Liberation, 54–5, 191
War of Resistance, 50, 53. See also
Sino-Japanese War, Second
Webster, Norman, 146
Wei Buren, 216
Wen Yiduo, 55
wheat sale, 158, 160, 161
Willis, Henry Parker, 30–1
Winnington, Alan, 83
Winter, Ernst, 167, 168, 237
Wong, G.Y., 105
Wong, K.K., 235, 244–5
Woo, Edward, 235, 244
Woodsworth, Dick, 139
World War II, 19, 20, 42–3, 49, 50,
54, 148, 258
Wuhan, 32, 34

Xia Fang ("down to the country-
side"), 93–5, 179, 196
Xiao Quangyan, 194–5
Xiao Quangzhen, 195
Xinhua News Agency, 88, 95, 169
Xinhui County, Guangdong
Province, 3, 102, 264